THE PREACHERS
OF SCOTLAND

THE PREACHERS OF SCOTLAND

From the Sixth to the Nineteenth Century

William G. Blaikie

THE BANNER OF TRUTH TRUST

THE BANNER OF TRUTH TRUST
3 Murrayfield Road, Edinburgh EH12 6EL, UK
P.O. Box 621, Carlisle, PA 17013, USA

★

Previously published by T. & T. Clark,
Edinburgh, 1888

★

First Banner of Truth edition 2001
ISBN 0 85151 805 2

★

Printed and bound in
Great Britain by
The Bath Press

CONTENTS.

CHAPTER I.—INTRODUCTORY.

CHAPTER II.—THE EARLY CELTIC CHURCH.

CHAPTER III.—PREACHERS OF THE REFORMATION.

Decay of Culdee Church—Extinction in twelfth century—No
notable preaching till Reformation—Sir David Lindsay's
taunts : Breakdown in pulpit of Archbishops of Glasgow
and St. Andrews—And of Bishop of Moray saying grace
at Rome—Only friars preached—Friar Arth at Dundee—
Friar Seton's escapade—A friar's preaching at Perth, and
its tragic results—Archbishop Hamilton's Catechism, an
attempt to supply place of sermons—Public speaking not
cultivated in Scotland — The earliest Scotch orator—
Notices of speeches in Scotch Annals—The Scotch dialect
as a medium of preaching—No Scotch Bible—Knox
accused of being too Anglified—Rollock preached in
Scotch—Moral condition of the country—Unprecedented
corruption of all classes, especially bishops and clergy
—Impurity, profanity, strife, and violence—Reputation
of Scotland for sorcery—Much of this cropped up after
the Reformation—Success of Gospel preaching—Patrick
Hamilton, first reformed preacher—His history, character,
doctrines, preaching, success, arrestment, trial, martyrdom
—Appearance of George Wishart fifteen years after—His
beautiful character—Notices of his preaching—Evangelis-

CHAPTER IV.—THE SUCCESSORS OF KNOX.

CHAPTER V.—THE COVENANTING PERIOD.

(PART I.)

What the Covenants were—The National Covenant—The
Solemn League and Covenant—Loyalty to Christ identified
with adherence to Covenants—Narrowing effect of this on
preaching, and on spirit of the Church—The Covenants
used for purposes of coercion—Otherwise pulpit powerful
instrument of moral and spiritual life—Prominence of
offices of Christ—Message of grace through His work
clearer, fuller, wider—Application closer—Current errors
as to popular sermons—"Sappy preaching." ALEXANDER
HENDERSON—A convert of Robert Bruce's—"The fairest
monument after John Knox that ever Scotland did enjoy"
—Charles I.'s compliment to him as preacher—Characteristics of his preaching. DAVID DICKSON—Regent in
the University of Glasgow—Christian work among the
students—Great spiritual success at Irvine—Revival work
—Professor of Divinity at Glasgow and Edinburgh—His
Biblical Studies and writings—His deathbed. ROBERT
BLAIR—His family—Remarkable autobiography and high
Christian experience—Regent in University of Glasgow—
Ministry at Bangor in Ireland—At Ayr—St. Andrews—

CHAPTER VI.—THE COVENANTING PERIOD.

(PART II.)

CHAPTER VII.—THE FIELD-PREACHERS.

CHAPTER VIII.—THE SECESSION PERIOD.

CHAPTER IX.—THE MODERATE SCHOOL.

Moderatism a reaction not a development—Opinions as to its
origin—Decline of Evangelical spirit—Divergence of views
on grace in the Church—Evangelical witnesses still found,
but prevailing current the other way—Decline of Ministry
in personal earnestness—Evangelical doctrine not openly
repudiated—Defects of Evangelical preaching needing to
be remedied—Spirit of refinement in eighteenth century—
Literary culture of Queen Anne's reign—Ancient plainness
and boldness of ministers becomes offensive—Puritan
opposition to amusement repudiated—Dr. Blair's pretext
when he borrowed novels—Dislike of rigid dogmatism in
pulpit—Desire for more culture in Church—More intercourse with society, more friendliness with literary and
cultured people—Law of patronage more rigidly enforced.
PRINCIPAL ROBERTSON of Edinburgh—His persuasive,
plausible eloquence—Becomes leader of Church, and
devotes himself to enforce law of patronage—His
policy reversed in nineteenth century—Aided by a
more determined man, ALEXANDER CARLYLE of Inveresk
—His autobiography—No trace of sympathy with objects
of Christian ministry—A thorough man of world—Gloried
in having delivered Church of Scotland from fanaticism—
His influence with Robertson—His unscrupulous and
unprincipled audacity. Dr. HUGH BLAIR—The model

CHAPTER X.—EVANGELICAL PREACHERS IN THE CHURCH IN THE EIGHTEENTH CENTURY.

xviii CONTENTS.

APPENDIX.

ON THE METHOD OF PREACHING ADAPTED TO THE AGE.

PAGE

A paper contributed to the *Homiletic Quarterly*, July 1878, in a Symposium with Professor Reynolds, Professor Murphy, Dr. de Pressensé, Canon Perowne, and Rev. J. Clifford, . 325

INDEX, ... 345

THE PREACHERS OF SCOTLAND

FROM THE

SIXTH TO THE NINETEENTH CENTURY.

———◆———

CHAPTER I.

INTRODUCTORY.

In no country has the pulpit of the Reformed Church taken a firmer hold of the people than in Scotland. All along it has been one of the factors of her history, one of the leading sources both of civil and spiritual influence. In days of struggle a free pulpit was contended for as for dear life. A ministry free to utter the message of Christ was indispensable, and if it could not be enjoyed under the arches of the cathedral or the roof of the parish church, it must be sought in conventicles and chapels, or even among the mountains and moorlands, with sentinels all round to give warning of the dragoons. The efforts and sacrifices needed to maintain it developed and exercised the spirit of independence, and were leading means of securing both the civil and the spiritual liberties of the country.

It may be granted that the pulpit of Scotland has been more for the masses than the classes. It has not attracted nor impressed the more cultured ranks of society in the

same degree as the middle and the lower.   Its power has
been most felt in the class pictured by Wordsworth—

> " A virtuous household, though exceeding poor !
> Pure livers were they all, austere and grave,
> And fearing God : the very children taught
> Stern self-respect, a reverence for God's word,
> And an habitual piety maintained
> With strictness scarcely known on English ground."

Its features have been stamped deeply on men like
William Burns, the father of the poet, James Carlyle, the
father of the philosopher, Hugh Miller, and David Livingstone. It has influenced not less powerfully a large class of
Christian women, whose sons have risen to honour, and
have never ceased to own their obligations to their
mothers.   It has made conscience and the fear of God a
great power in many a life, arrested with strong hand
the disorderly tendencies of our nature, and directed much
manly energy into the channels of wholesome industry
and holy endeavour.   Nor is its influence merely a
tradition of the past.   Wherever a preacher of fresh
robust gifts appears, a new life springs up at his feet.
Even ordinary life becomes brighter to toiling men and
women, when once a week they have a pulpit to gather
round, full of fresh life and spiritual power.   In the early
days of far-away colonies, the want of such a pulpit has
been felt by Scottish settlers a dreary thing.   Many is
the request that has sped homewards for an earnest and
rousing preacher. And when the request has been met, and
a powerful voice has been heard proclaiming the message
of grace, as in the pulpits of the fatherland, a new hope
has sprung up for the settlement, and a new guarantee
for all that makes a country stable, orderly, and happy.

No doubt there have been ups and downs in the
popular feeling, as there have been ups and downs in the
quality of the pulpit itself.   An ill-served pulpit must

always breed an indifferent people. But, generally, the enthusiasm created in the better periods has been strong enough to sustain the national feeling, and carry it over periods of collapse and decline.

The question naturally arises, to what has this power of the Scottish pulpit been due? Are we able to trace through its more effective periods, the presence, under varying forms, of any abiding elements of power? In the Reformation pulpit, in that of the Covenanting period, in the Secession offshoot, in the modern Evangelical revival, and in the several modifications of these types, is there to be found any identity of teaching, any identity of spirit, any common seed of life? If there be, it must be of some consequence to discover it. For among the things that are somewhat unsettled in the present day, the pulpit is one. Is its day done? Is the old form of it worked out? Or if there still remain in it the promise and potency of better days to come, how is this promise to be brought into play?

It is no wonder if thoughtful young men are pondering these questions. The pulpit of to-day is shorn of much of its ancient jurisdiction. The political sphere, once so free to it, is now all but interdicted. Trespassers here are prosecuted with the utmost rigour of public dis-approval. As a guide of public opinion, the newspaper has taken its place. The platform, the press, and the lecture-room have each cut off a slice of its domain. It is like the Pope at Rome, shut up in the innermost circle of its former kingdom. Even the religious press has become a rival in one sense, though a valuable help in another. Laymen and laywomen are taking on them-selves the function of religious teachers. The divinity that did hedge a preacher has vanished. The mass of church-going people deem themselves to be already fairly instructed in religious truth, and many are asking

whether church-going is really the best way to spend
the day of rest.   How is the pulpit to be sustained ?   How
is it to be freshened up ?   How is it to regain its old hold
on the people ?

In answer to such questions, specifics for reforming
the pulpit are heard on every side.   Drop the supernatural, say some, and run your preaching on the lines of
Modern Science.   Drop the contrast of sacred and secular,
say others, and bring all that is interesting in science and
history, in travel and in criticism, within the scope of the
pulpit.   Discard the fierce dogmas of Calvinism, is another
advice, and brighten your preaching with happier and
more generous views of human life.   Substitute life for
doctrine, say others, and especially the living person of
Christ for the doctrine of atonement; this will be like
fresh air and daylight in a confined chamber.   Hold
firm to the old ways, is an advice that comes from
others in weighty tones ; let your preaching convey the
great message of reconciliation through the blood of
Christ; fix this in your own soul as God's message to
your people, and let it sound out from you as such with
the mingled authority and affection of a prophet of the
Lord, and by God's blessing you will have as great
success as ever.

Our object in this course of lectures is to deal
historically with this question.   Accepting it as a fact
that the pulpit of Scotland has had periods of great
influence ; that it has nursed a powerful religious life—not
by any means perfect, but real and strong, converting
many souls, enlightening many eyes, and rejoicing many
hearts,—we desire to separate its enduring from its
changing attributes, with a view to determine how the
strength of that which abideth for ever may be combined
with the changing drapery of times and seasons.

From the Reformation to the present day the Scottish

pulpit has been passing through a course of development, and its history, as we shall see, is continuous from first to last. But long before the Reformation the missionary preachers of the ancient Celtic church had done a great work in the country. We cannot pass by that very interesting epoch in a survey of the preachers of Scotland. But we must treat it as a detached chapter, profoundly instructive, but without any specific links of historical connection with the Reformation and subsequent period. It is with the Reformation that the modern pulpit of Scotland really begins. And it is on the lines of the Presbyterian Church that its power has been chiefly shown. With the exception of Archbishop Leighton, who after all was more of a writer than a preacher, the Episcopalian clergy in the seventeenth century had little or no preaching gift. In more recent times neither the Roman Catholic nor the Episcopalian Church in Scotland has ever produced a great pulpit star. The feeble elegance of Archibald Alison is no exception. If we leave living men out of the reckoning, Methodists, Baptists, and Unitarians are in much the same category. Congregationalists stand higher, with a Wardlaw, a Lindsay Alexander, and a Pulsford on their roll. But the great power of the Scottish pulpit has been connected with its Presbyterian organisation. It has been in the main a Presbyterian pulpit, and this fact throws light both on its merits and its defects.

The evolution which may be traced in the history of Scottish preaching marks a progress from a ruder to a more cultured, and from a narrower to a more comprehensive type. First of all, we find it adapting itself to the condition of men startled, as on the Day of Pentecost, by a sudden sense of guilt and danger, and its great object is to unfold the scheme of grace—to answer the question, " Men and brethren, what shall we do ?"

Little can be said for any kind of preaching, be the circumstances what they may, where this great subject has not the leading place. A Gospel which has no doctrine of salvation from guilt and condemnation at its heart is no Gospel at all. But if this doctrine of salvation for the individual be the heart of the Gospel, it is not the whole. "The whole counsel of God" which St. Paul did not shun to declare to the Ephesians embraced much more. In the case of the Scottish Reformers, one of their chief objects was to defend the doctrine of salvation from all that seemed likely to impair its efficacy, first from the Church of Rome, and then from attempts to interfere with the Scriptural constitution and free action of the Church. To originate the divine life in the individual soul, through living faith in Christ; to develop that life, mainly on its divine side, through the power of the Holy Ghost applying the written Word; and to maintain pure and effective the machinery through which these objects were to be gained, was the great aim of the preachers of the Reformation, and of those who followed in their steps.

Nor did the pulpit of Scotland advance much beyond this in the sixteenth and seventeenth centuries. In the latter century it became more doctrinal, but always with the object of ascertaining more thoroughly the mind of the Holy Spirit, and bringing it to bear more fully on the life of man. The preachers were still defending a threatened treasure, and therefore they were still preachers of the warrior type. In protecting their treasure, they brought no little of their natural ruggedness into play. Their energies were often concentrated on the one object of defending a threatened Gospel, and in the struggle for this it went hard with the more passive and gentle graces of Christianity. The cause was so good that it seemed that the utmost vehemence in maintaining it might not only be pardoned, but was absolutely requisite. There was no little Philistinism on the side of the Church, and but little perhaps of sweetness and light. Men like Leighton sighed for something calmer, serener, heavenlier; but they did not take the right way to attain it. The cause of the Gospel of salvation remained under the guardian care of the warrior-preachers, and but for the stand made for it by them, especially by the Covenanters and field-preachers, it might have vanished from the land.

The eighteenth century was the first period of settled calm for the pulpit of Scotland. A reaction set in, and a new craving showed itself. Of war with the world the Church thought she had had enough, and likewise of vehement contendings for doctrinal truth. Might not a better relation be established with the world, and would it not be more wholesome and profitable to preach a practical Gospel, and thus get life to become more social, more pleasant, more human? Might not a more comfortable relation be established with philosophy and science, with literature and art, with culture and the ordinary amenities of life? The fatal error was that the "moderate" pulpit sought to accomplish these ends apart from the life-doctrine of Christianity—apart from its doctrine of salvation. The world was to be taken as it was, and made a friend of—it did not need to be first conquered to Christ. The Church was to bestow her blessing on all the forces and forms of culture around her, whatever might be the spirit in which they were carried on, and the objects at which they aimed. This moderate school had never much enthusiasm; at last all spirit went out of it, and it passed away.

The Secession kept alive the Gospel, nearly but not altogether on the footing on which it had received it from the seventeenth century. The doctrine of salvation was preached, and preached right nobly, but not in the keen warrior spirit of the Covenanters. There was more repose, more of the contemplative, more leading of men beside green pastures and still waters. But there was little effort to extend the sphere of the pulpit, to get it to educate character, to establish right relations with nature and humanity, to improve all that was improveable in man, to saturate the social and national life of the country with the spirit of Christ.

It was Chalmers that first apprehended the capabilities and the obligations of the pulpit in these directions, and by his remarkable genius gave it the corresponding set. No one can charge him with undervaluing the doctrines of grace, or with giving an inferior place to that message which has ever been, and ever will be, " the power of God unto salvation to every one that believeth." Yet many good men looked on Chalmers with suspicion as one whose loyalty to revealed truth was somewhat uncertain. It was because they deemed it incumbent on them to confine the pulpit to its old domain, and could not view without apprehension the relation in which Chalmers wished to place it to the more common interests of humanity and to the culture of the age.

At the present day we find in the Scottish pulpit several types of preaching.

1. We have a school with which it is a *sine quâ non* to reconcile Christianity with "modern thought." All preachers alive to the signs of the times must feel the necessity of reckoning somehow with this factor—the necessity of recognising reason and conscience in some capacity, and of assigning to modern science, historical, physical, and metaphysical, a place of some kind in relation to revealed truth. Unitarians and professed rationalists have no hesitation in making modern thought the ruling or predominant factor. They are led in consequence to eliminate the supernatural from Christianity, and reduce it to little more than a remarkable develop-

ment of natural religion. It is impossible to deny that, following the course of the *Essays and Reviews*, there is a tendency in some Presbyterian pulpits among us towards this view, the tendency being held in check by the obvious incompatibility of the position with an honest acceptance of the Calvinistic standards. But apart altogether from the merits or the demerits of its system, it is obvious that this school is in no true sense a development of the old pulpit of Scotland. It involves a complete break with the past; it repudiates the very foundation of the Reformation pulpit; it turns the eyes of the people wholly away from what used to be presented to them as the alpha and the omega of revealed truth.

2. There is the old Evangelical school, which holds firmly to the primary elements of the Gospel, and aims, to use a common phrase, at the conversion of sinners and the edification of saints. When accompanied with great emotional fervour—the genuine movement of a throbbing heart—this style of preaching is still a great power; for it deals with the very elixir of life, and brings to famished souls the finest of the wheat. But when the preacher is a commonplace man with a very ordinary soul, unable to throw a ray of fresh light on what has been said so often, unable even to present his message in that vivid form which a man's own experience makes so telling, the preaching is tasteless and feeble, and peculiarly unsatisfactory to the young. It is because there are so many commonplace evangelical preachers that the impression gets a footing among young men that this line of preaching is thoroughly exhausted, and that the preacher who would hold his audience must hie him "to fresh woods and pastures new."

3. We have a school in which little is made of Calvinistic doctrine, even of the great doctrine of atonement, but where it is sought to promote a full-orbed Christian

life, and a wide Christian culture. The preacher's great
desire is to get men to live as Christians; to make the
Christian spirit flourish and prevail everywhere.   He
desires to fill the heart with just conceptions of the love
and loveableness of God, to expound all that is involved
in His fatherhood, and make the relation real of a loving
Father and a loving child.   He labours to turn all life
into a service of God, and to get help for this from all the
legitimate pursuits and interests of men.   He desires to
establish a real brotherhood among all classes, rich and
poor, preaches readiness for service as the true clue to a
useful, happy, and honourable life, and encourages the
spirit that ever seeks to avoid inflicting pain, and delights in opportunities of giving pleasure.   The aims are
excellent, but surely a fatal error is committed, if it is
believed that these ends may be attained apart from a
fundamental change of relation to God through vital
union to Christ, or that the Christian life can be sustained
save by faith in Christ as the substitute of sinners, and
the regeneration of the Holy Ghost.

4. A fourth, and, as we believe, the best type of preaching among us, is that which takes something from both
the two last-mentioned schools, and is not altogether
regardless of the position of the first.   It starts from the
same facts as the Evangelical school, recognises man's
guilt and ill-desert, his need of mercy to pardon and
grace to renew, and aims, first of all, at establishing a
vital relation between the sinner and the Saviour.   But
beyond this it aims at applying Christianity in every
direction both to secular and spiritual life; it seeks very
specially to develop the spiritual life of the individual, but
it would baptize not only the individual, but the family,
the Church, the community in all its relations and operations into Christ.   It recognises the imitation of Christ as
the true flower and fruit of the Gospel, the crown and

consummation of all Christian teaching and training. Under Christ it seeks the improvement of all that is improveable in the human soul, and the enrichment of human life with every lawful joy which does not react injuriously on what is most vital and precious. It would correct the hideous distortions of modern commercial and social life by the infusion of the self-sacrificing spirit of Christ. It seeks a friendly relation with all that is best in art, science, literature, and general culture, these being viewed as manifestations of God, and designed to help on the great ends of life. Nevertheless, it demands a subdued and chastened attitude of spirit towards this present world, which to the Christian must ever be far more a school of training than a scene of enjoyment; and it leads the thoughts and feelings onward to another state of being, to be realised when Christ comes again, in whose presence alone there is fulness of joy and pleasures for evermore.

And with reference to modern thought, it endeavours to find for it its due place, but in marked subordination to the fact that Christianity is a supernatural revelation from God; that its lessons rest on divine authority; and that while reason is to receive, to explain, and to harmonise the body of revealed truth, it is not to usurp the throne, but to serve only as the handmaid of revelation.

We offer this sketch with some misgiving; the outline must be explained and filled up as we proceed. It is meant to indicate the true line of development of the Scottish pulpit; the aim with which it started three centuries ago, and the consummation toward which, in its best form, it seems to be now stretching.

CHAPTER II.

THE EARLY CELTIC CHURCH.

THE earliest period of Scottish church history is one of extraordinary interest and brilliant triumph; a time, too, of remarkable preachers, and, what is more, remarkable men.

Of the introduction of Christianity into Scotland we know hardly anything. It seems to have been due to the efforts of Roman Christians who were either soldiers in the invading army, or who, moved by the love of Christ, followed it to cast the seed of the Gospel into the furrows of war. But it is remarkable that no bright Christian star appeared in our sky, and especially no native star, till about the end of the Roman occupation, and that, when stars did appear, the brightest of them shone in parts of Scotland that had never been overrun by Roman arms. In what manner the early evangelists of Scotland and Ireland attained their remarkable spiritual life; by what means, from communities almost heathen and very savage, they emerged in all the beauty of holiness, of the highest type of Christian character, and were able to adapt themselves with such extraordinary success to the people to whom they preached, is one of the most interesting problems of our religious history. To us it seems that no period of Scottish church history has rivalled the purity, the beauty, the glory of its dawn. No men ever appeared

in our country more worthy to be called "living sacrifices," more thoroughly devoted to the cause of Christ.
They were not indeed free from errors, both in doctrine
and practice ; but better specimens of consecrated lives it
would be hard to meet with anywhere. Strange, that
while at this day the spirit of entire consecration is sought
by some of our most earnest people as the very crown and
flower of the Christian life, so many ministers of Christ at
the very dawn of our history should have reached and
maintained that glorious distinction.

In the fifth century, St. Patrick achieves a work in
Ireland which even at this day we look back on with
wonder. If he was born at Dumbarton, as Dr. Stokes
with other recent biographers thinks probable,[1] we may
claim him as our own countryman, and the obligations of
Scotland and Ireland to each other are balanced by the
fact, that Patrick, the great evangelist of Ireland, was a
Scot, while Columba, the great evangelist of Scotland, was
an Irishman. Of the kind of influence that made Patrick
a missionary, we can have little doubt. The herd boy
that was so impressed by the history of St. Paul, and who
felt that at his conversion he was re-made by the Lord
for the salvation of others ; who seemed to hear the echo
of the man of Macedonia's words in a call to himself from
Ireland, " Come and walk again among us," and who over-
came the opposition of his parents to his missionary
career by repeating words that he believed were spoken
to himself : " He who gave His life for thee—He speaks
in thee "—this man must have been cast in the spiritual
mould of St. Paul. What is called St. Patrick's Hymn,
which, notwithstanding some doubts as to its being his,
Drs. Stokes and Wright have inserted in a recent issue of

---

[1] *Ireland and the Celtic Church.* By G. T. Stokes, D.D., Prof. of
Eccles. Hist., Trin. Coll., Dublin.

his works,[1] shows very clearly the place Christ held in his
religious experience.   One of its passages runs :—

> " Christ with me, Christ before me,
>   Christ behind me, Christ within me,
>   Christ beneath me, Christ above me,
>   Christ at my right, Christ at my left ;
>   Christ in the fort,
>   Christ in the chariot seat,
>   Christ in the poop.
>   Christ in the heart of every man who thinks of me,
>   Christ in the mouth of every man who speaks to me,
>   Christ in every eye that sees me,
>   Christ in every ear that hears me."

The power by which he evangelised Ireland, preaching
to the people the gospel of salvation in their native
tongue, reclaiming them from their wildness, and putting
a new face upon the whole country, was as like that of
the apostles as anything known in post-apostolic times.
A man whose name has lived so long in the hearts of the
people, associated with the noblest qualities of the Christian missionary and patriot, must, apart from the legends
which superstition has added, have been a man of singular
magnetism, and a preacher of great spiritual power.

Contemporary with St. Patrick, but rather earlier,
another Scotch Evangelist, St. Ninian, is labouring in
Galloway and the south-west of Scotland with corresponding vigour and success.   Of his life we have little
trustworthy record, his chief biographer St. Ailred having
flourished six hundred years after him.   He speaks of him
as the son of Christian parents, intensely devoted from his
boyhood to the study of the holy Scriptures, delighting
in them with his whole heart, separating himself with
wonderful care from all that was evil and unholy, and

---

[1] *The Writings of St. Patrick.* By G. T. Stokes, D.D., and C. H. H.
Wright, D.D., 1887.

distinguished for a marvellous fear of God and love of man. Agreeable in manners, and reflecting from his countenance the joy and peace that reigned in his soul, he devoted himself to the conversion of the Southern Picts, and among them he effected a wonderful change. Few sons of Scotland ever made a deeper mark, or left a more honoured name than Ninian. The churches named after him attest his influence to the present day. Through all the mediæval ages his name retained its sanctity and its fragrance. When superstition enthralled the country, his tomb became a sacred spot, and till the Reformation, or near it, "bands of votaries of all classes, from the Court downwards," might often be seen "passing thro' Peebles or Ayr on their way to St. Ninians."[1]

But the sixth century is the great era of Scottish evangelism. The kingdom of Cumbria or Strathclyde, after its first acquaintance with the truth, seems to have relapsed to a great extent into paganism, and St. Kentigern, or as he is often called, St. Mungo, was the man who won it back to Christ. We see in him an ardent evangelist, practising the most rigorous asceticism, conspicuous for virtues of abstinence which caused him to be known as "a Nazarite of our Nazarene, the Lord Jesus Christ." Jocelyn, one of his biographers, describes him as "beautiful to look upon and graceful in form. Having a countenance full of grace and reverence, dove-like eyes, cheeks like the turtle dove, he attracted the hearts of all who beheld him. His cheerful expression was the sign of that inward peace, beaming out in streams of holy joy and triumph which the Lord bestowed upon him."[2] Through his preaching and holy influence he gained to Christ that whole district which became the

[1] *Historians of Scotland,* Introduction to Life of St. Ninian. By Bishop Forbes, p. lvii.
[2] *Ibid.,* Jocelyn's Life of St. Kentigern, ch. xviii.

diocese of Glasgow, besides doing much good beyond its limits.

But the fame alike of Ninian and Kentigern is eclipsed by that of Columba. His life divides into two periods, the Irish and the Scotch. It was A.D. 563, in his forty-second year, that he began his labours in Iona, the very time of life at which, about ten centuries later, John Knox first opened his mouth as a preacher. It is difficult to reconcile the account which some of his biographers give of his Irish life, including Count Montalembert, Professor Stokes, and Bishop Forbes (but not our own Dr. W. F. Skene), as the life of a wild, passionate, imperious Irishman, with the calm, gracious dignity that ever marked him at Iona.

He was the first missionary that ever crossed the Grampians, and the whole of the north-west Highlands of Scotland seem under him and his coadjutors to have been converted to the faith of Christ.

It is impossible even to glance at the labours of the many eminent evangelists who shared the spirit and extended the spiritual conquests of those whom we have named. Among the Irish, Columbanus and the two Finnians were of the highest rank. Wales contributed its share of stars to the Celtic firmament; and as for Scotland, not only was the work of Columba kept up in all its vigour for a considerable time by his immediate companions, but missionaries went forth to other parts of the world, and as Ebrard[1] has well shown, "in the sixth seventh, and eighth centuries, evangelised the largest part of Great Britain, Burgundy, Rhineland, part of South Germany, and Switzerland." In Scotland, not only Columba's name but the names of many of his followers still live in the names of churches and shrines. As Hill

[1] *Die Iroschottische Missionskirche des sechsten, siebenten und achten Jahrhunderts.* Von Dr. J. H. A. Ebrard, 1873.

Burton has remarked, in the records of those times the terms "saint" and "missionary" are interchangeable. "In the Gothic pages of the *Breviarium Aberdonense* we come one after another through a crowd of these ancient saints. The Celtic names preponderate conclusively, even though there was a considerable Teutonic element in Scotland."[1] The qualities ascribed to them in the Breviarium were more in accordance with subsequent Roman traditions than with the real facts of their lives. But the Church that bred them never owned the jurisdiction of the Church of Rome.

It is with the preaching of this noble band of Christian missionaries that we have to do in this chapter. Great preachers they were; preaching was indeed their great, almost their only, weapon. Unfortunately, any records of their work that have come down to us give us little account of their sermons. They tell us a great deal of their alleged miracles. Adamnan's Life of Columba, written within a century of the saint's death, is divided into three parts, which detail his prophecies, his miracles, and his visions respectively, but give nothing of his sermons. If we were to believe the half of it, he had little need to preach. Such supernatural appendages are characteristic of an author who had lost faith in the power of the Gospel message, backed by a holy Christian life; and to make out the greatness of Columba, magnified the fruits of his natural sagacity, or the answers of believing prayer, into stupendous marvels.

It is chiefly from incidental notices, and from what we know of the men and the manner of their life, that we gather what and how they preached. But the subject has never been formally discussed. There have been many battles over this Celtic Church, and profound researches to support the respective sides of the warfare.

---

[1] *History of Scotland*, vol. i. p. 264.

Its form of church government has been very earnestly and elaborately disputed. On one side it has been vehemently contended, and no doubt quite conclusively, that its government was not that of monarchical episcopacy. On the other side it is affirmed, and with much reason too, that neither was it identical with our modern presbytery. We agree with Mr. Hill Burton in the compliment he pays to the late Dr. M'Lauchlan, for the moderation with which he discusses this question, as compared with some earlier writers.[1]

What we have to do with is the preaching of the Celtic missionaries. Dr. Wylie, in his very graphic *History of the Scottish Nation* (vol. ii.), has given an ideal and somewhat elaborate sketch of what he conceives to have been a sermon of St. Patrick's. We can hardly accept of this as historically correct. It is too like the modern evangelistic address. But in St. Columba's time, the popular conception of the Gospel message had not yet been fashioned in the modern mould. Not till Anselm published his *Cur Deus Homo*, was the way of salvation so explicitly defined. There are, however, some materials which it will be well to bring together, to help us to determine the substance of the preaching of the Celtic missionaries, and to explain the impression which it made.

To estimate the precise nature of their work, it would be desirable to have some knowledge of the character, and especially the religious beliefs and spirit of the people among whom they laboured. But for this, too, the materials are very scanty. Few will be disposed to doubt that the Northern Picts were a very savage race. The country was poor and cold, and the features which afterwards brought it the designation "Ecosse la Sauvage,"[2]

---

[1] In *History of the Early Church of Scotland*, by Rev. Thomas M'Lauchlan, LL.D. See Burton's *Hist. of Scotland*, i. 403.
[2] *Les Ecossais en France.* Par F. Michel, i. 2.

had all their primitive ruggedness in Columba's time. It was the savage condition of the people that made residence in islands so necessary for evangelistic work. As for the Druidical religion, the old opinion regarding it seems now to have passed away—that it was administered under a comprehensive and elaborate organisation by an all-powerful priesthood. Druidical rites, and probably human sacrifices, prevailed; priests there must have been, but there is no trace of a powerful priestly organisation, and the people do not appear to have been held very tightly in the grasp of the old faith.[1] We hear of hardly any persecution of the Christians. The missionaries were allowed to prosecute their work with little opposition except from the priests. We do not read of massacres in Scotland like those which distressed St. Patrick in Ireland.[2] In this respect the lines fell to them in pleasant places, and they enjoyed a freedom from annoyance and anxiety which few missionaries in the like circumstances have known. The friendship of King Brude, the powerful ruler of the Northern Picts, acquired by Columba at an early period, no doubt contributed in a large measure to this result.

1. If we put together the scattered notices we find of the ministry of Columba and his school, the first feature to attract our notice on every side is *its thoroughly Biblical character*. It was most emphatically a ministry of "the Word." Indeed, the monks possessed hardly any literature but the Scriptures. Some of them had been at Rome, and were doubtless acquainted with the Christian writings of the time; but if they had these books in their little cells, they were for a purpose so subordinate that we never hear of them. What they read, what they copied, what they delighted in, was the holy Scriptures. What they preached was "verbum Dei." Of their

[1] Hill Burton's *Hist. of Scotland*, i. 210.
[2] See his *Epistle to Coroticus*, passim.

boundless devotion to the Scriptures we have a striking
proof in the fact that Columba, with his own hand, is
said to have transcribed the Gospels, and also the Psalms,
three hundred times ; and that on the last day of his life
he was engaged in copying the 34th Psalm ; when he
had copied the words, " they that seek the Lord shall not
want any good thing," feeling the touch of a chill hand,
he wrote, " Here I must stop ; what follows, let Baithene
write ; " after resting a little on his bare stone bed, he
went at midnight into the church, and, kneeling down
to pray, he calmly died.[1]

Writing of the preaching of St. Kentigern, Ailred says,
that he proved to the people of Strathclyde that Woden
was but a mortal man, and showed from the very beauty
of the visible creation that Almighty God, Three in One,
was the Creator of all things.   He then preached Christ
to them, and showed by the most true and lucid demonstrations that there is none other name under heaven,
believing in which men may be saved, but only the
name of our Lord Jesus Christ.[2]

But the writer from whom we obtain by far the most
minute account of the matter of the preaching of the
Celtic missionaries is Columbanus, sometimes called
Columba the younger, and not to be confounded with
the saint of Iona.   Columbanus, likewise, was an Irishman, who left his native country for evangelistic work ;
but instead of making for the shores of Scotland, turned
his steps to central Europe, and, if he did not found the
monastery of Bobbio in the north of Italy, presided over
it for a considerable time. A volume entitled *Instructiones*,
by Columbanus, has come down to us from these distant
times, and we may warrantably regard it as expressing
what was believed and taught by the Celtic Church.

---

[1] Adamnan's *Life*, ch. xxiv.
[2] *Historians of Scotland*, vol. v., Life of St. Kentigern, ch. xxxii.

The *Instructiones* or sermons are simple, practical, fervent exhortations, constantly dwelling on Christ, His love and His work, and striving to kindle a corresponding spirit, a spirit that would show the love of Christ glowing in the heart, and that would fill the life with charity and humility. He is never weary of urging how Christ by His death became our life, how if we are alive to God we must be dead to sin, and how the fruit borne in our life should bear some proportion to the price wherewith we are redeemed. A great price truly, when "the Lord died for the servant, the King for the minister, God for man."

Founding upon the views of this Columbanus, and reading into his sermons a little of the theology of more recent times, Ebrard has constructed a system of doctrine of the Celtic Church,[1] of which Hill Burton gives the following summary :—" It had a full right to be called an evangelical church, not only because it was free from the power of Rome, and always showed a determination, whenever the Roman Catholic Church came in contact with it, to appeal from the authority of Rome to the Holy Scriptures as the only supreme authority ; but above all, because its inner life was penetrated and stimulated by the inner form and substance of the evangelical church. . . . To the Culdees the Holy Scriptures were no text-book containing a list of lawful doctrines, but the living word of Christ. They taught with all sincerity the innate sinfulness of the natural man, the reconciling death of Christ, justification by faith without the aid of works ; above all things the worthlessness of all outward works, and regeneration as life in Him that died for us. The sacraments were to them signs and seals of the one grace through Christ, and as such held only a second place in their teaching. They denied the efficacy of

[1] See *Iroschottische Missionskirche, Die Heilslehre*, pp. 99-134.

saints, angels, and relics, and urged to a very pure and heavenly life." [1]

Mr. Burton, we think, and perhaps Dr. Ebrard too, have made the Celtic theology more systematic, and more distinctly Calvinistic than it was. We must remember, too, that Columbanus probably addressed his *Instructiones* to professing Christians, while Columba and his brethren had to deal with savages. In dealing with such men there are certain outstanding facts of revelation which all missionaries have found to be most efficacious, and we have every reason to believe that Columba's experience of them was the same. These are the great moral miracles of the Gospel history; how after man had rebelled against God, God made a wonderful plan, not to destroy him, but to save him; how Jesus Christ, the Son of God, came into our world, born of a Virgin, to execute that plan; how He did execute it by dying on the cross in the room of man; how He rose from the dead and is now in heaven, whence He is to come again to this earth, to gather all His people together, and dwell with them in glory, in holy and everlasting joy. The untutored heart is singularly open to the influence of wonder, and what the missionaries had to tell them was singularly fitted to excite this spirit. If there be still something to make men wonder in " the old, old story of Jesus and His love "; if even yet the history of the life and death of the Son of God can only be told rightly, when set forth as the wonder of wonders, we can almost picture to ourselves the strange look of these wild barbarians, when the missionaries, with tearful eye and trembling lip, told them of the manger of Bethlehem and the cross of Calvary. What else could have dispossessed the old gods from their hearts at a stroke, spite of all they had learned from their fathers? What else could

[1] Hill Burton, i. 404-405.

have turned these shaggy men and women, hardly less wild-looking than the cattle on their mountains, into devout and earnest followers of a crucified Jew?

There is still a place for the marvellous in the business of the missionary and the preacher. Many a savage has been arrested and awed by the burning glass, the mirror, the rifle, "the chip that could speak," as a South-sea savage called a chip of wood on which a missionary wrote a message to his wife to send him a certain tool. The spread of education and intelligence strips these things of their mystery, and reduces them to natural phenomena. As we get more and more enlightened, we are less and less carried away by wonder. In some cases, it seems to be wholly dropt out of men's religion. But it cannot be dropt without loss. It is a poor soul that is never awed by that great mystery of godliness,—God manifest in the flesh, as the Saviour of the guilty. Such a soul can never rise high above the level of ordinary feeling; it can know nothing of that uplifting power which breaks the attraction of earth, and bears one up as on eagles' wings, because every other feeling is absorbed by the marvellous truth, "The Son of God loved me and gave Himself for me."

2. But if the Columban ministry was remarkable as a ministry of the word, it was still more conspicuous as *a ministry of the life.*

Never, probably, in these islands, was there a body of men whose habits were in such thorough accord with what they preached and taught. In their lives they were simple, self-denied, abstemious. They were ever ready to help when help was needed. They always took side with those who suffered wrong, and sought to get redress for them from the mighty. Had there been over-burdened crofters in those days, driven by hunger and despair, we know on whose side they would have been. The sick, the poor, the aged were objects of their most affectionate care. The hearts of the missionaries themselves were steeped in the truths which they proclaimed. They seem to have had no desire for wealth, no longing for worldly consideration, distinction, or power. One wonders at the proofs one meets with of the intensity as well as the wide prevalence of this spirit. How thoroughly Columba himself was penetrated by it, is manifest from many things recorded of him. Waiting on the Lord, he renewed his strength. He had times of remarkable refreshing from the presence of the Lord, of glorious illumination by the Holy Spirit, when he might almost be said, like St. Paul, to have been caught up into the third heavens, and seen and heard things unutterable. For three days and nights, it was said, on one occasion, the grace of the Holy Ghost was communicated to him in so wonderful a manner that rays of surpassing brilliance issued through the chinks of the house, and strains of spiritual song were heard which had never been heard before.[1] Marvellous revelations of divine truth seemed to be made to him; but what impressed him most was, the new meaning that seemed to be given to the Scriptures, and even to parts of them that were difficult and obscure. He grieved that his disciple Baithene was not with him that he might have communicated to him, in all their freshness, the interpretations which had been vouchsafed to him in the sacred volume. Allowing for the tendency to exaggerate, and to introduce the supernatural in material form, we see clearly from these statements how close his communion with his Lord through the Holy Scriptures must have been, what revelations of the divine glory he got through the earnest and admiring study of them, and what remarkable spiritual power must have come to him thereby.

[1] Adamnan's *Life*, Book III. ch. xix.

Adamnan's account of Columba's appearance and mode of life is in full harmony with this view. " From his boyhood he had been brought up in Christian training in the study of wisdom, and by the grace of God had so preserved the integrity of his body and the purity of his soul, that though dwelling on earth he appeared to live like the saints in heaven. For he was angelic in appearance, graceful in speech, holy in work, with talents of the highest order and consummate prudence. . . . He could never spend the space of even one hour without study or prayer, or writing or some other holy occupation. . . . He was beloved by all, for a holy joy ever beaming on his face revealed the joy and gladness with which the Holy Spirit filled his inmost soul." [1]

" Charity," says another biographer, " was even stronger than humility in that transfigured soul. No necessity, spiritual or temporal, found him indifferent. He devoted himself to the solace of all infirmities, all misery and pain, weeping over those that did not weep for themselves. These tears became the most eloquent part of his teaching, the means which he employed most abundantly to subdue inveterate sinners, to arrest the criminal on the brink of the abyss, to appease and soften and change those wild and savage but simple and straightforward souls whom God had given him to subdue." [2]

It was as preached in this spirit and supported by such a life, that the message of salvation through the blood of Christ became to the Picts of Caledonia the power of God unto salvation. The tale in itself was marvellous, such as had never entered into the heart of man. Could it be that the great God whom they had offended was willing to treat them in a way so different

[1] Adamnan's *Life of St. Columba*, Pref.
[2] Montalembert's *Monks of the West*, iii. 152.

from the manner of men? If any doubts remained in their minds, the lives of the missionaries could not but scatter it. How truly had they learned the lesson of forgiveness! When they saw how good they were, and devout, and kind, and self-denying; when they contrasted the peace and joy in which they lived with the wild tumult of their own hearts, every doubt disappeared; they were won to Christ. Some historians have surmised that the people must have been partly Christianised before, otherwise the completeness and rapidity of the change cannot be understood. The completeness and rapidity of the change are accounted for by the marvellous reflection of the message in the lives of the missionaries. It is with no little shame for our degeneracy that we mark in these men, in combination with their intense aggressiveness, a gentleness and love appropriate to the calmest times. In these far-away islands, where between the roaring of the Atlantic waves, the howling of the wind in the glens, and the dashing of the snow-drift against the mountains, all the forces of tumult seemed to hold high revel, these men maintained a serenity of spirit that seemed the very counterpart of heaven. Admirably adapted for laying the foundation, they were not less fitted to give the last touch of beauty and refinement to the Christian edifice; and it would have been well for the Scottish Church if their spirit had been more common in many subsequent periods of earnest contendings, not always marked by the meekness and gentleness of Christ.

3. Further, this Columban ministry was *a ministry of poetry and song.* Singing psalms was not only an outlet for their devotion, but also a method of interesting and attracting the heathen. Speaking of the Irish practice, Montalembert says: "At that period, as ever since, the love and practice of music was a national passion with

the Irish. The missionaries, and the monks their successors, were also inspired by this passion, and knew how to use it for the government and consolation of souls." Then he tells a legend of a shepherd who, as he was one day keeping his father's flock in the forests of Kerry, was attracted by a procession of missionaries chanting psalms in alternate strophes, as they continued their course. Rapt by their psalmody, he followed them to the gates of their monastery, and waited till the chanting of their evening song was finished. The prince of the country, who had taken an interest in the shepherd and a liking for him, invited him to his palace, and offered him his sword, his buckler, and his lance, all the tokens of a brilliant warrior life. "I want none of your gifts," the shepherd always replied, "I want but one thing, to learn the chant which I have heard sung by the saints of God." [1]

Columba, too, was a great singer. He had a magnificent voice, capable of being heard at an enormous distance. On one occasion, when opposed by certain Druids, he intoned a psalm with such marvellous effect that his enemies were reduced to silence, and the surrounding spectators trembled before him.

Of Columba's gifts of poetry there are still proofs, for a few of his poems survive. With the Irish bards who at that time occupied a high place in the social and political institutions of Ireland, and who were to be met with everywhere, in the palaces and monasteries, as on the public roads, he lived during his Irish life in great and affectionate sympathy. After he settled in Iona, nothing seems to have stirred his vein of poetry like the thought of Erin, to which his heart turned with all imaginable love and longing. "From the high prow, I look over the sea, and great tears are in my grey eye when I turn to Erin—to Erin, where the songs of the

[1] *Monks of the West*, iii. 90, 91.

birds are so sweet, and where the clerks sing like the
birds; where the young are so gentle, and the old are so
wise; where the great men are so noble to look at, and
the women so fair to wed." [1]

The missionaries who went to evangelise Europe were
full of the same spirit. As Professor Stokes remarks of
the Continental Columba (Columbanus), he led in Burgundy a most simple life. We trace in him the same
love of nature and natural objects which we find in the
beautiful stories told of Columba. Everything is said to
have obeyed his voice. The birds came to receive his
caresses. The wolves instinctively shunned him. Crowds
flocked to the Irish teacher to learn the secret of a pure
and holy life. The Gallic bishops did not like his ways,
and strove to reduce him to conformity with theirs.
But he would not abandon his own. He asked of them
permission only to live in the forest. " Oh, let us live in
peace on earth, when we shall be together in heaven ! "

But what we are most concerned to notice at present
is the prominence given by Columba to song as a missionary agency. Of the power of that key to the human
heart, he and his comrades seem to have been well aware.
That which came upon us here a few years since with
the novelty of a surprise, must have been well known to
them thirteen hundred years ago. It was not as if they
substituted a musical entertainment for the Gospel; the
Gospel and the Scriptures ever held their place of supremacy; but they knew the power of music to touch and
open the heart, and though a subordinate, it proved a
valuable factor in their methods of evangelisation.

4. Finally, the ministry of the Columban Church was
a ministry of holy, courageous enterprise. Even at this
early period, the Scot had shown himself fond of travel
and ready for adventure; and now this feature of the

[1] Stokes' *Ireland and the Celtic Church*, p. 123.

national character was cordially consecrated to the service of Christ. It is surprising how little these missionaries thought of a journey to Rome, tedious, expensive, difficult and dangerous though it was. Some of them in the course of their lives were there oftener than once—St. Kentigern is said to have been seven times. In Ireland, Columba had travelled much. "Omnes regni provincias continuo peragrans, urbes, oppida, paga circumiens."[1] The words remind us of what we read in the Gospels: "Jesus went about all the cities and villages, teaching in their synagogues, and preaching the gospel of the kingdom." So addicted were some of the monks to travel and voyage that they got the name of the sailor monks. "Such was Brendan, an Irish monk, whose fantastic pilgrimages into the great ocean, in search of the earthly paradise, and of souls to convert, and unknown lands to discover, have been preserved under the form of visions." Seven long years he is said to have spent in search of the Fortunate Islands. Cormac, who was more closely associated with Columba, made three voyages in search of an island believed to exist in the midst of the ocean. In one of these voyages, his boat was carried by a strong wind out to sea fourteen successive days, and it was a kind of miracle that it ever returned.

If we remember that these boats were mere coracles, constructed of wicker-work, covered with hides, we shall understand what courage and faith were needed for such enterprises. Montalembert is of opinion that in thus putting imagination as well as the spirit of adventure at the service of the faith and of ideal virtue, these men and their achievements are worthy of being reckoned among the poetic sources of the *Divina Commedia*. They exercised a lively influence upon the Christian imagination during all the middle ages, and even up to the time

[1] O'Donnell's *Life of Columba*, p. 398.

of Christopher Columbus himself, to whom the salt water epic of St. Brendan seems to have pointed out the way to America. "I am convinced," said Columbus, "that the terrestrial paradise is in the island of St. Brendan, which nobody can reach except by the Spirit of God." [1]

The prevalence of this spirit of travel and enterprise in the Celtic Church prepared the way for its remarkable mission work in foreign countries. When we think of Columba and his brethren in that remote island of the West, so secluded even yet from the rest of the globe, we are apt to fancy them as quite cut off from the civilised world, and as living in ignorance of all that was happening in other countries, except perhaps their native Ireland. Very different was the real state of the case. Many men paid visits to Iona that had traversed England, France, Germany, Switzerland, and Italy ; and many a traveller's tale instructed and refreshed the brethren when other duties permitted them to gather round a stranger. Yet all was subordinated to the great purposes of their mission. They were ready to go to foreign lands if called to do so by the head of their order. In that church men were never wanting for foreign service. And so the lamp of the Gospel was lit with marvellous rapidity in many lands.

Of the remarkable spiritual influence of Columba and his friends it would be easy to give abundant proofs. But it is needless to prove what no one denies. Let a single instance indicate the means by which he prevailed. A pilot one day complains to him of his wife, who has taken an aversion to him. Columba calls her to him and admonishes her. She declares she will undergo any penance, go to any convent, or undertake any pilgrimage

---

[1] Montalembert, *Monks of the West*, Book IX. ch. vi. *Dictionary of Christian Biography*, art. "Brendan." Grubb's *Eccles. Hist. Scot.* vol. i. pp. 55, 56.

—anything rather than be affectionate to her husband. Columba sees how the land lies, and proposes that they should all three fast and pray over it. They agree; Columba spends the whole night fasting and praying. In the morning he asks the woman, with a touch of irony, what convent she now proposes to enter. " None," says the woman. " My heart has been changed during the night. I know not how, but I have passed from hatred to love." [1]

Of Kentigern, Ailred says that neither his foot, hand, nor tongue ceased from the execution of the work he had undertaken, from the working of miracles, from the preaching of salvation, till all the ends of the earth remembered themselves and turned unto the Lord. And he draws a picture of him being engaged in all kinds of good works, turning concubinage into marriage, reducing the wild people to law and order, and bringing the spirit of Christ to prevail over all manner of disorder and vice. [2]

Of Cadoc, one of the most distinguished of the Welsh saints of the sixth century, it was said that " to know the country of Cadoc it was only necessary to discover where the cattle fed in freedom, where the men feared nothing, and where everything breathed peace." [3] He was a chief as well as a saint, and was the protector of his dependants and neighbours, the guardian of the poor, the defender of women, and of all who were poor and needy, against extortion, violence, and oppression. The legends that surround the name of King Arthur no doubt have extended to Cadoc, who was his neighbour and his friend. But this whole class of legends bear testimony to the existence of a high moral tone in the British Church, and a chivalrous regard for justice and honour. They prove the presence of a remarkable spiritual force that mastered some of the strongest propensities of rough human

---

[1] Montalembert, iii. 254.   [2] *Life of St. Kentigern*, ch. xix.
[3] Montalembert, iii. p. 63.

nature, and purified society by the gentle influences of Christian love.

Perhaps we have drawn too flattering a picture, a picture which might lead some to ask, Were they human after all? We are far from thinking them perfect. Defects and errors might easily be pointed out in their church system, in their monastic vows, in their asceticism, in their worship, and in their beliefs. It must suffice here to refer to the very admirable lecture on St. Columba, in the Evangelical Succession Series, by the Rev. James Calder Macphail—a very sympathetic sketch of the man and his work, with a discriminating view of its imperfections and faults.

We have referred to the lack of material for a full history of this great movement. Notwithstanding this lack two things are very plain; in the first place, that the weapon wielded by the preachers was the great message of grace, the story of redeeming love, proclaimed alike by lip and by life; and in the second place, that the fruit of this proclamation was one of the most remarkable spiritual transformations that ever brightened the face of a country. We will not anticipate what we have yet to make good. But we believe it will appear that in no subsequent era of pulpit power in Scotland has the weapon essentially changed; nor will any period of our past history afford much encouragement to those who think that the evangelical weapon has now lost its edge, and that its proper place is among the querns and stone hatchets of a bygone age.

Note A.

St. Columba's Miracles.

Adamnan's *Life of St. Columba* is not properly a biography, but a kind of *éloge* in three parts :—I. Of his prophetic revelations ; II. Of his miraculous powers ; III. Of the visions of angels. As Adamnan wrote within a century of Columba, it is remarkable that supernatural legends should by that time have grown to so remarkable profusion. Some writers have questioned Adamnan's authorship of the treatise, among whom was Sir David Dalrymple (Lord Hailes). Dr. Reeves rather sneers at this, as if Sir David had done it for purposes of ecclesiastical controversy. Dr. Skene ascribes the prevailing belief in Columba's supernatural powers to three peculiarities :—1. His sonorous voice, of which Dallan Forgaill says—

> "The sound of his voice, Columcille's,
> Great its sweetness above every company ;
> To the end of fifteen hundred paces—
> Vast courses—it was clear."

Adamnan says it was miraculous. It did not seem louder than an ordinary voice, yet persons more than a mile away heard it distinctly. 2. Skill in interpreting signs of the weather. He watched with great care the indications of change in those parts, and was able to promise to his companion Baithene a south wind in the morning to enable him to reach Tiree, and to Columban a north wind, at the third hour of the same day, to carry him to Ireland. 3. Sagacity in forecasting probable events, and keen insight into character and motives. "How tales handed down of the exercise of such qualities should by degrees come to hold as proofs of miraculous and prophetic power it is not difficult to understand." To these explanations of Dr. Skene's it may be added that Columba was a man of prayer, and in deep sympathy with God, whose Word was his constant study, and of whose promises of help and guidance he must, like all likeminded men, have had frequent and striking experience. Further, there can be no doubt that in their preaching these early evangelists would dwell much on our Lord's miracles and prophecies. The supernatural in the great Master would be constantly presented to the people, and the opinion may have crept in that the servants of a Master who did such wonders must possess somewhat of His power. So far from these legends throwing doubt on the reality of the Gospel miracles, they ought to have the opposite effect. It was because the great Founder of Christianity was so manifestly, so gloriously supernatural, that the same quality came to be claimed for those of His servants who in other things resembled Him most. If there be not such a thing as genuine money, there will be no counterfeit money. If the Lord Jesus Christ had not stood out before the world as the Divine Son of God, if the evidence of this had not been overwhelming, and if the effect of it on men's minds had not been very powerful, there would have been no temptation to think that a measure of the same power must have fallen to all His most honoured servants.

NOTE B.

CULDEE BISHOPS.

The question of Culdee bishops is a singular one, and at some points the discussion becomes almost ludicrous. It has often been asked, How came it that Columba himself was not a bishop, but only a presbyter? To this it is answered that Etchen, Bishop of Clonfad, meant to make him a bishop, but by mistake conferred on him the order of a priest. There is a double wonder here; how should he not have been a priest before it was proposed to make him a bishop? And how should so ludicrous a mistake ever have occurred, or, if it did occur, how should it not have been rectified? "The monasteries of the Irish Church," says Stokes, "were always ruled by abbots, who were sometimes bishops, but most usually presbyters. . . . If not bishops, the abbots kept a bishop on the premises for the purpose of conferring holy orders." The notion is ludicrous—a bishop "kept" by an inferior ecclesiastic, "on the premises," like a carpenter or a messenger, to be at hand when needed for his job. Surely if a bishop is anything he is a supreme ruler, and not a servant of presbyters. Besides this, it appears to have been considered in the power of a single bishop to confer consecration. When Etchen made his blunder about Columba, there was no other bishop with him to confer the episcopal office. This, it is said, was valid, but not regular. The truth is, it does not seem possible to develop either one or other of our existing forms of church-government out of the Celtic practice. In the quality of simplicity, and in the absence of monarchical bishops, it had undoubted affinities to Presbytery. In the position of the abbot there was an approach to Episcopacy. High Churchism is utterly baffled in trying to find authority for its hierarchical notions; modern Presbyterianism is more at home, but finds it very hard to digest the abbot. The clear and very important lesson from the Culdee church-government is that it was not of Roman origin; it was the government of a church which went back to an earlier period, and bore clear marks of independence of Rome.

CHAPTER III.

I⊤ is not easy to ascertain the precise duration of what may be called the enthusiastic period of the Columban church. It would have been contrary to all experience for a community to remain age after age at the pitch of spirituality and fervour which marked it in Columba's time. It is instructive to remark that the decline of the church in missionary zeal ran parallel to its decline in character and influence, and likewise in independence. About a century after Columba, Adamnan, his biographer, and one of his successors, strove hard, but as yet in vain, to induce his brethren to adopt the Roman time for observing Easter. But it was in this way that the policy was introduced of substituting Roman for British practices which ended in the extinction of the Culdee Church. It was not till about the end of the twelfth century, and under the influence of King David I., that the work of demolition was completed. "Thus," as Dr. Skene has said, "the old Celtic Church came to an end, leaving no vestiges behind it, save here and there the roofless walls of what had been a church, and the numerous old burying-grounds to the use of which the people still cling with tenacity, and where occasionally an ancient Celtic cross tells of its former state. All else has disappeared; and the only records we have of their history are the names of the saints by whom they were founded, preserved in old calendars, the fountains near the old churches bearing

.their name, the village fairs of immemorial antiquity held
on their day, and here and there a few lay families holding
a small portion of land, as hereditary custodiers of the
pastoral staff or other relic of the reputed founder of the
church, with some small remains of its jurisdiction."[1]

During the long period of more than three centuries,
from the extinction of the Culdee Church to the Reformation, we find scarcely a trace of Christian preaching in
Scotland worthy of the name. That a dim tradition of a
lost spiritual paradise would linger in the scenes where
Columba and his successors had scattered such blessings,
with profound veneration for the men who had seemed to
live the life of heaven upon earth, and perhaps some relics
of that spirit of independence which they had fostered, we
may well believe; but no remnant of spiritual life
remained as a seed of future revival; no slain witness
rose from the dead or ascended into heaven; no phœnix
sprang from the ashes of its parent bird. The Scottish
church, now thoroughly Romanised, set herself with
determined malignity to resist that doctrine of salvation
by grace, which, under Columba and his brethren, had
filled the country with joy and peace. If poor Lollards
appeared in Kyle, delighting in the Scriptures and its
message of grace, or if a Paul Craw came from Bohemia
to testify what had refreshed the souls of many of his
countrymen, the stake and the fagot were quickly applied
to silence their testimony. When Adam Reid of Bars-
kimming was summoned before the King and the Archbishop of Glasgow, in 1494, to answer for heretical
opinions, he inveighed bravely against the bishops and the
church for " utterly forgetting the charge that Jesus Christ,
the Son of God, gave to His apostles, which was to preach
His evangell, and not to play the proud prelattis, which
all the rabble of you do this day."[2]

---

[1] *Celtic Scotland*, vol. ii. p. 417.   [2] Knox's *Hist.*, i. 12.

That preaching was a lost art on the part of the bishops and secular clergy before the Reformation, and was practised only by some of the friars, is abundantly proved by witnesses without number. In the poems of Sir David Lindsay of the Mount there is no more frequent reproach than that the clergy could not preach.

> " Great pleesure were to hear one bishop preech,
>   One dean, or doctor in divinity ;
>   One abbot who could well his convent teach
>   One person flowing in philosophy ;
>   I tyne my time to wish what will not be ;
>   Were not the preeching of the begging friars
>   Tynt were the faith among the seculars."

In the ordinary histories of the Reformation, we have found but two instances of attempts of bishops to preach, both of them sufficiently humiliating. Knox tells us that, in 1545, "when George Wishart began to offer God's word at Ayr, which was by many gladly received, Dunbar, Archbishop of Glasgow, by instigation of Cardinal Beaton, came to Ayr to mak resistance to the said Maister George, and did first occupy the kirk." Some of Wishart's friends wished to dispossess him, but to that he would not listen, but at the " Merkate Croce he made so notable a sermon, that the very enemies themselves were confounded. The bischope preeched to his jack-men, and to some old bosses of the town. The sum of all his sermon was, ' They say that we should preech ; why not ? Better late thrive than never thrive ; had us still for your bischop, and we will provide better for the next time.' This was the beginning and the end of the bischop's sermon, who with haist departed the town, but returned not agane to fulfill his promisse." [1]

Hardly less successful was John Hamilton, Archbishop of St. Andrews, in 1559. From *A Historie of the Estate of*

[1] Knox's *Hist.*, i. 166.

Scotland, printed in the *Miscellany* of the Wodrow
Society, we learn that when the Queen Regent was trying
to coerce the people of Edinburgh to restore the old
religion, the Archbishop of St. Andrews, on a day in
August, ascended the pulpit of the Abbey Church of
Holyrood, "and after he had vomited a little of his superstition, he declared that he had not been well exercised
in the profession [of preaching] : therefore desired the
auditors to hold him excused." [1] It is a remarkable fact
that two heads of the church, the Archbishops of Glasgow
and St. Andrews, should have earned so unquestionable
a title to be enrolled in the list of "stickit ministers."

There were even instances of prelates unable to get
through less difficult services.   Lindsay of Pitscottie tells
an amusing story of Andrew Forman, Bishop of Moray,
a very able man, who rendered signal service to the Pope
and to the King of France, when, with huge armies on
either side, they were on the eve of battle, by acting as
mediator, and preventing the bloody encounter.   The
Pope loaded him with honours, invited him to Rome, and
invested him with the dignity of legate ; in acknowledgment of which Forman gave a great entertainment to the
Pope and his cardinals ; but, being a poor Latin scholar,
when he began to say grace, he stuck at the word
Benedicito, expecting the guests to say Dominus; but as
they said Dans, he lost his composure and his temper,
and broke out in Scotch, "To the devil I give you all
false carles, in nomine patris, filii et spiritus sancti."
"Amen," quoth they. "Then the bishop and his men
leugh [laughed].   And the bishop showed the Pope the
manner, that he was not a good clerk, and his cardinals
had put him by his intendment [out of his intention] ;
and therefore he gave them all to the devil in good Scotch;
and then the Pope leugh among the rest." [2]

[1] *Miscell.* Wod. Soc., p. 67.   [2] Pitscottie, *Hist. of Scot.*, p. 166, 3d ed.

The only preachers, as we have said, were some of the begging friars, and their sermons, for the most part, were either on the miracles of the saints, or appeals for charity. Sometimes, however, a friar would go further; like William Arth, who at Dundee inveighed against the abuse of cursing, and reprobated the vicious lives of the bishops and clergy. He was required to repeat the sermon at St. Andrews. "His discourse of cursing" (says Knox) " was, that if it was rightly used, it was the most fearful thing upon the earth ; for it was the very separation of man from God ; but that it should not be used rashly and for every light cause, but only against open and incorrigible sinners. But now, said he, the avarice of priests and the ignorance of their office has caused it altogether to be vilipended ; for the priest whose office and duty is to pray for the people, stands up on Sunday and says, 'Ane has tynt a spurtill.' 'There is ane flaill stolen from them beyond the burn.' 'The goodwife of the other side of the gait has tynt a horn spoon.' 'God's malison and mine I give to them that knows of this gear and restores it not.'" [1]

Another preacher, Alexander Seton, a black friar, was accused of having said that "it behoved a bishop to be a preecher, or else he was but a dumb dog, and fed not the flock, but fed his own belly." In hot indignation, the Archbishop of St. Andrews confronted the friar with his words. With a sly touch of humour, Seton said that those who had ascribed these words to him were manifest liars. The bishop was charmed to hear this, and called for the knaves that had brought him the false tale. One after another maintained that they had heard the words, but Seton still affirmed they were liars. At last he gave his explanation. " My lord, ye may see and consider what ears these asses have, who cannot discern betwixt

[1] Knox's *History*, i. 38.

Paul, Isaiah, Zechariah and Malachi and Friar Alexander Seton. In very deed, my lord, I said that Paul says 'it behoveth a bishop to be a teacher.' Isaiah saith, that 'they that feed not the flock are dumb dogs.' And Zechariah saith, 'they are idle pastors.' I of my own head affirmed nothing, but declared what the Spirit of God had before pronounced, at whom my lord, if you be not offended, justly ye cannot be offended at me. And so yet again, my lord, I say that they are manifest liars that reported unto you that I said that ye and others that preech not are no bishops, but belly-gods." The bishop was greatly enraged, but as Seton was Confessor to King James V., and popular in the country, he was afraid to punish him at once. Knox says the grey friars were suborned to accuse him of heresy to the King, who would have been ready enough to go against one who dealt with him faithfully for his loose licentious life; but foreseeing trouble, Seton made his escape to Berwick, beyond the king's jurisdiction.[1]

Another sample of the preaching of the friars we find in connection with a well-known martyrdom which took place at Perth in 1543. A zealous friar, named Spence, was preaching on All-Hallow day, probably in St. John's church, and trying to prove that salvation could not be attained without the intercession of the saints. Robert Lamb, a merchant in Perth, one of his hearers, stood up, and holding out an English Bible, the reading of which had just been authorised by parliament, adjured the preacher to speak the truth from the Scriptures, otherwise that book would be a witness against him at the great day of the Lord." A great commotion arose, the women being much excited, and threatening Lamb with their vengeance for his disrespect to their beloved saints. The friar tried to proceed; a bailiff or policeman urged

[1] Knox's *History*, i. 48.

him to desist. " It must be fire and fagot," he said, " to daunton these heretics, not words." The bailiff's sister was so enraged that, unable to get close to Lamb, she flung her bunch of keys in his face, crying " false thief, false heretic." After all, Jenny Geddes was not the first woman to use that kind of argument. The conclusion of the story is horribly tragic. The cardinal and the clergy insisting on it, Lamb, with other four men, in spite of many remonstrances, were hanged outside the city walls, while Lamb's wife, for refusing to pray to the Virgin in childbed, as soon as the execution of the five was over, was taken to a pool at the side of the Tay, where, after she had committed her children to the charitable care of her neighbours, her infant was taken from her bosom, and she was drowned.[1]

But in truth there is no need for resorting to the testimony of disaffected persons to show how utterly the religious instruction of the people was neglected in Scotland at this time. In that very remarkable book which has lately been brought prominently into notice, *The Catechism of John Hamilton, Archbishop of St. Andrews,* 1552, we find most ample proof from the heads of the church herself, not only of the utter neglect of preaching, but of the prevalence of all the atrocious vices which have been charged on the Scottish ecclesiastics of the period. We refer to the edition of Hamilton's Catechism recently published under the able editorship of Mr. Law, of the Signet Library, Edinburgh, with a preface by the Right Hon. W. E. Gladstone. Hamilton was an illegitimate son of the Earl of Arran. He is often called by Protestant writers the " bastard bishop." In 1547 he succeeded Cardinal Beaton as Archbishop of St. Andrews, and was appointed papal legate. At one time he had leant to the cause of the Reformers, who appear to have expected him to join

[1] R. Scott Fittis's *Ecclesiastical Annals of Perth,* pp. 61, 62.

them; but holding by the old ship, he did as others have done—borrowed a leaf from the book of his opponents, and tried to throw life into his church by introducing some of their methods. In particular, alarmed at the popularity of Protestant preaching, he sought to provide for the people regular and sound religious instruction. But it would have been vain to call on the ordinary clergy to begin to preach to the people. The catechism was provided, much as the book of Homilies in the Reformed Church of England, to furnish material for popular instruction. It is a remarkable catechism in many ways. As Mr. Gladstone points out, the name of the Pope does not once occur in it. It is more biblical than we should have expected, as if it had been skilfully constructed to produce the impression that after all the food provided by the church did not differ much from that of the Reformers. That it might be popular it was prepared in the Scotch dialect, and the clergy were to read it consecutively, half an hour every Sunday and holiday. But here was a difficulty. Many of the clergy were miserable readers, and there was great fear of their so stammering in the attempt as to make the performance ridiculous. Accordingly they were enjoined to read it frequently in private, so as to become quite familiar with it; and in public they were to read it audibly, intelligently, and reverently; to articulate the words distinctly, to attend to the punctuation, and learn to impress the minds of their hearers by the animation of their voice and gesture, and by the fervour of their spirit. After all, these men of the old church were wise in their generation. But there was no time to apply their remedy, for the triumph of the Reformation was much nearer than they had imagined.

In other countries where the Church of Rome ruled, preaching had not sunk to so low an ebb. In England

and in France the pulpit had not been so neglected as it
had been in Scotland.   If, therefore, a pulpit was to arise
that would lay its strong hand on the mass of the people,
and powerfully influence not only individual and family
life but the political life of the nation, we should have
looked to one or other of these countries to produce it,
rather than to Scotland.   Nor did other things seem
favourable to a pulpit in Scotland.   The lowland Scots
are not naturally a fluent race.   The Irish Scots who
accompanied Columba had doubtless far greater facility
of expression than the men of the Reformation, nearly a
thousand years later.   Before the Reformation, the art of
public speaking seems to have received in Scotland no
vestige of attention.   We have been able to discover
hardly any memorable speech either from the bar, the
bench, the pulpit, the platform, or in parliament.   In
fact, for a striking specimen of early Scottish eloquence,
we must go back to the days of the Roman invasion.   It
is a notable circumstance, that out of the forty-six short
sections which Tacitus gives to the life of his father-in-law
Agricola, three are occupied with a report of the speech
which Calgacus (or Galgacus) delivered to the thirty
thousand Scots confederates who were drawn up on the
flanks of the Grampians to meet Agricola; and other two
with the speech of Agricola to his troops on the same
occasion.   Whatever we may think of the accuracy of
Tacitus' report, it is evident that the speech must have
been a memorable one, and made a great impression both
on his father-in-law and himself.   Notable it has proved
for many a succeeding age; for two of our best-known
Latin aphorisms, " omne ignotum pro magnifico," and "ubi
solitudinem faciunt, pacem appellant," are attributed by
Tacitus to this eloquent Scots soldier.   One should like to
know what these aphorisms are in the pure Celtic in
which the warrior spoke them.

The traces of eloquence to be found in our old Scottish histories and chronicles are few and far between. The speeches recorded are more frequently those of foreigners. Sir David Dalrymple, in his *Annals of Scotland*,[1] on the authority of Aldred (*De bello standardi*), gives part of a very eloquent speech, which he believes to be genuine, delivered by Robert de Bruce, an emissary of Stephen, king of England, to King David I. of Scotland, when their armies were facing each other on Northallerton Moor. The point of his eloquence was, the outrages committed by the Scottish army. In Fordun's *Chronicles of the Scottish Nation*, we have a very eloquent Eloge or Lament on King David I., by Baldred, Abbot of Rivaulx.[2] The fact of its being inserted at full length in the dry, bare chronicle of Fordun, shows the estimation in which it was held. In Hume's *History of the House of Douglas*, we find a powerful speech attributed to Archibald, fifth Earl of Angus, in connection with the advice and offer which gained for him the title of " Bell-the-cat." The extreme rarity of memorable speeches in Scottish annals shows that the nation was little gifted with eloquence. Individuals with strong natural gifts of speech will be found in any community, and appeared in Scotland, no doubt, from time to time ; all that we allege is, that before the Reformation they were very rare.

The dialect of English commonly used in Scotland about the time of the Reformation did not present any serious obstacle to pulpit eloquence. It was both a rich and an expressive dialect. Though it had not yet been much used in prose literature, it had found ample employment in the memorable writings of the Scottish poets of the fifteenth and sixteenth centuries. One fact, however, was against it—no translation of the Scriptures into the Scottish dialect was ever made. Tyndale's translation

[1] Vol. i. pp. 85, 86.　　　[2] Book v. ch. xxxv.-xlix.

was the version in common use, and it seems to have been much read, for in 1543, under the regency of Arran, who was not unfriendly to the Reformed cause, the Parliament of Scotland passed an Act authorising the reading of the Scriptures in the English tongue. This want of a Scotch version of the Bible was a great cause of the Scotch dialect passing into disuse in literature, although the tenacity with which in spite of this it held its ground in conversation for many generations attests its remarkable adaptation to the taste and needs of the people. It was also true of the Scottish dialect that it was capable of being easily transformed into the current English. We have a memorable instance of this in the case of John Knox himself. Knox did not write in Scotch, and, as far as we know, he did not preach in Scotch. One hardly expects to find him reproached by a Roman Catholic correspondent with having forgot the " auld plane Scottis whilk his mother lernit him," and with having introduced a " southeron " dialect which this opponent affected not to understand.[1] We are apt to think of Knox as surpassing all men in rugged diction as well as in rugged acts, and it is amazing to find his contemporaries taunting him with an anglified style. The truth, however, is, that Knox was both a learned and a cultivated man, familiar with Latin, English, French, and perhaps Italian, and that his long residence in England and the Continent enabled him to contribute considerable refinement in some points to the national life. There is a correctness, a simplicity, and a power in the style of his more careful writings far beyond the level of his age, and rendering them not wholly unfit to be compared with some of our best classics. One of his contemporaries who made much more use than he did of the Scotch vernacular was Robert Rollock, first teacher and first Principal of the University of Edinburgh. The

[1] See Law's Introduction to Abp. Hamilton's *Catechism*, viii. ix.

man whose office linked him to the literary culture of the day spoke broad Scotch in the pulpit ; the man whom many have regarded as the greatest savage of his age used the dialect of Latimer, Cranmer, and Queen Elizabeth.

There is yet another preliminary point to be brought out before we come to the pulpit set up at the Scottish Reformation. What was the moral and religious condition of Scotland previous to that event ? What kind of soil was it into which the preachers of the Reformation had to cast the seed of the word ? There are abundant materials for answering this question. Both church and state were steeped in corruption. Notwithstanding the air of chivalry thrown over King James v. in the *Lady of the Lake*, his character was scandalous, and his moral influence atrocious. With regard to the bishops and clergy, Sir David Lindsay's poems abound with the most odious pictures.[1] But, indeed, they made no secret of their wicked lives, and in no respect did the bishops show greater activity than in trying to obtain lucrative berths for their bastard sons, and high marriages for their daughters.[2] Dean Stanley, the last man to exaggerate wickedness, speaks of "the hideous and disproportionate corruption which took possession of the Scottish hierarchy during the last two centuries of its existence."[3] The proverb "like priest like people" was abundantly verified, especially in connection with the seventh Commandment ; and there came a relaxation of the law of purity from which in some parts of the country we have never recovered.

Whatever hospitality and kindness may have been dispensed by the monasteries, the clergy generally were greedy and exacting. The poor man of Ayr in the Satire

---

[1] See *Ane Satyre of the Three Estaits*, etc., *passim.*
[2] See David Laing's Notes on Knox's *Hist.*, i. 41.
[3] *Lectures on the History of the Church of Scotland*, p. 40.

of the Three Estates tells how, with a horse and three cows, he had contrived to sustain his frail old father and mother as well as his own family ; but when his father died, the laird seized the horse for rent, and the vicar one of the cows for corpse dues; when his mother died, the vicar took a second cow, and when, through sheer vexation, his wife followed, the third cow, with all the old people's clothes, was taken for her. A set of men called " pardoners " went through the country, like Tetzel in Germany, retailing indulgences for money. Profane swearing was fearfully prevalent. " One-half the conversation," says Mr. Chalmers, " both in England and in Scotland, was made up of swearing." In Lindsay's Satire there occur no fewer than forty-three forms of oaths with which ordinary conversation is intermixed.[1] The most sacred names, the most sacred objects, the most sacred aspects of the very work of Christ seem to be purposely chosen to garnish the most frivolous remarks. " By the rood ; " " by Him that wore the croun of thorn ; " " by Him that herryit hell ; " " by the mass ; " " by the sacrament "—are samples of a habit that showed how utterly the people had lost regard for sacred things. If the clergy were openly immoral, and the people profane, what hope was there of a revival of good preaching by the one, or of earnest, sympathetic listening by the other ?

Besides all this, Scotland had long enjoyed an unholy reputation for alleged traffic with the Evil One. Sorcery, witchcraft, and kindred superstitions had obtained such a footing on the soil that among our French neighbours our country was known as " la résidence favorite du Diable." [2]

On a more public stage the perpetual feuds and bloody encounters of the great nobles and their retainers,

[1] Laing's Edit. of *Lindsay's Poems*, ii. 299.   [2] Michel, i. 2.

that had desolated the country during the reigns of all
the Jameses, had generated a spirit unfavourable alike to
law and gospel, to secular industry and to spiritual life.
Hereditary enmities that after a time of bloody strife
went to sleep through sheer exhaustion, but awoke again
with new bitterness from the remembrance of the past ;
passions that took fire like tinder and shrank from no
deed of ferocious violence; rough words and rough deeds,
provoking irritable tempers that hurled them back with
interest on those from whom they came—such things
had little in common with the spirit of the Gospel, and
furnished little ground for the expectation that it would
have a favourable reception in Scotland.

And yet it sometimes happens, and it happened in
Scotland, that in a demoralised community, the message
of grace, when it falls fresh and bright on unaccustomed
ears, has a wonderful success.   For sin and misery go
together, and to sinners, guilty, helpless, and miserable,
the news of a free salvation has a marvellous attraction.
There is no community too sunk for the divine message
of the Gospel to raise it up.   But preaching that will
attract such a community must have in it a new element
of hope.   No mere turning round of an old kaleidoscope,
no mere burnishing up of a faded hope will give the
electric thrill.   The truth must come fresh as the morning star, sparkling with the dew of heaven.

But even then, whatever success the Gospel may have,
the old condition of the community will have an unfavourable influence in two ways.   In the first place,
"old Adam" will be very prone to show himself, even
where the new life has been implanted.   And in the
second place, the demolition of the old notion of salvation
by works will leave those who do not come under the
gospel of grace, without any moral force to move them.
When they find that good works do not save, but fail to

accept salvation by grace, they fall between two stools, and have nothing to hold them up. In the judgment of fair and intelligent men, therefore, it will be no proof that the preaching of the Reformers was a failure if much of the old ruggedness and wickedness remained even in leading men, and if a considerable section of the people, released from the restraints of the Romish Church, but not influenced by the spiritual forces of the Reformed, were as far from God and from goodness as before.

First among those who lifted up his voice in Scotland as a preacher of the cross was young Patrick Hamilton (A.D. 1504-1528), a youth of high connections and of royal lineage, and as gentle and amiable as he was high born.[1] In early boyhood he had studied at the University of Paris, where Erasmus and Budæus, breaking the fetters of mediævalism, had just opened for scholars new realms for research and mental enjoyment. His intellectual emancipation prepared the way for the spiritual, and though he had heard the unfavourable verdict of the Sorbonne doctors on the views of Luther, he had read with a glow of delight the splendid defence of Melanchthon against "the furibund decrees of the Parisian theologasters." Afterwards he had turned his steps to Wittenberg; had supped with Luther and his new married wife in the Augustinian cloister; had heard his hymns sung in loud chorus by fervent congregations; and had been charmed by his eloquence from the pulpit in the church of the Elector's castle. Thereafter at Marburg he had met with Tyndale and Frith; had heard the truth expounded with rare felicity by Lambert; and now he compiled a little treatise—the only one that has come down to us—under the name of *Patrick's Places*. So valuable was this treatise counted by Knox

[1] *See* Knox's *History;* Foxe's *Book of Martyrs; Precursors of Knox*, I. Patrick Hamilton. By Rev. Professor Lorimer, 1857.

that he gives it at full length in his History, as does also
John Foxe in his *Acts and Monuments.* With singular
clearness the key-note of the Reformation, " By grace are
ye saved," is sounded in *Patrick's Places,* yet with an
earnest desire to guard against Antinomian abuses.   And
now, his heart being full, he thinks of dear Scotland, and
dear Kingscavel, his family home, and he burns with the
desire to lead his friends and countrymen to the fountain
where he has drunk his fill.   In 1527, in his twenty-
third year, he returns; and first at Kingscavel, and then
in the neighbouring parishes, he proclaims the way to
heaven—salvation by grace.   Never did the silver trumpet sound more sweetly or more richly ; and as it fell on
the ears of men who had never heard it before, it was
at once recognised as the trumpet of heaven.   Knox
says, "The bright beams of the true light which by God's
grace was planted in his heart began most abundantly
to burst forth as well in public as in secret."   And
Spottiswood says, " Many gave ear to his preaching, and
he had a great following, both for his learning and
courteous behaviour to all sorts of people." [1]   Young,
graceful, gentle, and accomplished, he seemed the very
ideal of an ambassador of Christ.   Hamilton made a
wonderful impression.

But a message from the Archbishop summoned him to
St. Andrews.   A decree had gone forth against him, and
daring though it was to make a victim of one so popular
and so highly connected, the Church thought herself
strong enough to risk the step.   We have no time to
notice the shameful trial which ended in his being condemned to the flames.   Neither can we dwell on the
awful tragedy, the long agony but triumphant faith of the
young martyr in the flames, the six hours it took to con-
sume his body, and his gracious bearing while conscious-

---

[1] *History of the Church of Scotland,* i. 124.

ness lasted.   His murder was a great crime and a great
blunder in one.   Scotland sympathised with the gentle
youth so foully done to death at the age of twenty-four,
and whose life had been as pure as that of his murderers
was vile.   Curiosity was excited to know what he had
taught, and what were the contents of the little pocket
volume, the four Gospels, which he had handed to one of
his friends with solemn care.   His death gave a powerful
impulse to the cause of the Gospel, which now spread,
quietly but very successfully, throughout the country,
but especially among many of the gentry, and the middle
or trading class who were now rising to wealth and
power.

It was not till fifteen years after the martyrdom of
Hamilton, in 1528, that the voice of the next great
preacher was heard.   In many respects, George Wishart
bore a close resemblance to Hamilton.   Of gentle birth,
of remarkable scholarship—going beyond the lines of our
universities—and pre-eminent for all the gentle virtues,
for charity, humility, generosity and godliness, " Master
George of Bennett's," as he was called at Cambridge,
stood unrivalled.   At first his steadfastness to the new
faith seems to have wavered, but only for a time ; and
when he returned from Switzerland, and from intercourse
with the Reformers there, no man had clearer views or
higher courage.   First at Montrose, then at Dundee,
afterwards in Ayrshire and other places, and finally at
Haddington, he at once roused and satisfied the souls of
the people.   The pivot of his preaching, like Hamilton's,
was God's way of life for sinners, through the sole work
of Jesus Christ.   A pupil of Calvin's, he had learned the
value of expository preaching, and at Dundee he expounded the Epistle to the Romans.   Of the character of
his preaching we get a most vivid picture in Knox's
History, when he came to Mauchline in Ayrshire, and was

excluded by the sheriff from the parish church. Some of the people were for forcing an entrance, and among them Hew Campbell laird of Kingzeancleuch, but the gentle Wishart "withdrew the said Hew and said unto him, Brother, Christ Jesus is as powerful in the fields as in the kirk, and I find that He Himself oftener preached in the desert, at the seaside, and other places judged profane, than He did in the temple of Jerusalem. And so, withdrawing the whole people, he came to a dyke in the moor edge, on the south-west side of Mauchline, upon which he ascended. The whole multitude stood and sat about him; (God gave the day pleesing and hot). He continued in preeching more than three hours." What a scene it must have been! The preacher standing for three hours on a dike, declaring the message of divine love and grace, with a thirsty multitude round him drinking in every word from his lips! We need not ask who the preachers are on whom his mantle has fallen. "In that sermon," says Knox, " God wrought so wonderfully with him that one of the most wicked men in that country, Laurence Ranckin, laird of Scheill, was converted. The tears ran from his eyes in such abundance that all men marvelled. His conversion was without hypocrisie, for his life and conversation witnessed it in all time to come." [1]

The tragedy was repeated at St. Andrews; the stake was erected again, and another Archbishop Beaton, nephew of the former, the well-known cardinal, gloated on the ghastly scene. It was again a bold crime, but again the perpetrators outwitted themselves. Wishart's views were too widely spread and too firmly established to be suppressed by fire. The chief result of this murder was to substitute John Knox for George Wishart, as the man of light and leading for the country. Not a few nobles were now in favour of the reformed views, con-

[1] *History of the Reformation*, i. 128.

verted before any thought of sharing the spoils of the Church could have flitted across their minds. Scholars like George Buchanan, men of culture like Sir David Lyndsay, lawyers like Henry Balnaves, were ardent supporters of the cause. If the life of Wishart had been spared, if he had been able to take the part of leader of the Reformation, it is quite likely that we should have had a gentler type of religion than that with which Knox became identified. But Wishart might have been unable to cope with the difficulties of the situation. Wishart was to Knox as Stephen had been to Paul. In both cases the martyr's mantle fell on one of broader shoulders and robuster build. The shocking death of the earlier witnesses turned out rather for the furtherance of the Gospel.

It is specially to be noticed that both Hamilton[1] and Wishart were laymen. The fact was sometimes used against them as an argument for suppressing their heretical ravings. Their preaching was the result of no academic or ecclesiastical training, but of a fermentation of the Word of God in their hearts which propelled it outwards like jets of water from Geyser springs. What the subordinate features of their eloquence were, we do not know, and we need not inquire ; its essential feature was just what it had been in the days of the Columban Church,—the glad news of a free and full salvation, devised by the Father, executed by the Son, and applied by the Holy Ghost. And the secret of its popularity was, that it was food for starving men : it was the answer to the question, What must I do to be saved ? it was the way to peace and rest, to God and to heaven.

[1] Though Hamilton was titular abbot of the Abbey of Fearn in Ross-shire, he had no ecclesiastical training, and notwithstanding a statement of Frith to the contrary, he was not in orders. It has lately come out that he was married shortly before his martyrdom. (See Lorimer's *Patrick Hamilton*, p. 123.)

The connection of John Knox with Wishart is very interesting. It began apparently but a few weeks before Wishart's martyrdom. Longniddry House, in East Lothian, the residence of Hew Douglas, to whose sons Knox acted as tutor, was one of the friendly homes where Wishart had found a welcome. Though Knox was now turned forty, their meeting was like that of David and Jonathan, the soul of Knox was knit with the soul of Wishart, and he loved him as his own soul. Though his study of Augustine and other fathers had already taught Knox much of the doctrines of grace, it seems to have been through Wishart's preaching that the spark came that kindled his knowledge into a living flame. Knox loved and honoured him as his spiritual father; accompanied him in his tour in East Lothian, carrying a two-handed sword to defend him, and would have been with him when he was apprehended at the House of Ormiston, had not Wishart insisted on his going back to Longniddry, because one was enough for a sacrifice. It were a scene for a painter's brush to delineate—after the tidings reached Knox of Wishart's brutal murder, but of his triumphant bearing in the flames at St. Andrews—Knox, gazing from the windows of Longniddry House, or from some neighbouring height, across the Firth of Forth and over the East Neuk of Fife,—trying to fix the course by which the martyr's spirit had risen in its chariot of fire and smoke to the palace of the King, and wondering where a man would be found to wear the martyr's mantle. In those days even strong men were obliged to repress their indignation, however vehement and righteous it might be; but the impulse derived from the death of Wishart must have worked inwards and remained in Knox unspent to his dying day.

Knox, so far as we know his early history, was an exception to the rule that the child is father of the man.

Neither his childhood nor his early manhood gave any foreshadow of the part he was destined to play in the history of his country. Born of respectable parents in or near the quiet town of Haddington; educated at the University of Glasgow, an ardent student and a successful teacher, especially in logic and philosophy; attached, it is thought, for a time to some monastery or another, but leaving it to be a domestic tutor in the house of a country laird, and continuing there till he was upwards of forty: he seemed of all men least likely to be a great preacher or a great reformer. That he possessed any preaching gift seems to have been unsuspected alike by himself and his friends. After the murder of Cardinal Beaton, he had taken refuge with his pupils for safety at St. Andrews, and while there it was his practice to teach them a catechism in the parish church, and to give them a Bible lesson in the chapel of the castle. It was his admirable method of opening up the Scriptures to these young men that led to his being called, and when unwilling pressed, to become a Protestant preacher. The book of Scripture which he opened up to his pupils was the Gospel of St. John, a proof that at that time it was the more contemplative and spiritual portions of the Word that formed his favourite food. It is worthy of remark that as Knox began his ministry at St. Andrews, so he virtually closed it in the same place. Shortly before his death, owing to the disturbed state of Edinburgh, he removed for a time to St. Andrews, and again he opened up a book of Scripture, but on this occasion it was the stirring Book of Daniel that formed the subject of his lectures. In the interval, he had swung round from the contemplative student to the vehement warrior. But all the time he retained his fondness for the method of consecutive exposition of a book of Scripture in the pulpit. If he got the hint of this from Wishart, it agreed well with

his own idea. At Geneva his conviction of the excellence
of the practice had doubtless been greatly confirmed by
Calvin's unrivalled expositions. We find here probably
the genesis of that method of biblical exposition or lecturing which has always been one of the characteristic
features of the Scottish pulpit, and which has proved the
means of imparting to our countrymen a knowledge of
their Bibles probably unsurpassed in any other people.

   The first sermon that Knox preached bore on the notes
or marks of the true Church; it was an answer to Dean
Annand, and from the account of it given by Knox in his
History, it must have been a remarkable specimen of bold
statement and fearless accusation. For a short time he
continued to preach with much acceptance and great
success. At the end of the siege of St. Andrews in
1547, he was treacherously consigned to the French
galleys, where he seems to have been as barbarously
treated as the Huguenots often were, perhaps chained day
and night to the bench, in consequence of which he con-
tracted a severe illness. On his release in 1549 he was
appointed by the Privy Council of England preacher in
the town of Berwick, and in 1550 he was removed to
Newcastle. In 1551 he was appointed one of the six
chaplains of Edward vi., a striking testimony to his high
character and his preaching gifts. This led to occasional
residence in London, and intercourse with the court in
1552 and 1553. Though virtually at this time a member
of the Church of England, he declined promotion in it, but
only owing to its want of discipline, and though offered
the living of Allhallows, London, and also the bishopric
of Rochester, he preferred to remain simply a preacher.
On the accession of Mary to the throne in 1553, Knox
had to seek refuge on the Continent. In 1554, he received
a call from the English congregation at Frankfort, which
he accepted. Resigning that charge next year in conse-

quence of disputes about the English prayer-book, he seems for a short time to have ministered to the English congregation at Geneva. He paid a short visit to Scotland in 1555, and spent the winter there preaching in private. After another residence abroad of about three years, he returned finally to Scotland, in 1559, was elected minister of Edinburgh, and continued in that office till his death, in 1572. His ministry thus divides into four parts; first, for a few months in St. Andrews; thereafter for about four years in England; then about six years chiefly on the Continent; and finally, about thirteen years in Edinburgh.

What was the sum and substance of Knox's preaching? Some would give a very short answer to this question— furious ravings against the Church of Rome, and bitter denunciations of the rulers of the country, when they did not favour his schemes. It is easy to show that such a notion is simply out of the question. Unfortunately, we do not possess any collection of Knox's sermons. The only sermon ever printed with his sanction was one delivered on a public occasion when his words had been misrepresented. Such sermons as are particularly referred to in his History were sermons on public events of a similar character. But we have ample materials for determining the kernel of his ordinary message, the truths which most of all he sought to press home on the hearts of his hearers. Among the considerations bearing on this question are the following :—

1. Knox was the spiritual successor of Hamilton and Wishart, of whose message no one could mistake the tenor; they were evangelists, if ever men were. It was their mantle that Knox took up. It was their converts he had to carry forward, men and women whose souls, hungering for the bread of life, had been guided to the green pastures and still waters of the Word. How could Knox have been

so prized by them if he had not possessed great skill and great fervour as a preacher of the gospel of salvation ?

2. Knox's official writings, and especially his confession of faith and his liturgy, show that the evangelical doctrines were the very heart and kernel of his system. If the confession shows what he believed, the prayers show how he felt. In particular, they bear evidence of a very profound sense of sin. The order for public worship begins with an explicit "Confession of Sin," moulded on the ninth chapter of Daniel; and it contains likewise a very full and cordial acknowledgment of the rich grace of Jesus Christ; as in the very striking prayer at the communion table : "We present ourselves at this His table (which He has left to be used in remembrance of His death until His coming again), to declare and witness before the world that by Him alone we have received liberty and life ; that by Him alone dost Thou acknowledge us Thy children and heirs; that by Him alone we have entrance unto the throne of Thy grace ; that by Him alone we are possessed in our spiritual kingdom to eat and drink at His table; with whom we have our conversation presently in heaven, and by whom our bodies shall be raised up again from the dust, and shall be placed with Him in that endless joy, which Thou, O Father of mercy, hast prepared for thine elect, before the foundation of the world was laid. And these most inestimable blessings we acknowledge and confess to have received of Thy free mercy and grace, by Thy only beloved Son, Jesus Christ, for the which, therefore, we, Thy congregation, moved by Thy Holy Spirit, render Thee all thanks, glory, and praise for ever and ever."

3. In some of his pastoral letters, and especially those addressed to suffering and afflicted Churches, there is a very full and most tender exposition of the great saving truths to which he desired them to cling, and of the holy, blameless, undefiled condition of soul and body which he

implored them to maintain. Pre-eminent among these letters is that to his old congregation at Berwick, a copy of which is contained in the Morrice MSS. in Dr. Williams' library, London, which Professor Lorimer has given in the Appendix to his work entitled *John Knox and the Church of England* (London, 1875). It is in substance thoroughly scriptural and evangelical, and yet in tone most tender and pathetic;—the letter of one who apprehended that every conceivable trial would fall to the earthly lot of his beloved friends, and while rousing himself to set before them the glorious consolations on which they were to fall back, could never forget their heart-breaking sufferings, or fail to weep with them that wept.

4. With hardly less of tenderness and sympathy, the kindly soul of Knox is laid bare in his more private letters, and especially his letters to his mother-in-law, Mrs. Bowes. This lady, while eminently devout in spirit and most blameless in life, was afflicted with a most troublesome conscience; she was perpetually writing the bitterest things against herself; always dreading that she had drawn down on herself the wrath of God; and constantly driven, by every discovery of sin in her heart, to the conclusion that she was not a child of God. Knox shows himself amply acquainted with the way and working of the divine life in the human soul, and well able to meet her complaints. The free grace of God, the objective foundation it lays for the removal of guilt, he never ceases to bring forward; while he shows that the presence of sin in the heart is in itself no necessary sign of unregeneracy, and that sin bewailed, resisted, loathed, is rather a sign of grace. He is thoroughly alive to that high privilege of a Christian, conscious enjoyment of God's favour, and to the importance of ever trying to secure it. Sometimes he adverts modestly to his own spiritual condition. His conscience charges him with no

open violation of God's law; but he bewails an untold amount of weakness, coldness, unholy feeling both God-wards and manwards; yet he knew how to bring all to the fountain of sin and uncleanness, so that he, even he, could sing the hundred and third psalm. It was of such things that Knox used to preach at Berwick and New-castle, at Frankfort and Geneva, before he had anything to do with the politics and politicians of his native country; and no doubt they were the staple of his preaching at Edinburgh too.

5. The high reputation which Knox had among his brethren for personal holiness is another index to the character of his preaching. He was ever looked up to as a spiritual father, and numberless were the letters he received thanking him for help from those whom he had found in the fearful pit and the miry clay. The impression which he made on his brethren is thus expressed by one of his contemporaries:—"a man of God, the light of Scotland, the comfort of the Church, the mirror of godli-ness, and pattern and example to all true ministers in purity of life, soundness of doctrine, and boldness in re-proving of wickedness."[1]

It in no degree invalidates the force of these considera-tions that the most odious charges of immorality were circulated against Knox after his death. While he lived, no one breathed any such accusation against him. If any reader deems it worth while to examine the value of these charges, he will do well to read M'Crie's remarks upon them, in his Life, and likewise an article entitled "The Last days of Knox" in the *Catholic Presbyterian* for October 1880, written by Professor Mitchell, D.D., of St. Andrews, than whom no living man possesses a more thorough knowledge of the time.

But this is far from all that has to be said about

[1] Bannatyne's *Journal.*

Knox's preaching.   In those days, every man's preaching was coloured by the attitude he held to the Church of Rome.   For he had not only to deal with souls needing light and guidance, but with an all-powerful corporation, striving to retain them in its bonds, and breathing out threatenings and slaughter against all who tried to break them.   Of this corporation, this Church of Rome, Knox entertained deliberately the worst opinion.   As it was soon after the martyrdom of Wishart that he first publicly expressed that opinion, so it is likely that the atrocious murder of God's noblest servant and his own dearest friend went far to form it.   The Church of Rome was antichrist, and it was engaged as really as any of the confederates of the second psalm in plots against the Lord and against His Anointed.   No man had a stronger belief than Knox in the personality of the devil.   Satan was the unseen head of that army, the unseen director of all its cruel machinations against the truth and all its friends.   If he had this conviction at the beginning of his public life, it was not allowed to pass away by what happened as his life advanced.   He knew well of the deeds of the bloody Mary and her bishops, Gardiner and Bonner.   He knew the infamous and horrible atrocities perpetrated in the Low Countries under Philip and Alva. He knew what oceans of blood had been shed in France, and the very last year of his life was the year of the massacre of St. Bartholomew.   The cry of the persecuted Vaudois had pierced his heart; he knew of the deeds of blood and iron in Spain, in Italy, in Austria.   All this burned into him the invincible conviction that on the soil of rugged Scotland he was called to maintain mortal conflict with the Prince of Darkness.   Knox's fight in Scotland was like that of Michael the Archangel contending with the devil for the body of Moses.   This led him to set down every man who was against him as of

the devil's party; and more especially, when one who had
embraced the truth either went back altogether, or gave
any countenance to Romish worship, the indignation
and distress of Knox knew no bounds. It was backsliding
of the most serious and dangerous character; it was a
fearful peril to the soul; it intercepted the divine favour,
it prepared for the guilty party the judgments of an
offended God.

The degree of force brought into play by such convictions in a vehement nature like Knox's is beyond calcu-
lation. But this view accounts for the extraordinary
energy and persistency which he brought to the work,
and for much of that ruggedness of speech and of action
with which, both in the pulpit and out of it, he carried it
on. It made the culture of the gentler virtues all but
impossible; but it added all the more to the force and
vehemence of the movement. The power of assault and
invective of which he was master was fearful. It is not
in his *Blast of the Trumpet against the monstrous regiment of women* that we find his faculty of denunciation
in full force. That is a comparatively calm and tem-
perate treatise; full of quotations from Tertullian,
Ambrose, Augustine, Chrysostom, and other orthodox
authorities, and not unlike what some Conservative politician of our time might say in opposition to female
suffrage. But if we wish to see Knox's indignation at a
white heat, and to know what burning torrents of scathing denunciation he could pour out on those whom he
held to be the prime agents of the devil, and the mortal
enemies of his country, we should read his *Admonition
to the professors of God's Truth in England*,[1] written from
the Continent on the eve of Queen Mary's marriage with
Philip of Spain, and when the Bishops of Winchester and

[1] *Works*, vol. iii. p. 250.   See especially the apostrophe to
Gardiner, p. 298.

London were raging against the Protestants. It must be owned to be a very intemperate letter, much more fitted to damage than to help the cause of Christ. But it is full of eloquence, and when the writer turns from scathing the persecutor to comfort the believing sufferer, his words are not wanting in tender and gracious consolation.

While this habit of Knox's gave immense decision to his will and force to his words, it contributed to Scottish preaching certain elements which have often reappeared in the history of our pulpit. Identifying fidelity to Christ with one side of a public controversy, and treachery to Christ with the other, it tended to make evangelical preaching controversial, to foster a way of judging of men's spiritual state according to the side they took, and to introduce an element of bitterness, and a spirit of denunciation very detrimental to the purity and beauty of religion. Probably there is no country where the religious life of the people has had to be maintained in connection with so much ecclesiastical controversy as Scotland. It has been a necessity of our country, and it were very unjust to blame our fathers for contending earnestly, as they believed they were called to do, for the faith once delivered to the saints. But it is not less a fact that this necessity communicated a certain hotness and roughness to the religious life of Scotland, the consequence of which is, that as compared with some other communities of Christians, those of Scotland have been deficient in the gentler virtues—in forbearance, good temper, patience, charity. It is often thought that the possession of these passive virtues cannot be found without a feminine softness which takes away the bone and sinew from the character; but surely the combination of the active and the passive virtues may be found in Christ's Church, when it was found so remarkably in Christ himself; and the union of strength and gentle-

ness, both in the pulpit and out of it, is one of those
things which, if we cannot attain to at once, we should
at least strive after very earnestly.

A word may be added as to the character of the oratorical gifts shown by Knox in the pulpit. The common
impression on this subject is derived from a description
in James Melville's Diary, who used to hear Knox preach
at St. Andrews in the feebleness of his last days. The
hand of death was already on him ; when he returned to
Edinburgh his voice could not fill St. Giles's Church, and
a smaller one had to be fitted up for him. " In the opening up of his text he was moderate the space of an half
hour ; but when he entered to application, he made me
so to grew and tremble, that I could not hold a pen to
write. He was very weak. I saw him every day of his
doctrine (teaching) go hulie and fear, with a furring of
marticks about his neck, a staff in the ane hand, and good,
godly Richard Ballenden, his servant, holding up the other
oxter, from the abbey to the parish kirk, and by the said
Richard and another servant lifted up to the pulpit,
where he behoved to lean on his first entry ; but ere he
had done with his sermon he was so active and vigorous,
that he was like to ding the pulpit in blads, and fly out
of it." The well-known picture of Sir David Wilkie
gives us a similar impression of physical excitement.

But observe, this physical vehemence was only in the
application. It shows, however, how Knox kindled with
his subject, and how much of physical warmth he brought
to bear on his delivery. If we ask what were his great
oratorical gifts, the answer seems to be, a power of plain,
direct, pithy utterance, a useful faculty of iteration and
amplification, and great fervour of emotion, the fruit of intensely strong conviction. He was a prophet of the Lord,
inspired like all true prophets and all great preachers
with his message, which worked like a burning fire in his

bosom, so that he could not forbear. He had no special gift of imagination, no special faculty of illustration. Apart from his impassioned nature, he would have been but an ordinary preacher. As it was, the work done by him in the pulpit has never been surpassed. Apart from the spiritual results in individual souls, its bearing on the nation was unprecedented. As Froude has said, he created a nation, while he reformed a church. Speaking of Scotland before Knox, Thomas Carlyle says : " Scotland is a country without a soul; nothing developed in it but what is rude, external, semi-animal. And now at the Reformation, the internal life is kindled, as it were, under the ribs of this outward, material death. . . . This that Knox did for his nation we may really call a resurrection as from death. It was not a smooth business; but it was welcome surely, and cheap at that price, had it been far rougher. On the whole, cheap at any price, as life is. The people began to live ; they needed first of all to do that, at what cost and costs soever."

But even the personal influence of Knox was not limited to his age. For three centuries his name has been a name to conjure by. It has sent a thrill through the veins of numberless Scotchmen to be reminded that their country was the country of Knox. It has never helped to make any man a sneak or a hypocrite. It has stimulated manhood, courage, perseverance. Coupled with other names with which it readily associates, it has nourished the spirit of independence and brightened the fire of patriotism. And all this it has done under shadow of the Gospel of the grace of God. Nor has this influence been confined to his native land. In every country of the Reformation there have been men whose hearts have beat with higher hope, and whose sinews have knit themselves to higher effort, as they thought what by John Knox God did for Scotland.

E

CHAPTER IV.

THE SUCCESSORS OF KNOX.

THE pulpit of Scotland did not want for able and eminent preachers during the generation that followed the death of Knox. However some of them might differ from the Reformer in their dealing with public interests, they resembled him strongly in their attachment to Bible truth, and in striving to make the great message of grace the leading power in the lives of their hearers. Had it been otherwise, had no powerful voices been heard in Scotland repeating the proclamation which had sounded out first from Patrick Hamilton, then from George Wishart, and now, when the Reformed Church was triumphant, from its great champion and founder, evangelical truth might have either died away, or lost its distinctive character. But the great preachers of the next generation were strong enough men to have impressed the community, even if no Knox had been before them. As it was, following one who made such a mark, and giving forth the same truths stamped with their own image and superscription, they contributed to impart a character of permanence to evangelical preaching, to make it as it were racy of the soil, and to give an exotic and unnatural character to preaching on other lines. Now as before, the great ordinary theme of the pulpit continued to be the normal relation of sinful man to the holy God; how it was broken in Adam and restored in Christ; and in what way the new life of trust and obedience and all other Christian graces was to be begun and carried forward. Now also as before, the preacher would sometimes turn to the public life of the nation. He maintained his right to criticise and rebuke wherever he saw the civil ruler forgetting the authority of God, and acting in the affairs of the Church in opposition to the tenor of His word.

But a change is to be remarked in the aspect of public affairs from about the death of Knox. Knox's Edinburgh ministry embraced the whole period of the reign of Mary; even at the time of his death, imprisoned though Mary was, the efforts of her friends to restore her had made no small disturbance. The great danger to the Church and to the country had come at that time from the Church of Rome. The great fear was that through political intrigue, at the court of France and elsewhere, the cause of the Reformed Church might yet be overthrown. The most characteristic feature of the Church of Rome was the mass, which Knox believed to be rank idolatry, and fitted to draw down the judgment of God; and the great battle with Queen Mary had been whether she was to be allowed to celebrate this "abomination" within the realm of Scotland. It had been the object of the Reformers to rouse an intense public opinion against the mass, and against the whole Romish system as culminating therein. When poor Mary was out of the way, and the country had a Protestant king, the danger from that quarter was comparatively over. The peril to the Church now arose from projects of civil rulers interfering with her government and her freedom. The attempt of the Regent Morton to set up tulchan Episcopacy, followed by that of King James to place Episcopacy on a more permanent footing, occupied the Church for many a year. It was this policy, and the interference it was held to involve with the supremacy of the Lord Jesus Christ as the only Head of the Church, that was denounced, when public events were touched on from the pulpit.

But it does not appear that it was a usual practice to preach on political events. On days of public fasting, or at the opening of Synods or Assemblies, it was almost inevitable to give forth a note of warning to the offending rulers, or of encouragement to the resisting people. On ordinary occasions the subjects preached on were much the same as now. Lecturing on the Old Testament gave more frequent opportunities of a lesson by the way to weak-kneed rulers, as in the case of Robert Bruce's lectures on the sickness of Hezekiah. But the main effect of the ecclesiastical policy of King James on the pulpit was to direct the attention of the preacher more earnestly to the royal supremacy of Jesus Christ; to bring prominently into view the glorious person of the Saviour, seated on the throne of the Universe, far above all principality and power; and to claim for Him the highest homage, alike of rulers and of ruled.

Another important feature of this age bearing indirectly on the pulpit was the deep interest manifested in the cause of learning. It was the age of academic revival and enthusiasm. It was just two years after the death of Knox when Andrew Melville, who at the Universities of St. Andrews, Paris, and Poictiers, and at the Academy of Geneva, had become one of the most learned men of his age, came to Glasgow as Principal of the University. Six years after, he was transferred to St. Andrews, the University which was regarded by the Reformed Church as the most important in the country. The coming back of Melville was the occasion of a wonderful revival of academic life and reform of academic work. And Melville threw his heart likewise into the affairs of the Church, and was indeed the most conspicuous advocate of her liberties in the age that followed that of Knox. Lawson, who succeeded Knox as minister of Edinburgh, was also an academic man; he had been Sub-

Principal of the University of Aberdeen; he was the means of reviving the High School, and of inducing the Town Council to found the University of Edinburgh. Robert Rollock, one of the most powerful and useful preachers of his day, was first regent, first principal, and first professor of divinity in the new University. George Buchanan, who was now Principal of St. Leonard's College, St. Andrews, had been in his day imprisoned for heresy, had filled the Moderator's chair in 1567, and was closely and cordially identified with the Reformed Church. In fact, the Church of Scotland at this period was in more cordial alliance with the academy than it has ever been since, except perhaps in the days of Principal Robertson. Our great academic men did not stop short like Erasmus, did not content themselves with having secured the emancipation of learning from its mediæval fetters, and did not look coldly on the zeal and enthusiasm of the evangelical pulpit. From the academy the pulpit derived the benefit of all the culture of the age. But this connection in no degree impaired the distinctive message of the pulpit. There was no tendency to infuse into it the spirit of rationalism. The claim of Christianity as a specific and independent revelation was maintained in all its integrity; the pulpit acknowledged neither Jew nor Greek, circumcision nor uncircumcision, bond nor free; but Christ was all, and in all.

It will be proper now to notice briefly some of the most conspicuous preachers of the time immediately after the death of Knox.

For some years Knox had had for his colleague a minister with a remarkable history, of much decision of character, and considerable gifts—JOHN CRAIG. Craig had been a Dominican friar, had been suspected of heresy in Scotland, had gone abroad and entered a Dominican monastery at Bologna, where, chancing to

find in the library of the Inquisition a copy of Calvin's
Institutes, he was so impressed by it that he became a
Protestant. Escaping from the monastery, he became
tutor in the family of a Protestant nobleman in Italy;
but being arrested and tried for heresy, he was condemned to be burned, and escaped only through the con-
nivance of a soldier, to whom he had once done a
kindness. After many remarkable adventures, he reached
Scotland about the time when the Reformation had
triumphed. Long residence abroad had caused him to
forget his native tongue, and unable at first to use it in
the pulpit, he preached in Latin in the Magdalene Chapel
of Edinburgh. Afterwards he became minister of the
Canongate, and thereafter he was appointed colleague to
John Knox. His entire sympathy with evangelical truth
is apparent from the Catechism, still well known, entitled
*A Shorte Summe of the whole Catechisme, wherein the
Question is proponed and answered in few wordes, for the
greater ease of the commoune people and children.*[1] His
intrepidity of spirit was shown by his objecting to proclaim the banns of marriage between Queen Mary and
Lord Bothwell; and though, on the removal of one of his
scruples, he did make the proclamation, it was not without a protest, all the more creditable to him because the
influence of Bothwell in the city was then very great.
Shortly before Knox's death he gave umbrage to the congregation, and by mutual consent he left Edinburgh. In
1580, King James, then fourteen years of age, chose him
for his minister, greatly to the joy of the church. He
retained this office till his death in 1600, and seems
to have been well worthy of the designation of Row,[2] " a
famous and worthy servant of Jesus Christ."

[1] A facsimile of the rare first edition, in 1581, was printed in 1883,
with a biographical introduction by Mr. Law, of the Signet Library.
[2] Row's *Hist. of the Kirk of Scotland*, p. 457.

In 1572, when Knox was near his end, he proposed as his successor, JAMES LAWSON, one of his own spiritual sons, then Sub-Principal at Aberdeen. Lawson had been a fellow-student of Andrew Melville's at St. Mary's College, St. Andrews, and his distinction as a scholar appears at this day from a red line under his name in the books of the college, believed by the late Principal Lee to have been made by Andrew Melville himself. It was at the admission of Lawson to the High Church that Knox made his last appearance in the pulpit. Lawson was then thirty-two years of age; he died in London only twelve years after, having been driven from his country on account of his opposition to prelacy. If any should think that it must have been a Boanerges that Knox desired as his successor, no mistake could be greater. Lawson seems to have been quite remarkable for the tender pathos of his spirit. James Melville calls him " a man of singular learning, zeal, and eloquence, whom I never heard preach but he melted my heart with tears." In another place he calls him " a godly, learned man, of a wonderful moving utterance in doctrine, whom I delighted meikle to hear, and whom I never heard but with tears both of remorse and joy." Yet his intellectual powers and attainments were very high. " For gifts and estimation," says James Melville, " he was chief among the ministry." Professor Johnston, a contemporary, calls him in his Latin eloge :—

" Ingenio felix Lawsonius, ore diserto,
    Acer judicio, consiliisque gravis.
  Corpore non magno, mens ingens : spiritus ardens
    Invictumque decus pectoris atque animi."

In his *History of the University of Edinburgh*, Sir Alexander Grant says of him that he was " a man of culture and experience, as well as piety and earnestness."

It is to Lawson, as we have said, that both the High
School and the University owed their existence. First, he
pressed on the Town Council, and with success, to erect
a new building for the High School. Next, he and
others urged them to take steps for the institution of a
University. After some delay, a royal charter was
obtained in 1582, and in 1583, under Robert Rollock,
the work of the College began. Rollock, who was then
a regent at St. Andrews, twenty-eight years of age, was
well known to Lawson, and it was the thorough confidence that Lawson had in him, as a suitable man, that
induced the Town Council to offer him the appointment.

Lawson was a zealous Presbyterian, and opposed
strongly the schemes for Episcopacy. When the "Black
Acts" of the Parliament of 1584 were proclaimed at the
Market Cross of Edinburgh, Lawson, with two other
ministers, in face of an order by the magistrates to drag
from the pulpit any minister who should say a word
against them, went boldly and made a solemn protest.
Lord Arran threatened that he would make Lawson's head
to leap from his neck though it were as thick as a haystack.
Alive to his danger, he escaped to London, but falling
into a sickness, aggravated by a mean paper against him
issued by some of his people, he died there in the same
year at the age of forty-four. "As he lived most godly
and sincerely in the whole course of his life," says one
who was with him at the last, "speaking to edification,
far from all slanderous or vain and idle words (as none
with whom he ever had his conversation, yea, nor the
enemies of Christ and His Gospel which are without, can
be able to lay to his charge the contrary), so gave he an
evident proof that the true fear of God was deeply seated
in his heart." So full was his heart of the message of the
Gospel, that when he came to London he was disappointed that he got no opportunity to preach it; but

for the thirty-four days of his sickness, his deathbed became a pulpit, and by his words many were won to Christ, and many others confirmed in the truth. Before his death he asked his friends to sing the 103d psalm; "and when voice could not serve, his lips were observed pronouncing the words as they were sung."[1]

In the absence of any published discourses, these notices show clearly what manner of man it was that Knox desired as his successor, and what manner of preachers they were that moulded the Church of the Reformation.

Not unlike to her husband is the portrait that James Melville draws of Janet Guthrie, his wife. "For her rare and most sweet gifts of knowledge, devotion, tender and most zealous love towards God, His servants, and all that loved the Lord Jesus Christ, I cannot of duty and conscience but make mention of her, as a happy memorial to posterity . . . As ever person in that estate, she kythed [showed] the fruits of true Christianity not only at that time, but all the days of her life to her death, living as a true widow of such a husband, in fasting, prayer, meditation, and exercise of the works of mercy and love, instructing the ignorant, sweetly admonishing offenders, comforting the afflicted, visiting the sick and diseased in body or mind, and persevering in prayer with them unto the end; so that her refreshment and recreation was to take pains in these exercises. Thus she lived in Edinburgh seven or eight years after our return, a remarkable mirror of godly widowhood, and died with as great missing of the godly in all degrees, especially the poor, as any woman that I ever knew."[2]

Both Knox and Lawson had been connected with St.

---

[1] *Account of the Death and Funeral of Mr. James Lowson*, Miscel. Wod. Soc. i. 449.

[2] *Autobiography and Diary of James Melville*, pp. 219, 220.

Andrews, and so also were the next brace of preachers of whom we have to speak—ROBERT ROLLOCK and ROBERT BRUCE. For St. Andrews, which had now Andrew Melville as Principal of the New College, was at that time and afterwards a great centre of warm evangelical influence. St. Andrews bred the men, and Edinburgh provided the pulpits. Rollock, who is best known as the first Principal of the College of Edinburgh, on which office he entered in 1583, was likewise a very eminent, powerful, and useful preacher. Besides instructing his students in the ordinary branches of knowledge, he took a particular interest in their religious training, assembling them all from week to week, and from some text of Scripture earnestly counselling them to follow the ways of holiness. In the divinity students, of whom he obtained charge at an early period, his interest was profound. " I can scarcely describe," says a contemporary biographer, "the assiduity, the watchfulness, the laboriousness, with which he set about training in divinity such of his former pupils as had applied their minds to the study of the sacred writings."

In a way somewhat strange, Rollock became one of the ministers of Edinburgh. It was the practice for many of the people to assemble early on Sunday mornings in one of the churches, called the New Church. How this came about we are not told ; all that we know is that the pious heart of Rollock was concerned to see them idle while they might be listening to the word of God. With great self-denying zeal he began to preach to them—the hour of service being seven in the morning—a thing that had never been done in Edinburgh before. Rollock seemed to have no other thought than that of occupying usefully a portion of time liable to be thrown away. But his brethren and fellow-citizens were so impressed with his gifts, and so full of admiration for the man, that they per-

suaded him to undertake the pastoral office; and at length
Rollock gave his consent. His preaching was attended
with a remarkable degree of spiritual power and impres-
siveness, and the most learned and cultivated class were
as much impressed as the ignorant. Their minds were
illuminated as with a heavenly light, and their feelings
wonderfully stirred up—the result of the clear and
practical way in which the preacher presented the truth,
and of the deep sympathetic action of his own heart,
moved by the Spirit of God, in unison with the truths
which he proclaimed.

The late Dr. W. M. Gunn, editor of the edition of
Rollock's works published by the Wodrow Society, draws
a pleasant picture of one of these morning services in the
New Church, where Rollock preached. We have space
only for the substance of it. Let us in imagination
transport ourselves to the New Church on some Sabbath
morning in 1596. It is the early hour of seven. We
enter with a great company of worthy burgesses and
students, and not a few of the barons and judges of the
land. Though only in his forty-second year, he is
already worn out with labour, but he preaches with great
fervour and eloquence. The sermon is on regeneration,
of which he gives a faithful exposition in the Scottish
dialect, concluding with a very earnest exhortation to
parents to strive, as they have been the instruments of
the generation, so to be the instruments of the regeneration of their children.

Rollock was to Knox somewhat as Melanchthon was to
Luther. The one full of fire and vehemence, the other
equally in earnest, but more mild and gentle. The one
emphatically a warrior, the other emphatically a pastor.
In the public conflicts with the King, Rollock was thought
by his brethren to have shown a temper too yielding and
accommodating. It is instructive to remark how men so

unlike in temperament as Knox and Rollock should have
been so devoted to the same work.   But just as we see
the power of their common Master arrresting and con-
trolling men so unlike in temperament as Peter and Paul,
James and John, so in this common enthusiasm of
Wishart and Knox, Robert Rollock and Andrew Melville,
for the evangelical message, we have evidence of the
unseen power that inspired them, one and all.

The opinion which James Melville had of Rollock was
not altogether favourable : "a good, godly, learned man,
but fellon [extremely] simple and pusillanimous, so that
he was easily carried with counsel."   This was said with
reference to some concessions which Rollock had wished
to be made to the King, in the contests about the church.
Nevertheless, in an elegiacal sonnet on his death (which
event took place in 1598-9, in his forty-third year),
Melville very emphatically commends him, and shows the
place which Jesus Christ held, alike in his life and in his
preaching.

> " On Christ thy heart was wholly set and stayed,
>   Of Christ thou ever thought, thou spake, and wryte ;
>   With Christ thou wished all thy works arrayed,
>   In Christ, in life and death, was thy delight."

Rollock's style of preaching was very plain, earnest,
and lively, addressed straight to his hearers, and thoroughly
adapted to the average capacity.   It may be interesting
to quote at random a few of his expressions showing the
peculiar pith with which religious truth could be put in
the Scottish dialect.   Discoursing on 2 Cor. v. and on
the efficacy of the blood of Christ applied by faith to
the soul, he says, " Albeit it was ane sinful soul, yet as
soon as the Father blinks upon it, wompled and wrapped
up as it were in the blood of Jesus, immediately He bids
it pass to glory."   The power of grace in regeneration is

such that " sa lang as thou livis heir, (fra the time thou
has gotten ane spunk thereof,) piece and piece it eatis up
the auld cankerit nature." To Christians too eager about
their earthly good, he says, "either sall thou be ruggit
[torn] fra it, or it shall be ruggit fra thee." True faith
must be fruitful, and that too in secular life ; " if I see
not gude deidis in thy awin calling, all thy wordis is but
wind." Speaking of a gross sinner as a child of perdition he says, " I will never count of him but as a mad,
tint, lost bodie." St. Paul, casting down imaginations
and every high thing, is " the fechter of ane strange battel,
the warriour of the Lord Jesus Christ, to win prisoners to
Him, to tak Kings and Princes by the lug, and lead them
to Christ." When the soul is indulging in imaginations
" she is sitting in her castle building her rampart, and
casting her fosses around her, and snaring herself in her
ain net. And let thee be, thou misters [needest] not ane
other to trap thee, thou wilt trap thyself, pride thee in
thy ingyne as mickle as thou will ; gif thou has nae mair,
wae is thee ; it shell fetter thee and tak thee in the girne
as sickerlie as ever thou saw ane bird fangit in the net
of the fowler." The familiar dialect, the current turn of
expression, as well as the intrinsic power of the old
Scottish dialect, lent additional force to the message thus
conveyed, and sent it closer home to the business and
bosoms of high and low.

In 1587, four years after Rollock came to Edinburgh,
there began to be heard the voice of another young
preacher, who like Rollock was the son of a Stirling-
shire laird, and an alumnus of St. Andrews. Robert
Bruce, second son of Bruce of Airth, one of the
ancient Barons of Scotland, and a connection of the royal
Bruces, born in 1559, was one of the very ablest men,
one of the greatest leaders, and one of the most successful preachers of his time. He had been designed for the

profession of the law, the position of his family being
so high that he could aspire to the office of a Lord of
Session, but such was the intensity of his spiritual experience, and of his conviction that he was called to
serve Christ, that renouncing all other projects he gave
himself up to the ministry of the Gospel. To do this
involved a great social sacrifice. In telling of his experience to James Melville, he said, that at first he
resisted what looked like a call to the ministry, but
such was the torment of his conscience that rather than
endure the same again, he would go through a fire of
brimstone, half a mile long. One awful night at Airth
in 1581, it pleased God to smite his conscience and
place all his sins before him, so that not a circumstance
of time, place, or expression was omitted. He heard the
devil accusing him audibly, not always truly, but whatever he did say that was true found an echo in his
conscience, so that he was pressed down as it were to
the lowest hell. " Always, so far as he spoke true, I
confessed, restored God to His glory, and cried God's
mercy for the merits of Christ ; yea I appealed even to His
mercy, purchased to me by the blood, death, and passion
of Christ. This court of justice holden upon my soul, it
turned of the bottomless mercy of God to a court of
mercy to me ; for that same night, or ever the day
dawned, or ever the sun rose, He restrained these
furies and these outcries of my just accusing conscience,
and enabled me to rise in the morning." [1]

Bruce could refrain no longer. He spoke to his father
about going to St. Andrews and studying for the ministry,
and after much difficulty he at last got his assent. When
we find that his preliminary experience was of this
profound character, indicating at once the depth of his
nature, and how it was penetrated by grace to its

[1] *Life and Works of Robert Bruce* (Wodrow Society), p. 8.

inmost core, we need not wonder that his ministry became one of remarkable power. And it should never be forgotten that it was men of this type, men who themselves were profoundly exercised by the truth, and who preached what had been burned into their very souls, that moved the heart of Scotland, and raised up so many confessors and martyrs among her sons.

So early as 1585, when he had been but two years at St. Andrews, Bruce was dealt with by James Melville to become the successor of Mr. Lawson in Edinburgh, who had died the year before. We can hardly conceive a stronger testimony to the splendid ability and mature Christian character of the man, than that, when only half his divinity studies were over, he should have been deemed by so sagacious a man as Melville qualified for the highest charge in the Church where Knox and Lawson had done their work. As a student he had shown wonderful gifts and great activity in explaining Scripture; opening up book by book, now with his companions at their meals, now in gatherings of students, and now in the morning service on the Lord's day.[1]

In 1587 he came up to the General Assembly, and was with difficulty persuaded to preach in Edinburgh. Soon after, the Council and people of Edinburgh applied to get him as their minister. He was very unwilling, his earnest desire was to be settled in some quiet place, but the pressure was too great, and a sort of compromise was effected by which he continued to preach, although not ordained. In the spring of 1587-8 an extraordinary Assembly being called in consequence of the invasion of the Spanish Armada, he was chosen moderator, probably the only probationer, and the only man under thirty, that ever held that office. He was again moderator in 1592.

For eight or ten years he was in high favour with the

[1] Melville's *Diary*, p. 148.

King, to whom he proved himself of great service by advice and assistance in troublous times. When the King went to Norway for his wife, and the Romish party, taking advantage of his absence, were stirring up feuds and commotions, Bruce was eminently useful in maintaining the peace of the community, for which service he obtained the King's cordial thanks in many letters from his Majesty. Afterwards, in the closing year of the sixteenth century, he fell under the King's displeasure, because, with several of his brethren, he was unable to do all that James required, in exposing the Gowrie conspirators. The truth is, that the faithfulness of Bruce in opposing the King's schemes for the restoration of Episcopacy, and in urging on him his duty to God, had offended him, and he was eager to get quit of him.

Bruce, after being confined in the castle, was banished from Edinburgh, and never allowed to return. Before this an income which had been given him from the revenues of the Abbey of Arbroath had been meanly taken from him and given to a nobleman. His life was spent now in this place, now in that, till at last, in his old age, he was allowed to reside on his paternal estate of Kinnaird, in the parish of Larbert, where, as there was no settled minister, he did the duties of that country charge. His death took place at an advanced age in 1631. Bruce of Kinnaird, the celebrated African traveller, was his lineal descendant. It is of Robert Bruce that the touching story is told that when he was dying, and felt the light fading, in order that he might die literally grasping God's word, he asked his daughter to turn up for him the eighth chapter of the Romans, and lay his finger on the last two verses: " I am persuaded that neither death nor life . . . shall be able to separate us from the love of God which is in Christ Jesus, our Lord."

It is distressing to think that a man like James VI.

should have had the power, out of the most miserable motives, to spoil so noble a life. If, like Richard Baxter, Bruce did splendid work, banished and thwarted as he was, it was but the shadow of what, like Baxter, he might have accomplished, if he had enjoyed but the most ordinary encouragement for ministerial labour.

The testimonies of his contemporaries to his influence are most striking. Fleming, in his *Fulfilling of the Scripture*, says of him, " Whilst he was in the ministry at Edinburgh he shined as a great light through the whole land, the power and efficacy of the Spirit most sensibly accompanying the word that he preached. He was a terror to evil-doers, and the authority of God did so appear in him and in his carriage, with such a majesty in his countenance as forced fear and respect from the greatest in the land, even those who were avowed haters of godliness. Yea, it was known what awful impressions King James himself had of him, and once he gave that testimony before many that he judged Mr. Bruce was worth the half of his kingdom."[1]

John Livingstone says of him, " No man in his time spake with such evidence and power of the Spirit; no man had so many seals of conversion, yea, many of his hearers thought that no man since the apostles spoke with such power. He had a notable faculty of searching deep in the Scriptures, and of making the most dark mysteries most plain; but specially in dealing with every man's conscience. He had a very majestic countenance, and whatever he spake in public or private, yea, when he read the word, I thought it had such a force I never discerned in any other man."

Among his spiritual children was Alexander Henderson, who played so conspicuous a part in the future history of the Church. In his unconverted days, Henderson had

[1] Wodrow's *Life of Bruce*, p. 143 (Wod. Soc.).

F

been intruded into the parish of Leuchars, against the will of the people. Hearing that Bruce was to preach one day in his neighbourhood, curiosity led him to the church, but shame bade him conceal himself in the obscurest corner. There the arrow of conviction found him and pierced him to the quick, when Bruce gave out as his text, "He that entereth not by the door into the sheepfold, but climbeth up some other way, the same is a thief and a robber." Henderson left the church a new man in Christ Jesus.

Under his ministry the very scenes of his banishment often became like the garden of the Lord. In recently tracing from the Moderator's chair the rise and progress of the Reformation in the Highlands, Dr. Gustavus Aird, of the Free Church of Scotland, dwelt on the work of Bruce, while in banishment at Inverness, as quite marvellous in spiritual results. When setting out, he was observed to pause, while preparing to mount. "I was receiving my commission from my Master," said Bruce, "to go to Inverness, and I got it from Himself before I put my foot in the stirrup, and thither I go to sow a seed that shall not be rooted out for many ages." Multitudes of all ranks would come from great distances to hear him, even crossing arms of the sea; and the blessing of heaven was so great that a sensible impression was made on that whole district of the country.

The secret of Bruce's power is brought out in an incident narrated by Livingstone. "When he preached at Larbert, he used, after the first sermon, when he had taken some little refreshment, to retire to a chamber in a house near the kirk. I heard that one day, some noblemen being there, and they having far to ride home after the afternoon's sermon, desired the bellman to go hearken at the door if there were any appearance of his coming. The bellman returned and said: 'I think he shall not come out the day at all, for I hear him always saying to another that he will not nor cannot go unless that other go with him, and I do not hear the other answer him a word at all.' The foolish bellman understood not that he was dealing with God."

What then was the character of Mr. Bruce's preaching? We will not dwell on some features which it had in common with most of the preaching of the age, its close adherence to Scripture, the prominent place of the doctrines of grace, or the earnestness with which it pressed on Christians the prosecution of the walk and warfare of faith. In exposition it is often most luminous, as, for instance, in his sermons on the sacraments, of which he takes the view that they are aids to faith, and which he so commends and glorifies, that while we see how rich and full of blessing they are as means of grace, we find nothing ascribed to them of magical quality. His chief homiletical qualities may be expressed in two words— luminousness and liveliness. Whether he preached in Scotch or not, we do not know ; his sermons are published in English, with just a flavour of the old dialect. But one cannot but be struck with the excellence of the style. It is simple, idiomatic Saxon, racy of the soil. He is homely, sensible, Scriptural, his own soul charged with great Gospel truths which it is his obvious and earnest purpose to transfer to the hearts of others. No metaphysical distinctions, no elaborate arguments, no flights of fancy does he indulge in, but plain speaking on solemn truths which every man's conscience tells him concern him profoundly. Everything is genuine and earnest. We do not mean that in this style of preaching Bruce differed essentially from his contemporaries, but only that he attained greater excellence in it. For all through this period and long after, the style of popular and effective preaching was essentially the same. Plain, lucid, and

direct, it was the preaching of men whose very souls were
saturated with Scripture, and who poured out the fruits
of their meditations with an emotion and a force that
arrested and overpowered the souls of their hearers.

We have been so much with Edinburgh preachers in
this chapter that we seem to have forgotten that Edinburgh was not Scotland. We must indulge ourselves
with an excursion to the country, and find out what kind
of sound the trumpet is giving there. We select three
counties—Ayr, Fife, and Midlothian.

The minister of Ayr is a remarkable man. JOHN
WELCH was one of those men of intense devotion, who, if
he had lived in the early ages of Christianity, would undoubtedly have been reckoned among the greatest saints
of the Church. Yet nothing seemed less likely in his
boyhood and early youth. Born about the year 1570, at
his father's place, Colliston, in Nithsdale, Dumfriesshire,
he joined a band of border-robbers, and became familiar
with all the wild work of border warfare. But the pleasure of such a life was very shortlived. His clothes
reduced to rags and his conscience sorely troubled, he
arose and went to his father; not, however, to be welcomed
like the prodigal son, but to encounter frowns, threatenings, and reproaches. At length, the father was so far
softened by the intercession of a female relative and by
the tears of the boy, as to yield to his request, for Christ's
sake to give him one more chance, and send him to
college. The request was complied with, and ere long
Welch emerged, one of the holiest ministers the Christian
Church ever had.

At Selkirk and Kirkcudbright, his first charges, the
people were too wild to endure his holy teaching and
faithful reproofs. In the impetuosity of his new and
intense spiritual experience, he seems to have forgot that
the wisdom of the serpent was one of the things which

his Master commended to His servants. At Ayr he showed more tact, and had more success. Welch married a daughter of John Knox, and it is told of her that when on one occasion she waited on King James to ask that her banished husband might return to Scotland, the King asked about her, and she told him whose daughter she was. " Knox and Welch !" exclaimed the King, " the devil never made a match like that." A good deal of banter passed between them, the King at last saying that her husband might return if he would submit to the bishops. Mrs. Welch, lifting her apron and holding it up before the king, replied, " Please your Majesty, I'd rather kep his head there."

Like many others who have had a striking conversion, Welch was a man of intense spiritual conviction and burning emotion. We are apt to fancy, from his joining a border band, that his nature must have been rough and hard ; but that false step may have been taken in boyish thoughtlessness, or under the advice of some companion, and the horror of conscience which it bred shows that it was not congenial to him. In fact no man seems ever to have had a more susceptible and fervent temperament ; his heart was just a fountain of emotion, and when grace took possession of it, it gushed with tenderness, and poured itself out in the most fervent entreaties to men, and wrestling prayers on their behalf to God. At Ayr he preached every day, studied diligently, and spent a third part of his time in prayer. Often, when he first went there, bloody riots occurred in the streets : Welch would rush between the combatants, with a helmet on his head, but no sword, and entreat them in Christ's name to be reconciled. It was not easy to overcome the practice, but at last he succeeded, and Ayr became a peaceable habitation. In respect of spiritual fruit, he was highly successful. David Dickson, who was afterwards minister of Irvine, and who had great encouragement in his own ministry there, used to say that the gleaning of the grapes of Ayr in Welch's time was equal to the vintage of Irvine.

Welch was one of those ministers who, for holding an assembly at Aberdeen in 1605, in opposition to the wishes of the king, were first confined in Blackness Castle, and then sentenced to death, a sentence which was afterwards commuted to banishment. He went to France. It is said that in fourteen weeks he was able to preach in French, but that when he got very warm with his subject he was liable to go wrong; to prevent which he made an arrangement with some young men that they were to stand up when he became too excited. When Boyd of Trochrig was at Saumur, Welch preached before the University there, which he did with great self-composure; when Boyd asked him how he could be so bold, he replied that he was so filled with the dread of God that he had no fear of man at all. His physical courage seems not to have been less than his moral; for when the town of St. Jean d'Angely, where he was minister, was besieged, he distinguished himself by his bravery; a cannon-ball having once struck the bed where he lay, he would not leave the room till he had given thanks for his preservation. In an extreme moment of the siege, when he was carrying powder to serve a gun, a ball from the enemy carried both powder and ladle out of his hands, whereon the undaunted minister took off his hat, filled it with powder, and carried it to a gunner beside him, who discharged the gun with such precision that it dismounted the enemy's cannon. If he had the tenderness of a woman, he did not want the courage of a man.

A volume of thirty-five sermons preached at Ayr in 1605, a little before his imprisonment and banishment, has come down to us. They are altogether in the evan-

gelical vein, some of them on very solemn aspects of the
Gospel. They are simple and earnest expositions of
Bible truth, but, as in similar cases without number,
they seem to have owed their most impressive qualities
to the tone of profound emotion in which they were
delivered. The preacher cannot reach that tone of
earnestness in which he would fain preach. " O that the
Lord would fill my heart," he exclaims, " with this truth,
that I might eat it and drink it, and feed upon it continually, and that He would fill me with the spirit of
exhortation, that I might exhort you to meditate on this
truth both day and night, that the remembrance of that
Day (the day of judgment) might never go out of your
hearts ! O that you would do it, even for His sake, that
left you His heart's blood to slocken that fire that will
burn both the heavens and the earth ! O hear, hear !" [1]

One thing is to be specially noted ; he does not omit
the ethical department of preaching. We should hardly
have expected that in one of his sermons, from the text,
" When he came to his disciples he found them asleep,"
he should give a brief practical application of each of the
ten commandments. But he regards the neglect of these
as one of the temptations to sleep to which Christ's
servants are exposed, and therefore he urges them to
consider them. His idea of holiness is not merely the
performance of religious duties, or the enjoyment of
religious privileges, but embraces a minute regard to
every specific precept of the decalogue.[2]

In these sermons Welch does not make much reference to the church politics of the day. But he was far
from viewing them with indifference, or thinking that
they had no vital relation to the Gospel of Christ. He
opposed the royal measures with heart and soul. While

---

[1] *Sermons* (on Rev. xx. 11), p. 8.
[2] *Sermons* (on Matt. xxvi. 40), p. 167.

confined in Blackness Castle he wrote a most fervent
letter to the Countess of Wigton, full of rapturous
admiration and delight toward the Lord Jesus Christ,
and expresses himself eager for the scaffold, the axe, or
the cord, that would bring to him the most glorious hour
of his existence.   In the very heart of these outpourings
of enthusiastic love for Christ, he brings in the especial
cause of his imprisonment, which was that he maintained
Christ to be the head of the Church, and that the Church
was free in her government from all other jurisdiction
but His.[1]   And he speaks of this headship as if not to
maintain it were base and horrid apostasy, a shameful
degradation of his glorious Lord.   His view of these
contendings and sufferings is explained by his sense of
the infinite glory of Christ, and the obligations to Him
of the Church which He had redeemed.   Livingstone
says of his preaching that it was spiritual and searching,
his utterance tender and moving, and that no man could
well hear him without weeping, his delivery was so
affecting.   For gracious saintly influence the name of
Welch is to be coupled with those of Samuel Rutherfurd,
Richard Baxter, Robert Leighton, and Robert M'Cheyne.

Nor did his influence cease with himself.   His son,
Josiah Welch, was a most devoted and successful preacher
in Ireland, and his grandson, another John Welch, great-
grandson of John Knox, was one of the most memorable
of the field-preachers of Scotland in the days of the
Covenant; a preacher of wonderful power and popularity,
for whom, with a price on his head, Claverhouse and
others searched for many a year, but who, by a miracle
of vigilance, eluded all their efforts, and at last died on
his bed.

The Fifeshire minister, for whom we must find a
place in our picture, is DAVID FERGUSSON of Dunfermline.

[1] See *Select Biographies*, Wodrow Society, vol. i. p. 23.

Fergusson was not college-bred. He began life as a glover, but, fired with the Reformation spirit, went to school and came forth a powerful preacher. He was one of the earliest ministers of the Reformed Church, was Moderator of the Assembly oftener than once, and died in a good old age. He found Dunfermline a wild rough place, but left it greatly changed. He was of a type of character of whom the Scotch Church has produced not a few specimens, an earnest minister, and yet a great humorist. Dunfermline was a frequent resort of King James vi., and the King greatly enjoyed a chat with the amusing minister. When the house of the Master of Gray, who was reported an apostate, was shaken by an earthquake, the King asked him why that house alone should be shaken. "Sir," said the minister, "why should not the devil rock his ain bairn?" Another time the King asked him, "David, why may not I have bishops here in Scotland as well as in England?" He answered, says Rowe, "mirrilie (it was his way), 'Yes, sir, ye may have bishops here, but ye must remember to make us all equal; make us all bishops, or you will never content us; for if ye set up ten or twelve loons over honest men's heads to knock us down, and give them in rent more thousands than honest men has hundreds, we will never be content. We are Paul's bishops, Christ's bishops: hold us as we are.'"[1] A collection of Scotch proverbs was published by David Fergusson, which still holds its place in our literature.

Fergusson represents a class of ministers that have had no little effect on Scottish life, as Dean Ramsay's *Reminiscences* show; thoroughly devout and serious, and in their main ministrations impressing their people profoundly with the dread realities of sin and salvation; yet finding outlets in the intervals of serious talk for a play-

[1] Rowe's *History of Kirk of Scotland*, pp. 418, 419.

ful humour which relieved the strain of earnest feeling, and contributed in the end to the great effect. It is only when the example of such men has been followed by others, having a smack of their humour but none of their devoutness, that mischief has been done. According to Buckle, the earnest ministers of Scotland were a set of gloomy fanatics, in whose eyes all humour was a hideous sin, and who were never pleased unless men were miserable. When one finds Buckle committing himself to such a stupid statement, one does not wonder that he should have placed Spain and Scotland in the same category as the most degraded, priest-ridden countries of Europe.

JOHN DAVIDSON was minister of Prestonpans in East Lothian. He was remarkable for a combination of fervour and courage. When minister at Liberton he fearlessly, on the appointment of the Assembly, pronounced sentence of deposition in 1638 against the Archbishop of Glasgow. At one time he had been imprisoned by the Regent Morton; afterwards, when the Regent himself was under sentence of death, he sent for Davidson and begged him to forgive him, as he forgave him for what he had said against him. Davidson was moved to tears, being at once surprised and delighted to find that his old enemy was resting by faith on the same foundation as himself—the atoning work of Christ. Once and again, Davidson was in collision with the King, and on these occasions, as well as from the pulpit, he addressed his Majesty in a tone and manner which we cannot justify. His own brethren became frightened at his boldness, and it was deemed prudent to remove him from Edinburgh, where he had been minister, to Prestonpans. There he distinguished himself not only for his diligence and faithfulness, but also for his liberality in building, from his own resources, a manse and a school.

In 1595, the terror of Philip II. of Spain, which had subsided for a time after the destruction of his Armada, broke out anew. The Privy Council imposed a tax, and asked the aid of the General Assembly to gather it in. On the motion of Davidson, it was resolved that humiliation for sin was the first and the best preparation for the defence of the country against a hostile attack. Carrying out this resolution, but not opposing the request, the Assembly met, to the number of 400, and Davidson was the preacher. After reading the 13th and 34th chapters of Ezekiel, he called on them to compare themselves, "their learning, zeal, godliness, multitude, days, time, occasions, and helps, or rather wants with the prophets of former days, as in the two chapters read; and see how much greater privileges they had, and why among their multitude *pro ratâ* there might not be as many false prophets and as few true and sincere as were in these days." In application he was very effective, so that, as Calderwood says, "within an hour after they entered the kirk, they looked with another countenance than that wherewith they entered." And then as if the arrows of heaven had pierced every heart, the whole assembly was melted in sobs and tears; the scene was unprecedented, such as had never been witnessed since the Reformation. A sermon followed from Luke xii. 22 : " Take no thought for your life," " with rare assistance of God's Spirit ; " and such was the impression, that when the Moderator desired the brethren to hold up their hands to testify their entering into a new league with God, a forest of hands was extended, and only one man despised the proceeding.

Davidson was perhaps the rudest of all the ministers; yet the occurrence of this day showed him to be a man of immense spiritual power. And here we see the secret of the influence of the Scottish pulpit.

CHAPTER V.

IN entering on the Covenanting period of the history of the Scottish pulpit, it may be well to call to mind what the Covenants really were.

Many persons have the idea that they consisted of a fanatical protestation against "black prelacy," with a solemn vow, before Almighty God, by every available means to sweep every vestige of it from the soil of Scotland. But the truth is, that the National Covenant came into being long before prelacy became a burning question, or even a question at all in Scotland. The Covenant in its first shape and intention was simply a band or bond for securing the Protestant cause against the wiles of the Papists; as may be seen from a covenant sworn at Stirling in 1559 :—" We, foreseeing the craft and sleight of our adversaries, who try all ways to circumvene us, and by privy means intend to assault every one of us, particularly . . . *thereby to separate us one from another*, to our utter ruin and destruction,—for remedy thereof we faithfully and truly bind us,[1] etc." The " National Covenant," subscribed by the King and all classes in 1580, was directed simply against popery, and even when this Covenant was renewed at the great Presbyterian crisis of 1638, and subscribed in the Grey-

---

[1] Rev. D. C. A. Agnew, in *Catholic Presbyterian*, June 1881.

friars' Churchyard, in some instances with the blood of the subscribers, popery was still, as before, the object against which it was directed.

The Solemn League and Covenant of 1643 was a different document, and in it, undoubtedly, prelacy was joined to popery as the object of attack. In the course of time a change of policy was introduced in reference to the purpose of the Covenants. At first, they were voluntary engagements, into which like-minded men entered for the protection of their common cause against the efforts of their opponents,—efforts which were directed to separating them from one another and crushing them piecemeal; and in so far as this was their object, it was legitimate and praiseworthy. But ere long it became the policy to enforce the Solemn League and Covenant, to compel men to swear it, whether they approved of it or not; it became a test of office, and an instrument of coercion, so that not to take it exposed one to temporal loss, and still more to social ostracism. Out of this policy arose most serious evils. The spirit of intolerance was fostered, and the consciences of men were demoralised. And whereas the policy embodied in the Covenants at first embraced the three kingdoms, but soon became utterly hopeless in England and Ireland, the difficulties, anxieties, and complications that arose in Scotland were as trying to men's tempers as they were perplexing to their judgments. In the end of the day the result was, that popular though the Covenants had been, they were allowed at the Revolution settlement to pass without recognition; greatly to the mortification of the Cameronian party, who had fought for them through thick and thin, at a cost of substance and suffering which covered their struggle with glory; but rather to the relief of those who, while grateful for the way in which the Covenants had rallied the friends of the Gospel,

deprecated their use as instruments of coercion, and
mourned the evils which had arisen therefrom.

It needs not to be said that in some respects this
state of affairs had an unfavourable influence on the
pulpit.   More than ever, loyalty to Christ came to be
associated with adherence to a certain outward course—
to the policy of the Covenants ; and disloyalty to Christ
with opposition to that cause.   Adherence to the Covenant came to be regarded with some as equivalent to the
whole duty of man : if men were only strenuous Covenanters, it mattered little in other matters what manner
of spirit they were of.   Not that the truly godly and
enlightened men of the party propounded or approved
any such doctrine ; the best preachers, as we shall see,
took occasion to warn their hearers against it.   But as
human nature goes, a tendency in this direction arises
naturally when any outward form, whether of doctrine
or of practice, becomes a shibboleth, demanding the
allegiance of all the faithful.   Men clamour about testify-
ing for " principles " as if that were the end of religion,
forgetting that principles (*principia*) are but the begin-
nings, and that the true use of principles is to help on
a life and character resembling those of our Lord and
Saviour.   In the struggle for the Covenant, as often in
later struggles for creeds and testimonies, there was a
tendency to forget that the essence of true religion is
conformity to the will, and resemblance to the image of
Christ.   Amid the strife of polemical warfare, this end
is often forgotten ; for if the symbol that expresses the
matter at stake be but strenuously contended for, the
spirit of Christ, which alone is of true value in the sight
of God, is apt to be overlooked.

Moreover, the practice of coercing men into signing
the Covenants interfered with that spirit of ready, hearty
service without which nothing can be well-pleasing to

God. And the whole circumstances of the time created a tempestuous atmosphere unfavourable to the temper of sweetness and serenity which goes so far to constitute the beauty of holiness. And when the Presbyterians themselves divided into revolutioners and protesters, and came to hurl against one another the denunciations they had formerly levelled at their foes ; when the indulgences offered by the King became the occasions of fierce reproaches against those who accepted them, the effect became still worse, and it seemed as if the Prince of Peace had departed from the soil of Scotland.

With this qualification, we are the more free to claim for the pulpit of this period the honour of having contributed in many substantial ways to the moral and spiritual life of the country. It never seemed to be more powerful than during the thirty years that ran from about A.D. 1630 to near the restoration of Charles II. in 1660. Never was its spirit more thoroughly or more powerfully biblical. It accepted with the utmost cordiality the message handed down from the Reformation pulpit; it saw in every man by nature an immortal being, severed from God and doomed to destruction ; it lifted up Christ, in all the riches of His threefold office, as the only fountain of redemption and recovery ; and it echoed Christ's word, " Ye must be born again," as the germ of that great transformation by which men are fitted for heaven.

While it thus accepted the legacy of its predecessor, it made the message of grace clearer, fuller, wider. It dwelt more copiously on the work and person of the Son of God ; it exhibited more clearly the glory and riches of the plan of redeeming mercy. It went over a greater breadth of Scripture; it dwelt with much affectionate complacency on the all-sufficiency of Christ, who is made of God to His people both wisdom and righteousness, sanctification and redemption. It entered more minutely into that mysterious conflict of flesh and spirit by which the divine life has to be advanced in the soul ; into all the hindrances to spiritual progress, as well as the helps and encouragements of the spiritual life. More than that, it brought the message of the Gospel more closely home to the soul and conscience of each hearer, and pressed him with more personal earnestness to accept the divine overtures of mercy. More than ever, the Scottish pulpit of this period exemplified the combination of heat and light. Many persons have the notion that in those days the Scottish taste in sermons was for long, dry, logical discussions, with innumerable heads and particulars, wearisome beyond endurance to any but a dry, hard, Scotch, theological intellect. And thinking of such discourses, prolonged to the extent of one or two hours, or even more, they find it impossible to understand how, out of purgatory, men could have been found to endure such a protracted penance.

Quite a mistake. The Covenanters did like a compact structure of bone and sinew, of heads and particulars, but it would have been poor preaching if it had not been brightened up and commended by much warmth and earnestness of feeling on the part of the preacher. As they expressed it, they liked " sappy " preaching. And indeed it is one of the lessons for preachers of every age, very specially derived from Scottish experience, that to be effective, preaching must not be hard and cold, however able, but warm and hearty, glowing in every sentence with the warmth of the preacher's soul. In the course of time the sermon did fall into ruts ; the method of heads and particulars, uses and applications, which had come quite naturally to the earlier preachers, became a restraint and a bondage ; but those who tried to cast it off could not escape the imputation of affecting innovations, as if they were wiser than their fathers. But for real efficiency, for attracting interest, producing impression, and moulding the character of the people, the pulpit of the seventeenth century hardly knows a rival.

We have adverted to some things in the public aspect of the times that were against it; let us notice one that worked strongly in its favour. We have already seen that to meet the efforts of the Crown to substitute government by bishops for government by presbyters, the Church was thrown upon the doctrine of the supremacy of the Lord Jesus Christ, and the obligation thence arising to pay supreme regard to His will as expressed in His Word. As Alexander Henderson expressed it, her great endeavour was "that all things be done in God's house according to God's will." But in course of time the Church found her jurisdiction interfered with in other matters besides that of government. The five articles of Perth, carried in 1618 by a corrupt Assembly under royal intimidation, belonged, several of them at least, to a more sacred category. The attempt by the State party to force a new liturgy on the Church, the use of which should be binding under the highest penalties, showed a determination to set aside Christ's authority, and tyrannise over His heritage even in the most sacred region of worship. By the force of reaction the Church was thrown upon the more full assertion of Christ's claims as Head of the Church, and the glorious privilege of the Church to follow her divine Head. The more this truth was thought of, the more glorious did it seem. Every vision of the Apocalypse acquired new interest when it was remembered that the true Head of the Reformed Church of Scotland was no other than the glorious King exalted to such honour there, the Lamb in the midst of the throne, having on His head many crowns, and surrounded by elders and living creatures, and thousands of thousands

G

crying with a loud voice, Worthy is the Lamb that was slain! The men of those times did not, like so many now, deem it enough to recognise Christ's headship over themselves personally; they joined to that, with all the ardour of their nature, His headship over the whole Church. To repudiate the one was as great a crime and as great a folly as to repudiate the other. To deny Him His place as King in Zion was to imperil their personal relation to Him almost as much as to deny His atonement or His mediation.

We see evidence of this intense conviction, for example, in every page of Samuel Rutherfurd's *Letters*. The glow of adoration toward the person and the work of the Redeemer bears equally on His relation to the Church and His relation to the individual believer. The more that one delighted to think of His grace in relation to one's-self, the more was one bound to see to it that He sustained no insult and no injury in His wider dominion. For the believer to join with those who gave over His authority as King of Zion to earthly sovereigns was about as wicked as to join with those who set aside His personal authority, that they might serve the devil, and the world, and the flesh. In this way the controversies of the day disposed the preachers to be ever looking to a risen and exalted Saviour; and to remember Him who had gone into heaven, and was at the right hand of God, angels and authorities and powers being made subject to Him.

If we proceed now to notice in detail some of the men who were most conspicuous as preachers in this period, we are arrested first of all by the great Church leader of the time—ALEXANDER HENDERSON, who was born in 1583 and died in 1646, and was successively minister of Leuchars in Fife and of Edinburgh. The part which he bore in the overthrow of prelacy and restoration of presbytery in 1638 is well known; and in the negotiations

and arrangements which followed that event. He had
gone into the ministry without experience of divine grace
in his own heart, and without any real interest in spiritual
work. In fact, he had been forcibly intruded; for the
people of Leuchars having locked the door of the church,
the presbytery on the day of ordination were obliged to
enter by a window. The striking manner of his conversion under the famous Robert Bruce has already been
referred to. His heart was now as thoroughly with the
presbyterian party in the Church as formerly it had been
with the prelatical. Of his great abilities it is unnecessary to speak; they would have fitted him for any post
in the country. Originally distinguished as a teacher of
philosophy, his mind was well trained and well balanced,
and there was a completeness about his character that
left hardly a morsel of ground for criticism. As Dr.
M'Crie has said, "he was enriched with an assembly of
endowments that have rarely met in one man." [1]   Robert
Baillie's testimony to him is still more striking :—" He
was the fairest monument, after John Knox, of incomparable memory, that ever the Church of Scotland did
enjoy." [2]

If Henderson's fame as a preacher is not the very
highest, it is only because it was eclipsed by his remarkable ability as a Church leader. But as a preacher, too,
he was very popular; a proof of which is the fact that
when engaged in negotiations with Charles I. at New-
castle in 1646, the King complimented him as the best
preacher in the town. What strikes one most about his
sermons is their calm tone and their eminently solid and
scriptural character. There is not a trace of that wild
fanaticism which has so often been represented as the
outstanding quality of the preaching of the Covenanters.
Henderson has come in for his full share of that

---

[1]. *Life of Henderson*, p. 61.   [2] Baillie's *Letters*, iii. 12.

abuse which has been so abundantly poured on the memory of Covenanting preachers. He has been stigmatised as fanatical and barbarous, and one would imagine that he must have raved and ranted in the pulpit after the style of Sir Walter Scott's Kettledrummels and Proudtexts. Yet, as Dr. M'Crie has said,[1] the three sermons which he preached before Parliament show that he possessed not merely good sense and learning, but also a rich imagination and a refined taste. And he quotes the account of him given by Grainger, a member of the English Church, who cannot be suspected of partiality:—"Alexander Henderson, the chief of the Scottish clergy in this reign, was learned, eloquent, and polite, and perfectly well versed in the knowledge of mankind. He was at the helm of affairs in the General Assemblies in Scotland, and was sent to England in the double capacity of a divine and plenipotentiary. He knew how to rouse the people to war, or negotiate a peace. Whenever he preached, it was to a crowded audience, and when he pleaded or argued he was regarded with mute attention."[2]

Yet here was the great leader of the Covenanters in their earlier period, allowed to be the ablest man in the Church, occupying the conspicuous position of minister of Edinburgh, one whose chivalry had rushed against the fabric of prelacy in 1638 and overthrown it, one who had been a leading member of the Westminster Assembly, and who had preached in Westminster both to Lords and Commons. Surely if such a man did not give its tone and character in a very marked degree to the preaching of his day, all experience and all history are belied. We remark in his preaching a carefulness of treatment, the fruit of a conscientious, painstaking habit, even when he was serving a small rural congregation. We note his

[1] *Review of Tales of my Landlord*, p. 97.   [2] *Ibid.*

great fidelity to Scripture, his hearty recognition of his
office as a preacher of the Word, whose main function
was simply to transfer to his people what God had given
in germ and substance in the Scriptures. We note his
profound honour for our blessed Lord, in whose presence
this man of intellect, this ruler of men, is as humble, as
utterly self-abased as if he were literally a babe. We
see that lucidity and simplicity which comes of mastery
of his subject, and of knowing how best to present it to
the ordinary mind. We see the working of an imagination which is more homely than poetical, more intellectual
than emotional, but which answers its purpose, makes
truth more vivid, and lodges it among the living fibres of
the soul. We see likewise the inevitable habit of regarding a right attitude towards the great Church question of
the day as the urgent duty of every loyal servant of
Christ. Were they to be told that the Scriptural government of the Church was a subordinate matter, and that
one might quite well stand aloof from those who were
banded to maintain it ? This were just as if in a ship a
leak were to spring up in one end, and those in the other
end were to stand aloof, were to refuse to stir, because it
was not come to them. " No, all should join together to
mend it again, and so to hold out the water. We are all
of us in one house, under one roof, and therefore when
the fire is begun in one end of the house, wilt not thou
rise to help to slocken (quench) it, because it is not come
to thee yet ? Certainly this is great madness, for it will
come to thee next, if thou stay in the house, and the fire
be not quenched. Can there be any safe when a leak is
struck up in the ship, if it be not helped ? Will not all
be burnt who are in a house when fire enters into it, if so
be that it be not slockened ? Now, are not all of us
members of one body in a ship and in a house together ?
Indeed that we are ; and certainly we do not the duty of

Christians, nor stands it with piety and equity, except all of us stand for the defence of religion, and every one of us of one another in a good cause." [1]

Perhaps we have a still more characteristic specimen of the pulpit of this period in another preacher, DAVID DICKSON of Irvine, who, if he fell short of Henderson in vigour of intellect and capacity of ruling, surpassed him in unction and emotion, and in a certain charm of manner which gives great personal influence. " Mr. Dickson," says Wodrow in his *Analecta*,[2] "had the happiest and gainingest way of winning upon the affections of gentlemen and others, and commending religion to them, of any man in his day." He instances the remarkable tact with which, at the famous Assembly of 1638, he complimented the Commissioner, the Marquis of Hamilton, after he had dissolved the Assembly in the King's name, and had called on them all to disperse. Dickson rose and said that the noble Marquis was much to be commended for his zeal and faithfulness in carrying out the instructions of his master the King; and he would propose him as an example for their imitation; and as their spiritual King had work for them to do, he would propose that they should sit still and attend to *their* Master's business. Dickson was born in 1583, and died in a full old age in 1663, an exception in point of longevity, to the great mass of his brethren, few of whom, owing partly to the troubles of the time, reached the age of threescore and ten. He was the only child of godly parents, who had been married a considerable time without having offspring; David, like Samuel, had been "asked of the Lord;" like him, too, dedicated from the first to the ministry; and he resembled him, moreover, in that union of kindliness and godliness which enabled

[1] *Sermons by Alexander Henderson*, pp. 161-2.
[2] Vol. ii. p. 116.

him to serve his Church and his country so earnestly during a long lifetime. At the University of Glasgow, after finishing his studies, he became one of the regents or professors; indeed it is one of the honourable marks of the Scottish pulpit that the most eminent preachers were usually men of learning, men who had shown an unusual aptitude for the culture of the time, and had assimilated the intellectual food provided at the Universities in a degree beyond the common. To our refined men of sweetness and light they are of course Philistines; but it is certain that they were less Philistine than any other class of the time.

Filled with evangelical zeal of the warmest type, Mr. Dickson laboured much to promote piety among the students, and working hard with Boyd of Trochrig, Robert Blair, and other devoted men, he was singularly successful in this endeavour. Work like that which we have seen lately among our university students is of old date in connection with our colleges, and bore as bright and blessed fruit in those days as it has done in ours.

In 1618 Mr. Dickson was ordained minister of Irvine, and remained in that charge twenty-three years. About four years after he was settled, he was banished by the King to Turriff in Aberdeenshire, on account of his testimony against the five articles of Perth; but next year he was allowed to return. His ministry was of the most fervent evangelical type. Wodrow says of it, "Multitudes were convinced and converted, and few that lived in his day were more honoured to be instruments of conversion than he. People under exercise and soul-concern came from every place about Irvine and attended on his sermons, and the most eminent and serious Christians from all corners of the Church came and joined him at his communions, which were indeed times of refreshing from the presence of the Lord; yea, not a few came from

distant places and settled at Irvine, that they might be
under the drop of his ministry." [1]

On Monday, which was the market-day at Irvine,
Mr. Dickson preached regularly, and the church was as
crowded as on the Lord's day. "At these week-day
sermons," says Livingstone, "the famous Stewarton sickness began, about the year 1630, and spread from house
to house for many miles in the strath, where Stewarton
water runs, on both sides of it." This was probably the
first manifestation in Scotland of those physical disturbances, in connection with earnest religious emotion,
which have occurred both before and since, in various
places, in similar circumstances. Dickson ascribed them
to the direct agency of the devil, and did his utmost to
discourage them. The Scotch ministers generally set
their faces against them, and it is remarkable that when
it was known that a minister was against them they seldom
appeared. In Ireland, both then and during the more
modern religious movement of 1858-9, the physical
symptoms were left more to their own course, and were
much more frequent; but even in Ireland in the seventeenth century, some of the Scotch ministers set their
faces strongly against them, and with the same result as
in the congregations at home. We all know how ready
some critics are to make sport of any movement which is
attended more or less by such eccentric conditions; it is
at once ascribed to sheer fanaticism; but the careful
medical inquirer will take a more discriminating view.
Granting that these manifestations are merely a form of
hysteria, two things may be affirmed of them: in the first
place, they have their origin in a powerful excitement of
the nervous system through some very real movement of
the soul; and in the second place, they appear chiefly in

[1] Account of the Life of Mr. David Dickson (*Select Biographies*,
vol. ii., Wodrow Society).

persons of weakly constitution. It would be ridiculous to infer that any movement which was attended by such conditions was downright fanaticism. Even in the strongest physical frames there is a close connection between mental experiences and physical manifestations; what is laughter, what are tears, or groans, or sighs, what are clenched fists, or clenched teeth, or the face suddenly turned to heaven, or the wringing of the hands, but the expressions of a most genuine emotion of which the soul is the seat? And if in weak natures the emotion sometimes overcomes and prostrates the nervous system, it is no more a proof that the movement is hollow or fanatical, than the fact of a flooded river overflowing its banks is a proof that rivers generally have no good thing about them.[1]

Wodrow speaks very highly of Dickson's preaching. "I have," he says, "some of the sermons preached at Irvine taken from his mouth. They are full of solid substantial matter, very Scriptural, and in a very familiar style, not low, but exceedingly strong, plain, and affecting. It is somewhat akin to Mr. Rutherfurd's in his admirable letters. I have been told by some old ministers that scarce any body of that time came so near Mr. Dickson's style and method as the Rev. Mr. William Guthrie, minister of Fenwick, who equalled, if not excelled him there." It is remarkable that in preaching, Dickson was greatly influenced by his surroundings. At Turriff, he needed days to prepare his sermons for the hours he had required at Irvine, and ascribing this to the malice of evil spirits, he used to say that the devils of the north were much worse than those of the west. When he became a professor of divinity, he fell off in sweetness and force; no wonder, he said, for I have lost my books; he missed pastoral intercourse with his people, the knowledge which he thus acquired

[1] See article on Revivals [by Principal Rainy], *North British Review*, Nov. 1860.

of their wants, and the encouragement to further preaching from learning how they had been helped before.

In 1639 Dickson succeeded Henderson as Moderator of the General Assembly. In 1641 he was called to the Chair of Divinity in the University of Glasgow. In 1643 he was appointed by the Assembly to draw up the Directory for Public Worship. About 1650 he was translated from the Chair of Divinity in Glasgow to the same Chair in Edinburgh. While filling these two offices he did much to mould the rising ministry of the Church after his own high pattern, and prepare them for the sufferings they were soon to encounter. In the unhappy division between Resolutioners and Protesters, Dickson took the side of the Resolutioners, though, according to Stirling, as recorded by Wodrow, he lived to see that he was wrong.[1] He was more jealous of any deviation from the traditional mode of preaching than we should have expected. The customary mode of treating a text was to give reasons, doctrines, and uses. Some men of independent mind, like Hugh Binning, discarded this method, exposing themselves thereby to the censure of Mr. Dickson, who would remark that the tricks of rhetoric did not save many souls. Robert Douglas, one of the ablest ministers of the Church, was likewise in the habit of preaching without doctrines, which some called " skimming the text." [2]

But, as Dr. Walker has said, " The true glory of Dickson is his devotion to Biblical studies. He set his heart on a Scotch commentary on the Scriptures. His plan was to assign particular books to men competent for the work, and to him we owe it that we have Ferguson on the Epistles, Hutchison on the minor prophets, on Job and the Gospel of John, Durham on the Song and Book of Revelation. Dickson himself put his hand to

[1] *Analecta*, vol. iii. p. 10.   [2] *Ibid.* i. 166.

the work. We have his English notes on Matthew and the Epistle to the Hebrews. His exposition of the Psalms is not unknown to Christian readers still."[1] Indeed Mr. Spurgeon emphasises it, amid many others, as a rich volume dropping fatness, one which he had read and re-read, and which he regarded as invaluable to the preacher.[2] The idea of a popular Scotch commentary at that early period was highly characteristic of the school of preachers now before us. If there was any conviction deeper than another in their hearts, it was that the Holy Scriptures contained the whole counsel of God, and that the business of the preacher and pastor was to transfer the Scriptures in all their fulness to the hearts of his hearers. With equal profundity of conviction they felt that the Lord Jesus Christ was the supreme glory of Scripture. Their eagerness to do honour to Christ inclined them to a Christology which found Him in almost every verse. If modern exegesis compels a less universal Christology, we ought at least to honour the spirit that gave to the Lord Jesus Christ a place of such transcendent glory, and that deemed a discourse hardly worth the preaching if it did not exalt the person and shed abroad the fragrance of the Son of God.

It is a common impression that both in preaching and in prayer the preachers of those days were tremendously long. Whatever may have been true on particular occasions, it does not appear from their published discourses that at ordinary times they preached longer than we do. In prayer, Dickson was often remarkable for brevity. But like the prayers of St. Paul, his devotions if short were singularly full of matter. On one occasion, Mr. Guthrie, minister of Fenwick, having come to visit him, when at family prayer, Mr. Dickson asked Guthrie

[1] *Theologians of Scotland*, pp. 14, 15.
[2] *Commenting and Commentaries*, p. 84.

to pray, but he declined. " Mr. Dickson went away," said Guthrie, " and prayed about ten words ; but I confess every word that he uttered would have filled a firlot ! " [1]

When King Charles was restored, and prelacy along with it, Dickson was far advanced in life. He refused the oath of supremacy, and as a consequence was driven from his Chair. " His heart," says his biographer, " was broke with the heavy change on the beautiful face of the Reformed Church." Probably it was not less oppressed by the bitter strife between Resolutioners and Protesters that had raged in the Church itself. He died very soon after, at the age of eighty, and in dying said, " I have taken all my good deeds and all my bad deeds, and cast them through each other in a heap before the Lord, and fled from both, and betaken myself to the Lord Jesus Christ, and in Him I have peace." His farewell to his family was beautiful. He called them together, said something to each, and gravely and solemnly pronounced the apostolic benediction ; then he put up his hand, and closed his own eyes, and immediately expired in the arms of his son, without any struggle or apparent pain.

Another preacher of the same school, hardly less eminent than Dickson, was ROBERT BLAIR, first of Ayr, and afterwards of St. Andrews. He was born in 1593, of good family, it is said, but his descendants gained more distinction than his fathers ; he was grandfather of the Rev. Robert Blair, the well-known poet, author of *The Grave* ; and great-grandfather of Dr. Hugh Blair, and of Lord President Blair of the Court of Session. In an interesting, artless narrative of his early life,[2] Blair has given us a careful account of the rise and progress of religion in his soul. Among the subjects of his profound

---

[1] Wodrow's *Analecta*, iii. 9.
[2] See *Autobiography and Life of Robert Blair* (Wodrow Society).

study, faith in Jesus Christ was conspicuous, and through
much meditation on Scripture he arrived at a singularly
full and elevated conception of the riches of grace stored
in His person, and through faith made available for men.
From his earliest childhood he had sought the Lord with
extraordinary diligence, and had found the usual ground
for peace and joy in believing; but in the year 1622,
when about twenty-nine years of age, he experienced a
remarkable addition of spiritual blessing,—what in our
days would be called a second conversion, in consequence
of the greatly enlarged views he was led to form of the
stores of grace contained in Christ. "I perceived," he
says, "that many that make use of faith in order to their
justification, made not directly use thereof in order to
sanctification. . . . I had not, before that, made use of
faith as a mean and instrument to draw holiness out of
Christ, the well of salvation, though it may be I had
both heard that, and spoken it by way of a transient
emotion; but then I learned to purpose that they who
receive forgiveness of sins are sanctified through faith in
Christ. . . . By this new discovery I did find a patent
door made for provision and furniture in and from Christ
my Lord." It is remarkable that when Blair received this
great increase of spiritual power, he made a special study
of the question of church-government, and like most such
men of his time became more resolutely bent on maintaining presbyterianism, as a duty to his Lord and Saviour.

At the time of this change Blair was a regent in the
University of Glasgow, and the first result to others of
his new experience was his urging the students under his
charge "to study piety and to be diligent in secret seeking
of the Lord;" in which endeavour the Lord was pleased
to bless him greatly. But to one who had been caught
up to the third heaven, and had shared, as it seemed, the
experience of the blest, the teaching of philosophy be-

came very irksome, it was "like sand between his teeth."
He began to think that philosophy was even an obstacle
to all spiritual good.   The good sense of the man, however, and the view he was led to form of the mind of
Christ, kept him steady in this difficulty ; he saw that
" duty in a lawful calling was service acceptable to God
by Jesus Christ when His immediate service was not
slighted, but consciously attended to;" further, he was
encouraged " to intermix holy ejaculations to God with
all his reading, meditating and teaching of philosophy ; "
and thirdly, he enjoyed opportunities which he greedily
embraced to teach the grounds and urge the practice of
true piety, and thus he got comfortably to the end of
his academic occupation, which indeed was not far off.

Mr. Blair's first sphere of ministerial labour was at
Bangor, in the north of Ireland.   The Ulster colony had
recently been formed, and many persons from the adjacent
parts of Scotland had settled there ; but in the great dearth
of ministers, and the great need of the colony for spiritual
guidance, Blair and others were induced to settle among
them.   The ministry of these men was attended with
singular blessing ; the awakening that followed was the
chief means of putting on Ulster the stamp which it has
ever since retained.   But the resolute attitude of Blair
against episcopacy brought him into grievous trouble from
the bishops, so that he was obliged to leave Ireland.
With a ship-load of emigrants he set sail for New England, but though the ship had come within sight of
Newfoundland, she sustained such damage from a storm
that notwithstanding the courageous efforts of a passenger
named Andrew Agnew, who, " suspended by ane tow
warked up to the neck in water, trying to repair her," her
head had to be turned, and the party came back to this
country.   Blair got a call to Ayr, where he was highly
beloved and esteemed.   The Assembly of 1638 ordered

his removal to St. Andrews, where most of his future life was spent. In 1662 he shared the fate of his brethren who would not take the oath of supremacy. After a time of wandering he settled at Couston in Aberdour parish, where he died in 1666 in his seventy-third year.

There were several things in Blair that would make a worldly critic set him down as a fanatic, one whose ministry would have given birth only to wild sentiments and an unwholesome feverish life. He had a remarkable faith. He believed in the possibility of drawing certain blessings from God by the exercise of faith as really as water is drawn from a well by bucket and chain. He believed in the possibility of close intimacy with God by prayer, so that one might speak to God, and hear God's reply. He believed in the supremacy of the spiritual world, and looked on all earthly interests as but the scaffolding through which the one abiding object was gained, the one great temple was reared. Could such a man be anything but a fanatical preacher? Let us see. It bears on the question to remember that he had had the best academical training, and that for several years he had been a teacher of philosophy. It is an undoubted fact that the labours of Blair and his brethren had a most blessed effect on the tumultuous colony of Ulster, and served to make that province what it has ever since been. It is moreover an undoubted fact that Blair bore a reputation for wisdom above all his contemporaries, and that the very aspect of his countenance was in keeping with this, for he was conspicuous for a calm, majestic expression, the very furthest extreme from wild fanaticism. It was as a compliment to his wisdom that the General Assembly, in the arrangements for the popular commentary, assigned to Blair the books of Proverbs and Ecclesiastes, a task which he accepted with complacency, and at which he is known to have laboured hard, though his commentary was never published. Blair was chaplain to King Charles II., and in Oliver Cromwell's time, when he was called before the Council, it was intended to deprive him both of place and pension; but he conducted himself with such wisdom in their presence that their president remarked it was well he was a minister, for if he were a politician, he would give them a world of trouble. There was no minister in all Scotland whom it would be more difficult to convict of fanaticism. No man was held in more honour by the Church at large—a proof this what kind of pastor the ministers generally looked up to as a model, and that it was to such a standard as his that amid many defects and imperfections they endeavoured to come up.

The name that comes next is one that claims special regard—SAMUEL RUTHERFURD. In some ways, Rutherfurd was to the Covenanting movement what John Bunyan was to the Puritan—its poet-theologian and preacher. In two respects however, Rutherfurd differed from Bunyan—in his comparative neglect of his poetical gift, and in his bringing into play, with heart and soul, gifts of a profounder kind, which have not increased his popularity, but for which he believed that the times had more need. For Rutherfurd was one of the most manifoldly gifted men of his day. Born in Roxburghshire about the year 1600, he studied at the University of Edinburgh, and like so many of his able contemporaries, at the end of his curriculum he was chosen a regent of the college, and spent some years in that honourable office. In 1627 he was settled at Anwoth, on the banks of the Solway, where his labours were attended with much blessing. Banished thence to Aberdeen, where many of his celebrated letters were written, he was appointed Professor of Divinity at St. Andrews, in that memorable year 1638. It is hard to say whether it was wise in him to leave the pulpit for the chair. If he had continued a working minister, he would have written fewer controversial books, but he would have done great wonders among the people. The latter part of his life was crowded with troubles. He died in his sixty-first year in 1661, on the very edge of the great persecution.

Rutherfurd was remarkable in three respects, as a controversial theologian, a preacher, and a devotional writer. From his earliest days he was a profound student, and the great business of his writings was to defend Calvinistic doctrine, Presbyterian polity, and constitutional government. The union in him of a subtle scholastic intellect and multifarious scholastic learning, that placed Thomas, and Scotus, and Bradwardinus, and all the rest of them at his finger-ends, with that seraphic imagination which made his letters like apples of gold in frames of silver, was a phenomenon without example even in those remarkable days. The sagacity that in his *Lex Rex* brought to light the true principles of constitutional government, and marked out the ground which has ever since been maintained in constitutional struggles, placed him in the first rank of political thinkers.

In his learned works, Rutherfurd paid no attention to the graces of style, nor did he bestow much pains on lucidity of order or simplicity of plan. His theological works, in little quarto volumes of very yellow paper and close clumsy type, are sufficiently repulsive in appearance to modern readers ; and when you open them, and instead of being carried to the gates of heaven find yourself in the labyrinths of scholastic distinctions and controversies, you have great difficulty in holding on.

As a preacher, however, Rutherfurd was highly popular and effective. He was the first Scottish preacher in whom the poetical temperament had free and full development, and the first to discover what a relish there was in the common mind for that way of treating religious

H

subjects. If he had only bestowed more pains on
preaching as an art, if he had put his imagination under
restraint as Bunyan did, and cultivated the same purity
of taste and style, his sermons must have attained the
highest place among the permanent memorials of the
pulpit of his day.

But Rutherfurd's fame rests chiefly on his *Letters*.
The mere by-play of his genius, the outcome of his hours
of relaxation when the bow of the student was unbent,
and the Christian pastor, out of the abundance of his heart,
strewed words of comfort and encouragement over the
path of his fellow-pilgrims—this, after all, is the work
which has come down fresh and living to our day. " So
far as I know," says Dr. Walker, "they are the only
letters two centuries old which are still a practical reality
in the religious life of Scotland, England, and America.
And criticism cannot get rid of the fact that they continue
to retain their hold of human hearts, that they have won
a place for themselves beside such books as Augustine's
Confessions and Thomas à Kempis."[1] The grace and
glory of Jesus Christ is their great subject, and their
object is to encourage the happy spirit of steadfast trust
in Him, even when all the waves and billows of public
and personal trial are passing over. It was an exciting
time ; and a full gushing heart like Rutherfurd's could
not but pour itself out to Christ's suffering people in
the warmest words of admiration for his Lord and in
the spirit of firmest trust.

And the theme that lay at the heart of his letters
was also the theme of his most characteristic sermons.
The love and the loveliness of Christ was what Rutherfurd delighted most to proclaim. It was a subject on
which he felt he needed to place no restraint on himself ;
the more exuberantly he handled it the better ; to prune,

[1] *Theologians of Scotland*, p. 7.

to trim, to modify what he had to say on such a subject would be almost mean. The heart could not burn too impetuously, the emotions could not surge and bubble up too vehemently when the theme was the love of Christ that passeth knowledge. His most characteristic sermons are therefore the outgushings of a heart excited to its utmost passion, and an imagination soaring to its utmost height. Yet they are by no means rhapsodical. They are mostly conversational in tone, familiar, easy to understand, easy to follow; using the most common similitudes, they are homely, sometimes even to the verge of vulgarity. But his quaint words and similitudes are often very telling. Take by way of sample the following from a sermon (from Song of Solomon v. 36) in a volume recently published.[1] "Pride, lust, laziness and security are the meikle water [the deep river]; the saints are the short-legged horse, and down they go." "Take Christ at the right stot [moment in His movements]. When His hand is thrusting itself down upon your heart, you should thrust your hand on above it, and thrust His stamp and His burning iron even down to the bone, that there may be great letters left behind, and all your life after you may bear Christ's mark." "*My hands dropt with myrrh upon the handles of the lock.* That is, the Lord left the smell of His words that flowed from his sweet lips. As well smelled as myrrh whereof the holy oil of the sanctuary was made. And not only that, but a smell of the effectual working of His grace was left on the lock of my heart, my will and consent, which made my hands, that is, my actions, to smell sweetly. We see when Christ is gone Himself he leaves a sweet disposition of obedience behind Him that will do His turn. His grace rubbed and scoured the lock, and made

[1] *Quaint Sermons* of S. Rutherford, hitherto unpublished, with a Preface by the Rev. A. A. Bonar, D.D., 1885.

it gleg [ready] and easy to open. Christ's fingers, wherever
they come, leave drops of grace behind them."

Sometimes Rutherfurd's appeals are highly poetical and
most effective. Witness this burst of true poetry in connection with the experience of Jesus when he said, " I
thirst." " O wells, O lochs, O running streams ! Where
were you when my Lord could not get a drink ? The
wells and lochs answer, ' Alas ! we dare not know Him ;
the Lord hath laid a fence on us ; we are arrested ; we
dare not serve Him.' Oh to hear the wells say, We will
give Herod and Pilate a drink, but we will give Christ
none ! Give me leave to say that there is none on earth
brewed for Him ; nothing but a drink of gall and vinegar.
The wells say, We will give oxen and horses drink ; but
never a drop for the Lord of glory. For all His service
done at Jerusalem, for all His good preaching, for all His
glorious miracles—not so much as a drop of cold water !
Fie on you, famous Jerusalem ! Is this your stipend ?
Is this your reward to your great high-priest ? No, not
so much as the beggar's courtesy, a drink of cold water,
to your dear Redeemer, Jesus ! But by this, Christ hath
brought drink for all believers." [1]

There are some to whom the unpruned lusciousness
of Rutherfurd's preaching, its gush of emotion, and frequent tone of rapture, are not acceptable.[2] But whatever
may be said against this as a universal method, and of
the necessity of mingling with it a quieter and more

---

[1] Rutherfurd's *Communion Sermons*, p. 289.
[2] One thing must be noted in connection with the printed sermons
of Rutherfurd and other preachers of this period ; they are seldom
printed as the preacher delivered them, or even as they were found in
the note-books of their hearers. Rutherfurd, like most of the popular
ministers in Scotland, made much use of the Scotch dialect ; but his
editors have usually been horrified at these expressions, and have
turned them into orthodox English. In this process much of the pith
of his language has evaporated. An exception occurs in the case of
the *Quaint Sermons* already referred to, in which the expressions in the

didactic strain, and likewise a more ethical element, there is no doubt that such preaching, when warm from the heart, is highly effective for spiritual ends. It is to be remarked, however, that Rutherfurd is not the minister who was regarded by his contemporaries as the most successful in spiritual work. David Dickson of Irvine, William Guthrie of Fenwick, and perhaps John Livingstone of Ancrum were more remarkable for the greatness of their spiritual harvests.

Wodrow's well-known anecdote of a London merchant's visit to St. Andrews and Irvine gives a vivid view of the three preachers, Blair, Rutherfurd, and Dickson. On his return, the merchant's friends "asked him what news he brought from Scotland. He answered he had very great and good news to tell them, and they wondered, because before that time he had been quite a stranger to religion. He told them that at St. Andrews he had heard one Mr. Blair preach, and, describing his features and the stature of his body, he said that man showed me the majesty of God, which was Blair's peculiar talent; then, added he, I afterwards heard a little fair man preach (Mr. Rutherfurd), and that man showed me the loveliness of Christ; then I came and heard at Irvine a well-favoured, proper old man with a long beard (which was famous Mr. Dickson), and that man showed me all my heart. He was most famed of any of his time to speak to cases of conscience. And they say that Englishman became an excellent Christian.

Scotch dialect are preserved. This we owe to the Rev. J. H. Thomson of Hightae, a most loving and painstaking editor. Mr. Thomson informs us that he has found many gross mistakes in current editions of Rutherfurd. For instance, in one place the church is described as "black as the moon." The reader has to think of the moon when invisible, but this makes a sorry simile. Mr. Thomson, examining a MS. copy, finds the true reading to be "black as a moor." It is much to be hoped that Mr. Thomson may find encouragement to publish more of these old writings in a better dress than hitherto.

The whole General Assembly of the Church of Scotland could not have given a better character of these three men."[1]

Of the same school with Rutherfurd was JOHN LIVINGSTONE, born 1603, died 1672.[2] His father was minister first of Kilsyth and then of Lanark, and was connected with the noble family which bore the title of Lord Livingstone, and afterwards Earl of Linlithgow. At first Livingstone doubted whether he had a call to the ministry. It was the practice in those times among God-fearing men to set apart a time for pondering doubtful questions amid prayer and fasting; and in a cave near Cleghorn wood Livingstone sought for light, and obtained it so fully that he felt that if he did not give himself to the preaching of Christ, he would have no hope of salvation. It is remarkable that he had no recollection of a time when he underwent a change tantamount to conversion. The new life seems to have dawned imperceptibly upon him. He tells of himself how once in a time of revival, being concerned that he had no such experiences to recall as those of some who were present, he made it his prayer that he might have them; and that during his sleep he got an impression of God's wrath so terrific as to make him feel what a fool he had been for asking what if given he would have been unable to bear. He was still a probationer without charge, and in his twenty-seventh year, when a neighbouring minister engaged him to preach at his church at Shotts, on the Monday after the dispensation of the Lord's Supper. The night before, he says, he had been with some earnest Christians who spent it in conference and prayer. Between eight and nine in the morning, when

[1] *Analecta*, iii. 3, 4.
[2] See his Autobiography (Wod. Society, *Select Biographies*, vol. i.); Wodrow's *Analecta*, etc.

meditating on his sermon, he had such a fit of fear, that
he was wondering whether he might not steal away and
leave the work for another to do. But such a proceeding
would have shown distrust of God, and he resolved to
preach. His text was Ezekiel xxxvi. 25, 26 ("A new
heart also will I give you," etc.), and after preaching an
hour and a half, he made the application "with such
liberty and melting of heart" that five hundred persons
ascribed their conversion to that sermon. It was a remarkable proof of the connection between the state of
the preacher's own heart and the highest spiritual
success. Livingstone used to say, "I found that much
study did not so much help me in preaching as the
getting my heart brought to a right disposition; yea,
sometimes I thought that the hunger of the hearers
helped me more than my own preparation."

Notwithstanding the high place as a preacher he thus
gained in his native land, it was not in Scotland but the
north of Ireland that Livingstone had his first charge.
His experience there was very delightful, so far as the
spiritual result of his services was concerned, but he
was made very miserable from the interposition of the
bishops, notwithstanding that "Dr. Usher, called primate
of Armagh, ane learned and ane godly man, altho' ane
bishop, interposed in his behalf." The testimony of
Livingstone to the remarkable harmony among the
Scotch ministers in Ulster, their earnest devotion to
their work, the wonderful interest of the people in
religion, and the striking transformation of their character, though many had been the wildest and roughest
of men before, attests powerfully the practical efficacy
of the doctrines of grace rightly received. In fact it was
this spiritual awakening that laid the foundation of the
prosperity of Ulster. But through the interference of
the bishops, Livingstone was compelled to retire. He

was in the ship with Blair that tried to reach New England, but was driven back, and he has given a graphic narrative of the voyage.

With the more favourable times for Presbyterianism, after the proceedings of 1638, Livingstone found Scotland more open to his labours. For ten years he was minister at Stranraer, where he was eminently useful. Thereafter he was translated by the General Assembly to Ancrum in Roxburghshire, where he enjoyed similar tokens of spiritual success. He was distinguished as a preacher for his pathos and his great power of melting hearts. At the Restoration he was banished from Scotland, and found a refuge in Rotterdam, where he died in 1672.

Livingstone has sometimes been represented as a specimen of Covenanting fanaticism. He was a revival preacher of the most earnest type. But, as Dr. Walker has pointed out, the employment to which he betook himself when banished to Rotterdam, and deprived of all opportunity of preaching, was hardly suitable for a fanatic.[1] The truth is, he knew well several Oriental languages, and had some knowledge of French, Italian, and Spanish. The occupation to which he set himself was to revise the Latin version of the Old Testament, and print the Hebrew and the Latin side by side in parallel columns. The work was accomplished, but the friend who was to bear the expense of the publication having died, it never saw the light. Whatever may have been the defects of these covenanting ministers, they were not deficient in the learning of the time. And with all their fervour in preaching, they were shrewd, careful, self-controlled men. The fanaticism for which they are so much blamed was the fanaticism that springs from a most profound appreciation of the solemn words

[1] *Theologians of Scotland*, p. 20.

of our Lord, " What is a man profited if he shall gain the whole world and lose his own soul ? "

Livingstone's opinion has been preserved on the difference between English and Scotch sermons. He thought the sermons of English ministers were like their knives, very beautiful to look to ; " but," says he, " there are some of your Kilmarnock whittles that, though they look not soe fair on it as your English knives, yet have a better edge, and will cutt as weel and much longer than they will doe ! " [1]

[1] Wodrow's *Analecta*, ii. 262.

CHAPTER VI.

THE COVENANTING PERIOD.

(PART II.)

THE covenanting period in Scotland was so rich in remarkable preachers that it is not easy to find a place even for a brief sketch of all the men of mark that represented the pulpit of the time. But if we accept the testimony of contemporaries, there was no man that for popularity and power in the pulpit surpassed WILLIAM GUTHRIE, minister of Fenwick, near Kilmarnock.[1] William Guthrie must not be confounded with his relative, James Guthrie, minister of Stirling, the "famous Guthrie" of the Martyrs' Monument in our Greyfriars' Churchyard, one of the first victims of Charles II., hanged on pretence of treason in the same week in which the Marquis of Argyll was executed, and whose head remained for years fixed to the Nether Bow Gate. He is less liable to be confounded with his brother, John Guthrie, who also was eminent as a covenanting preacher.

William Guthrie, minister of Fenwick (born 1620, died 1665), was proprietor of the estate of Pitforthy, near Brechin; but in order that he might be wholly free from worldly cares for his work as a Christian minister, he made over the estate to one of his younger brothers. His conversion in early youth was of that marked kind where a time of great spiritual distress is succeeded by a

---

[1] See Dunlop's Memoir, *Select Biographies*, Wodrow Society, vol. ii. Wodrow's *Analecta*, etc., etc.

condition of extraordinary happiness. At the University
of St. Andrews he studied philosophy under James
Guthrie, the martyr, to whom we have just adverted;
and divinity under Samuel Rutherfurd. Fenwick was a
newly erected parish, and William Guthrie was the first
minister of it,[1] and when he was settled in it the people
were in a state of lamentable rudeness and ignorance,
living in neglect of God and religion. According to
Dunlop, they were all persuaded by Mr. Guthrie to
attend public ordinances, and to set up and maintain
the stated worship of God in their families, and there
was scarcely a house in the parish that did not furnish
some fruits of his ministry, some real converts to a
Christian life. One of his contemporaries says that he
so secured the affections of the public that they turned
the cornfield of his glebe into a little town, every one
building a house for his family upon it, that they might
live under the drop of his ministry. Another says he
converted and confirmed many thousands, and was
esteemed the greatest practical preacher in Scotland.
In prayer too he had a marvellous gift, sometimes praying a long time, and getting so near to God, and so
melted for sin, and urging such earnest Gospel pleas for
divine blessing, that some used to say it was worth
coming a long distance for the prayer alone.

To have met Guthrie in one of his moods of relaxation, one would not have guessed what aptitude he had
for the office of the ministry. He was of a social and
affable manner, equally at home with high and low, hand-
some in face and figure, with a wonderful flow of humour,
fond moreover of fishing and fowling, to which he had

[1] The church is still standing, much as it was when he occupied
it. The old sand-glass that used to serve as a warning to the preacher
when it was time to end, and other antiquities, are still extant. And
in the churchyard are several tombstones over the bodies of martyrs
of the Covenant.

often to resort for delicate health; indeed, so like the
Thomas Guthrie of our own age, that, on the principle of
heredity, one is strongly predisposed to believe that the
one was the ancestor of the other.   Yet neither his love
of humour nor of sport seems to have interfered with
his heavenly-mindedness; for, even amid the glee and
hilarity of a fishing party, he would invite his companions to some secluded spot, that they might join in
pouring out their hearts to God. It is said that in his
early ministry he introduced himself in his sporting
capacity to some careless people in the parish, who
would have turned from him at once had they known
him to be the minister; and finding they had never yet
been in the church, he rallied them on their laziness,
and got them to promise to go and see what like it was.
When they came, to their amazement, their sportsman
friend entered the pulpit, and delivered a sermon that
brought the truth home to them as they had never felt
it before.

In every several department of ministerial duty Mr.
Guthrie was a pattern. His preaching had a marvellous power; it was thoroughly scriptural from first to
last, delivered with all the ardour and tenderness of one
in dead earnest over his people; commended and applied
by "allusions and illustrations adapted to the capacity of
the meanest;" and delivered with a liveliness and power
which secured the interest and attention of all. He was
most regular, industrious, and successful in visiting and
catechising, while his dealings with the bereaved and
afflicted were full of tenderness and sympathy, very
edifying, and much appreciated. In the public business
of the Church he never spared himself, and while joining
with the Protester party, he endeavoured to mollify the
bitter spirit which too often marked the controversy. He
had a remarkable gift in conversation, and even while

giving full play to his vivacity and humour, knew how to maintain the honour of his Master, and administer the word of rebuke, without driving from him the men of mark into whose company he was sometimes thrown.

With all these various gifts, he was no mean theologian. He was well acquainted with the original languages of Scripture, and he was the author of the well-known little treatise, *The Christian's Great Interest.* It is said that the great John Owen was once asked whether he had ever heard of him. " Heard of him ? " was the reply, " that little book of his is my *vade mecum,* and there is more theology in it than in all the folios that I have written." Though suffered to remain in his parish longer than the other covenanting ministers, chiefly through his friendship with the Earl of Eglintoun, Guthrie was at last driven from it in 1665. He did not long survive his expulsion, but died the same year at the early age of forty-five, from an attack of gravel, to which cruel disease he had long been subject, like many more of the ministers of that period.

Of the preaching gifts of Guthrie, we of later times have hitherto had most inadequate opportunities of judging. In his lifetime an anonymous volume was issued, being notes of sermons on Isaiah lv., which was commonly ascribed to him ; but it was most unsatisfactory, and it was to vindicate himself that he published the book by which he is still known—*The Christian's Great Interest.* A similar volume was published after his death, purporting to be sermons by him on Hosea xiii. 9 (" O Israel, thou hast destroyed thyself," etc.) ; but his widow issued an advertisement warning the public that they were not authentic, and not a fair representation of his views. In an edition of his Works published at Glasgow in 1771, there are five sermons ; and in the volume of Lectures and Sermons preached chiefly in the time of persecution by eminent ministers, edited by John Howie of Lochgoin, and published in 1779, there are no fewer than seventeen.

But all these collections are exceedingly faulty. We must remember not only of Guthrie, but of many other ministers of the period, that they did not publish their own sermons, nor receive from the printer proofs and revises till every rugged phrase had been corrected, and every obscure sentence made luminous. The fondness of the Scotch people for good preaching was shown, among other ways, by the eagerness with which they wrote notes of sermons, struggling with might and main to lose no good thing their minister said. Many a man under the influence of this passion, learned a sort of shorthand of his own, which enabled him to preserve more or less the whole substance of a sermon. If one had lived in those times one would have been surprised to see, at some field-preaching, this man and the other with his inkhorn slung to his button-hole (for pencils did not exist in those days), taking out his little manuscript book as soon as the text was given out, and in spite of the cold that chilled his fingers, driving a stumpy goose-quill over its pages with unabated zeal, until the preacher closed the Bible and ended his last exhortation.

Now it is one or other of these collections that has usually formed the basis of the published sermons, and it is easy to account in this way for ruggedness of style, for want of connection, for one-sided statements with qualifying words omitted, and for the uncouth, unfinished form of the whole. Guthrie, too, is one of those who have suffered from the conversion of their quaint Scotch expressions into very flat English. In his case, as in that of Samuel Rutherfurd, the gentleman already referred to, Mr. Thomson of Hightae, has been able to undo some of the mischief of these Anglifying editors, and to restore

his own image and superscription to his sermons. A
sermon of Guthrie's as presented in Howie's volume and
then in Mr. Thomson's manuscript are as different as an
old church painted and plastered according to the taste
of last century, and the same church in its original integrity.

Here is the way in which a sermon opens on the
Syrophenician woman. "Oh! but it is a mickle matter
to take God up right in our addresses to Him. There is
many folk within the Church that hath been praying to
Him these twenty years, that are but babbling, and
cannot open a mouth to Him; yet here is a woman of
Canaan, who at the time is without the Church, that
comes and speaks like a print book to Him. . . . She
calls him both Lord and Son of David. She puts cannily
these two together. Oh happy are they who hold these
two together in profession and practice!" Speaking of
her suit, he says: "The first thing in it, is—Have mercy
on me! O Lord, give me the pardon of my guilt! and
then there is less ado. If once I had that, I wot well
there is the less behind. Many a sore head, heart, leg,
side and arm has the people of God, and yet readily, ye
will aye hear them first on this string, Lord, have mercy
upon me, and forgive me my sins." He is very strong
in pressing that there is but one charter, one covenant
for men, embracing both spiritual and temporal mercies
together, and that it is ridiculous to ask for temporal
mercies without having accepted Christ as the fountain
of pardon. "God hath put all the mercies of His people,
both spiritual and temporal mercies, all enduements, yea
all things, no worth the shoes [i.e. not excepting the
shoes] that ye wear on your feet, all these are put in the
charter of the covenant. There are not two covenants or
two charters. Ye are all mistaken that's going to the
covenant for spiritual things, and not for all ye stand in

need of. Hout! ye are all gowks, for all mercies are comprised in that one charter." With reference to the Headship of Christ, Guthrie was far from content to apply it to the government of the Church; he shows how gloriously it includes every needed blessing: "Christ Jesus is appointed heir of all things, Head over the Church, and over all things to her, and to her bairns. Forsooth? Is He? Yes; He is Head over health and over sickness, over riches and over poverty, over consolation and over terror and sorrow to thee, and Head over well and woe to thee; so that whatever concerns His Church or thee that is truly one of His, is unquestionably in the hand of Him who is the faithful and true witness."

One gets a new idea of the preaching of the time from many of these sermons. The preacher appears in closest contact with the mind and soul of even the least cultivated of his hearers; he speaks to them in their own language, dramatises the scene so that they may see it, brings a rattling shower of questions every now and then to play upon their consciences, keeps them close to Christ, and shows them how exceedingly rich and nourishing are the pastures of Scripture. His soul breathes in all that he says, and his fine voice expresses fully all the varying emotion of his soul.

Yet no man could with less reason have been called a fanatic. And certainly no man was further removed from that type of character which writers like Buckle, Morison, and even Sir Walter Scott held to be the Covenanter type,—fierce, narrow, bigoted, and gloomy. A fairer estimate of the ministry of Scotland would find no small measure of geniality and even hilarity associated with their earnestness. However it may clash with the notions of theorists, it is a fact, as some one has put it, that in the human soul the fountain of tears and the fountain of laughter lie very near to each other. An anecdote of a dinner party at which Mr. Guthrie and Mr. James Durham (a much graver man) were present, illustrates this connection. " Mr. Guthrie was exceeding merry, and made Mr. Durham smile, yea laugh, with his pleasant facetious conversation. It was the ordinary custom of the family to pray after dinner, and Mr. Guthrie was desired to pray; which he did with the greatest measure of seriousness and fervency, to the astonishment of all present. When they rose from prayer, Mr. Durham came to him and embraced him and said, ' O William, you are a happy man; if I had been so merry as you have been, I could not have been so serious, nor in any frame of prayer for eight-and-forty hours.' "

And yet, grave though JAMES DURHAM [1] was, compared with William Guthrie, it is certain that of all the outstanding preachers and theologians of this age none was spoken of habitually with more respect and reverence by his contemporaries. In the church, Durham became a minister of Glasgow, professor of divinity in the University, and thereafter chaplain to the king. He was also a voluminous writer, and some of his practical works, such as his exposition of the Song of Solomon, his seventy-two sermons on the fifty-third chapter of Isaiah, and his work on the Apocalypse, were for many a day among the favourite books of devout people in Scotland. A treatise on *Scandal* goes deep into some of the most important questions relating to the visible Church.

Few men have more assiduously fulfilled the injunction than James Durham—" work while it is called to-day." He was born in 1622 and died in 1658, at the early age of thirty-six. But even of that short life it was but the latter portion that was given to the service

---

[1] See Life prefixed to the treatise on *Scandal;* Wodrow's *Analecta;* Stirling *apud* Wodrow.

of Christ. Durham was proprietor of the estate of
Powrie in Forfarshire, and in his early days he held a
commission in the army. When on a visit to the house
of his wife's mother in the parish of Queensferry, he was
invited by her to accompany the family to church on the
Saturday before the communion. A mere soldier, and
caring little about church matters, he was very unwilling
to go, but after some pressure, he went. The earnestness of the preacher impressed him, and next day he went
in a much more suitable frame. Mr. Melvin, minister
of the place, preached from 1 Peter ii. 7, " Unto you that
believe He is precious," and Durham's heart "was so
impressed that he went in deep earnest to the table and
joined himself to the Lord in an everlasting covenant
that was never broken." He had no thought however of
leaving the army, and it was some time after, on the eve
of a battle, that Mr. David Dickson, riding past, heard
some one praying, and finding that it was Durham, dealt
with him very earnestly to induce him to consecrate
himself to the ministry. Twice, during the battle,
Durham made a remarkable escape, and in testimony of
his gratitude he resolved to do as Dickson had urged.
Licensed in 1647, he was immediately called to be a
minister of Glasgow, and in 1650, when Dickson was
transferred from the divinity chair of Glasgow to that of
Edinburgh, Durham was appointed to the former. He
did not hold that office long, for the same year he was
nominated chaplain to King Charles; but though his
devout, learned, and earnest character procured the king's
respect, there was little congeniality between them. In
1651 he was called to be minister of the Inner High
Church, Glasgow, in which office he had for colleague
Mr. John Carstairs, father of the celebrated Principal
Carstairs. He was minister of the inner church, when
Andrew Gray (to be spoken of hereafter) was minister of

the outer. Wodrow tells of a communion Sabbath when an immense crowd flocked to the outer church, and the inner was comparatively empty till it filled up from the overflowing of the other. Nevertheless, preaching from Matthew xxii. 5 (" the remnant made light of it "), Durham made a deep impression both on saints and sinners; it was one of the greatest days of power known in the church. The intensity of his studious habits impaired his constitution, and he died after little more than ten years' service in the ministry.

Some of the books that have been named furnish us with much ampler records of his pulpit work than we possess of most of his contemporaries. If we were to characterise them in a single sentence, we should say that the one theme which predominates in them all is Jesus Christ and Him crucified. His whole ministry was directed to the object which had been so successfully accomplished in his own history by Mr. Melvin of Queensferry—commending Christ. His sermons for the most part are long, with little sparkle or play of genius, yet they were immensely relished, and very useful. They are constructed on a plan which had now become the ordinary method in Scotland—some observations to begin with, then a statement and enforcement of the doctrines in the text, and in connection with each doctrine, a series of uses, or practical applications. Undoubtedly this method, cumbrous though it was, conduced materially to fulness and explicitness in the handling of subjects.

But if it be asked wherein lay the attractiveness of such sermons as Durham's ? the answer is,—Not in any remarkable faculty of illustration, for of that he had very little ; not in poetical or imaginative touches, for his mind was essentially grave and prosaic. If we compare his exposition of the Song of Solomon with that of St. Bernard, for example, in the eleventh century, we find a great contrast. Bernard gushes with emotion and sparkles with poetry ; Durham, much fuller of instruction, is comparatively dry and tame. The elements of his popularity were, first, the plainness of his style ; it is conversational throughout ; the sentences short and fitting, and the whole so manifestly addressed to the audience that they could not but attend. And second, the exceeding earnestness of his heart ; the intensity with which he felt, and manifestly felt, all that he uttered ; the deep solemnity with which he spoke. The order of his mind was exceedingly grave and devout. It is said that while engaged in lecturing on the Revelation he used to devote two days of each week to prayer and fasting, that he might be guided to the right interpretation. Perhaps it was the great solemnity of Durham's disposition that cast a temporary shadow over his deathbed. "Brother," he said to his colleague, Carstairs, "for all that I have preached and written, there is but one Scripture I can remember or dare grip unto ; tell me if I dare lay the weight of my salvation upon it ? It is, " Whosoever cometh unto me I will in no wise cast out." " You may depend on it," said Carstairs, "though you had a thousand salvations to hazard." A little after he cried out, " He is come, He is come ! "

Among the younger ministers of this period there were two who gained the highest distinction, although their period of service was exceptionally short. These were HUGH BINNING and ANDREW GRAY.

Hugh Binning,[1] eldest son of John Binning of Dalvenan, a considerable landed proprietor in Ayrshire, was born in 1627, had a very deep and earnest spiritual struggle in his boyhood, was a distinguished and most

[1] Life, prefixed to Works ; Wodrow's *Analecta ;* Brown of Whitburn's Memoir.

diligent scholar, and at the age of nineteen, after a very keen competition, was elected Professor of Philosophy in the University of Glasgow. As a teacher of philosophy he was very successful, and here first his independent character showed itself; for " he was the first to reform philosophy from the barbarous terms and unintelligible distinctions of the schoolmen, and the many vain disputes and trifling subtleties which rather perplexed the minds of the youth than furnished them with solid and useful knowledge." Ending his career as professor at the age of twenty-two, he was thereafter ordained minister of Govan, near Glasgow.. Notwithstanding his strong turn for philosophy and learning, Binning became a remarkable preacher. His deep spirituality and constant sense of the divine presence gave him unusual power. He was more a preacher for the educated few than for the common people. It is a proof of his being ever ready for his Father's service, that on the morning of the day on which he was to be married, thinking it right to attend the week-day sermon in a neighbouring church, the minister pressed him to preach himself, and notwithstanding his peculiar circumstances, he complied. In the dispute before Cromwell in Glasgow in 1651, Binning, by his learning, his mastery in debate, and fervent eloquence, entirely overpowered the opposite party, and filled even Cromwell with astonishment.

In the debate—then, alas, so active in the Church—between the Resolutioners and Protesters, Binning took the side of the latter, but without the bitterness that was so often shown, as appears from his treatise on *Christian Love*, which was meant as an Eirenicon. This exposed him to the not very friendly criticism of some of the other side ; even so good a man as David Dickson must have a fling at what he called his new-fangled conceit as a preacher. It is disappointing to find Dickson, with reference to his style, make the remark, that the tricks of rhetoric did not save many souls. The explanation of this is, that the same independence of mind which emancipated Binning as a professor from philosophical formality emancipated him as a preacher from similar artificial rules. Discarding the prevalent method of doctrines and uses, he preferred to let his thoughts run in a continuous stream, and his sermons are often undivided. His English, too, is a considerable improvement on the current style. The fervour and liveliness of his spirit bore him along, and carried his hearers with him. Mr. Durham used to say there was no speaking after Mr. Binning.

He appears to have had a broader and more comprehensive mind than many of his contemporaries. He not only continued his studies in philosophy, but, having great delight in nature, he was a naturalist too, and he had learned that there is a place for such things in the kingdom of God. Buckle, Dean Stanley, and other writers, complain of the intellectual narrowness of the Scotch divines of the seventeenth century. As a fact there is some ground for the complaint; they were so absorbed with the direct application of revealed truth, that for the most part they did not apprehend its wider relations, nor concern themselves with the inquiry how it was to be affiliated with the other departments of human knowledge. Even when we admire, we do feel the sameness of topic, the limitation of sphere. But in Binning we perceive the budding out of a larger soul. It is impossible to say what he might not have effected if he had reached the ordinary term of life. But what happens so often in providence happened then—the very man who seemed to be most necessary to guide the Church in a forward movement was cut down. He died of consumption in the year 1653, at the early age of twenty-six.

A deathbed remark has often been repeated, as if he felt he had made rather too much of philosophy, "to a dying man one line of the Bible is worth more than all human learning."

Of ANDREW GRAY [1] we may safely say, that never in the history of our country did a man of his years make so deep a mark. He was the youngest son of Sir Andrew Gray of Crichie, and brother of the first Lord Gray; and his wife was a daughter of Baillie of Jerviswood. He tells that, when a boy, in going one day between Edinburgh and Leith, he observed a poor beggar go into a field, and, behind a great stone, pour out his heart in prayer. The boy was greatly struck by the earnestness and fervour of the beggar. "There," he said to himself, "is a most miserable creature, in the most destitute of all conditions, while I have everything I need, and yet I never made such an acknowledgment of my mercies as that poor creature who does not lie under one-tenth of my obligations." He was but nineteen years of age [2] when he was ordained a minister of Glasgow, and his life closed in 1656, little more than two years after.

Nor was his career the mere flash of a meteor, for he left a record of very substantial work. His knowledge of Christian experience was wonderfully extensive and minute; he knew well the joys and troubles, the helps and hindrances, the temptations and the delusions of the Christian life. He had a remarkable power of probing the conscience; as James Durham remarked, he could make men's hair stand on end. He laid down a high standard of practical religion; he would be called at the present day an exacting preacher. He not only called on Christians to mortify their lusts and resist temptation,

[1] Wodrow's *Analecta*; Stirling, *apud* Wodrow; Baillie's *Letters*.
[2] Baillie makes him a little older—twenty-two at ordination.

but he urged them likewise to beware of all that insensibly lowered their tone, diminished their spiritual strength, and thus made them less able to resist temptation. It is a clear sign of spiritual earnestness when one is not satisfied to know that in certain courses there is no positive sin, but must see that they do not weaken one's spiritual force, that they do not dispose one to a habit of careless self-indulgence. It is because earnest Christians look carefully to this, that they are often misunderstood by the world, and are supposed to denounce harmless things as sinful, when all that they mean is, that they have found such things spiritually relaxing, tending not to brace but to weaken their moral and spiritual fibre.

We remark of Gray as of Binning, that he severed himself in a great degree from the cumbrous forms and methods which had come to be associated with orthodox preaching. In the letters of Robert Baillie, Gray, Binning, and Robert Leighton are spoken of with a considerable spice of bitterness on account of their "new guise of preaching, contemning the ordinary way of expounding and dividing a text, of raising doctrines and uses. Gray is said to run out in a discourse on some common head, in a high, romancing, unscriptural style, tickling the ear for the present, and moving the affections in some, but leaving little or nought to the memory or understanding."[1] If we had not had Mr. Gray's sermons to guide our judgment, this criticism of Baillie's would have been damaging to his memory. Thoroughly puritan in his theology, Gray had the courage to speak with more natural freedom and natural life than many of his contemporaries; thus bringing on him the censure of the worshippers of use and wont. The ordinary Covenanter pulpit had acquired a formal set, which many supposed

[1] Baillie's *Letters*, iii. 258.

essential to faithful preaching. Gray was like many young men of our own time who are repelled by the three-headed division of a sermon. But in forming for himself a more natural channel, he took care, as all young preachers ought, to be not less scriptural or less solid than his predecessors were; and often, at the close of his sermons, in warning sinners and exhorting them to accept the offer of Christ, he rises into a strain of impassioned appeal that has been rarely equalled in any age.

There are yet many names that might be dwelt on, eminent in their day for pulpit gifts and power. There is GEORGE GILLESPIE, more remarkable as a Church leader and theological author, a man of the most remarkable gifts, but likewise a distinguished preacher, though we are unable now to form a judgment of his preaching power, in consequence of a volume of sermons, which he had prepared for the press, never having been published.

Hardly less eminent as a Church leader than Gillespie was ROBERT DOUGLAS,[1] whose singular fate it has been to be represented in our own times by Dean Stanley as a pioneer of the "moderate" party in the Church of Scotland.[2] Singular in many ways, he was singular in the mystery that hung over his birth; and even Stanley does not disdain to refer to the rumour, which was current in the days of Bishop Burnet, and also of Wodrow, that made his father a natural son of Queen Mary, borne by her to Sir George Douglas, keeper of the castle of Lochleven. This rumour, however, so far as Queen Mary is concerned, wants confirmation. Robert Douglas was a man of singularly majestic appearance, like Robert Blair of St.

[1] Kirkton's *History of the Church of Scotland;* Wodrow's *History;* Wodrow's *Analecta;* Chambers's *Eminent Scotchmen.*
[2] *Lectures on the Church of Scotland,* p. 103.

Andrews, of both of whom a minister of the name of Tullidaff used to say that he could never look on their faces without a feeling of awe. In early life he was a chaplain in the army of Gustavus Adolphus, and it is said that when travelling with the army, having no book with him but the Bible, he committed the whole of it to memory. Gustavus Adolphus had a very high opinion of him ; he had never known, he said, a man of so great wisdom. "He might be a counsellor to any prince in Europe. For prudence and knowledge he might be a moderator to a general council, and even for military skill he could very freely trust his army to his conduct." [1] If Douglas had not been a man of high principle, he might have been Archbishop of St. Andrews when Sharp was appointed ; he spoke to Sharp very plainly, and when he saw he was bent on accepting the post, he bade him take it, and God's curse along with it. Douglas was the preacher on the occasion of the coronation of Charles II. at Scone, and it was he who on that occasion presented the covenant to be sworn by the king. He is described by Wodrow as "a great State preacher, one of the greatest we ever had in Scotland, for he feared no man to declare the mind of God to him. Yet he was very acceptable and easy to be conversed with. Unless a man were for God he had no value for him let him be never so great or noble." Douglas was a member of the Resolutioner party, and did not leave the Church in 1662. He had been a minister of Edinburgh, but as an indulged minister, he served at Pencaitland in East Lothian, where he died in 1674.

What could have induced Dean Stanley to fix on Douglas as an embryo "moderate"? His chief reason, if we may judge from its being given in italics, is connected with "his theology," for he is said by his con-

[1] Wodrow's *Analecta*, i. 84 ; ii. 136 ; iii. 82.

temporaries to have had *a singular way of preaching,
without doctrines, which some called "scumming the text."*
"Without doctrines!" He must have been against all
dogma, the Dean evidently fancied, a latitudinarian of the
most genuine type! Whereas the whole meaning is,
that, like Binning, Gray, Leighton, and others, he discarded the method of dividing his discourse into "doctrines and uses," and preferred to elicit his teaching in
a more simply expository method from the text. Could
Dean Stanley ever have read the sermon of Douglas on
the occasion of His Majesty's coronation?[1] If ever
sermon was at the very antipodes of the spirit and
manner of the "moderate" school so dear to the Dean,
and of whom he would make the preacher the remote
ancestor, it is the sermon of Douglas on that occasion.
Did ever moderate preacher express the wish in the ears
of the king, that he might truly be humbled for his own
sins, and the sins of his father's house which had been
great? Did he ever recommend to the king to take
some hours for reading the Holy Scriptures, as a good
means to make him acquainted with God's mind, and
with Christ a Saviour? Did he ever say, "If a king will
be a suitable reformer, he must be reformed himself?"
Or did he ever impress the duty of prayer in words so
plain as these :—" Sir, you have many difficulties and
oppositions to meet with; acquaint yourself with prayer,
be instant with God, and He will fight for you. Prayers
are not in much request at court; but a covenanted king
must bring them in request. I know a king is hardened
with multiplicity of affairs, and will meet with many
diversions; but, sir, you must not be diverted. Take
hours and set them apart for that exercise. Men being
once acquainted with your way will not dare to divert

---

[1] In *A Collection of Sermons, etc., at renewing and subscribing the
National Covenant of Scotland,* etc., etc. Glasgow, 1742.

you. Prayer to God will make your affairs easier all the day. I read of a king of whom his courtiers said, *He spoke oftener with God than with men.* If you be frequent in prayer, you may expect the blessing of the Most High upon yourself and upon your government."

Is it conceivable that Dean Stanley misunderstood an anecdote which Douglas related to the king in order to recommend " moderation "? Owing to infirmity an old and valued counsellor applied for leave to retire from the service of a king of France, which being granted, the king required him to sit down, and write some advice that would be useful for him in governing the country. The counsellor would fain have been excused, but the king insisting, left him with pen and ink and a sheet of paper. After due deliberation, the aged counsellor wrote in large fair letters at the head of the sheet the word *modus ;* and in the middle of the sheet the word *modus ;* and at the end of the sheet the word *modus.* He folded the paper and gave it to the king; meaning that the best counsel he could give to him was that he should keep temper in all things. " Take this counsel, sir," said Douglas to the king, "and be moderate in the use of your power. The best way to keep power is moderation in the use of it." [1]

Another distinguished preacher was ANDREW CANT.[2] He was so bold in his speech, that fearing the conse- quences, the Church did not allow him to accept a call to Edinburgh. Very likely he was one of the wild men with whom Bishop Burnet tells us that Douglas did not always agree. He was minister in succession at Newbattle, Pit- sligo, and Aberdeen. Baillie tells us that he was " ane

---

[1] *Sermon* (in volume), p. 481.
[2] Wodrow's *History* and *Analecta ;* Calderwood and Row's *His- tories ;* Baillie's *Letters.*

superexcellent preacher," whose courage was equal to any ordeal, and who dared to vindicate his loyalty in church in presence of Cromwell's officers, even when some of them, provoked by his outspokenness, were advancing to the pulpit with drawn swords to stop him.

There is a whole bevy of preachers too, mentioned by Livingstone,[1] many of whom had probably little more than local celebrity, but who bear witness to the great variety and individuality of gift and manner that characterised the time. For young men in those days were not all tumbled into the same ecclesiastical mint, to get their individuality obliterated, and to come out one and all with the same image and superscription. Livingstone speaks of John Gillespie, Kirkcaldy, as a " thundering preacher," —probably there were many such ; of Scrimger of Kinghorn as a man of most tender heart, and most pressing in his dealing with the people ; of Dykes of Kilwinning, who could get more out of a passage when he was combing his hair than some men would in a day ; Smith of Maxtoun, who knew all the psalms by heart, and was somewhat of a terror to divinity students ; Ker of Lyne, who would ask questions from the Catechism of every beggar that came for help, but was generous in his charity when he got good answers ; Josias Welsh, son of John Welsh, afterwards settled in Ireland, whose searching methods procured for him the nickname, " Cock of the Conscience ; " Dury of Dalmeny, a man of most wonderful invention and rare gift of preaching; Greg of Newmills in Cunningham, who preached with such animation and struck the two fingers of his right hand so vehemently against the palm of his left that the blood was known to come out from the tips of his fingers. It is evident that

[1] See his *Memorable Characteristics* (Wod. Soc. *Select Biographies*, vol. i.).

this was one of those periods in Scotland when great preachers appeared in a galaxy, and stars of the second and third magnitude were almost too numerous to be counted.

But there is one man of this period whose soul was like a star and dwelt apart, and yet, by universal acknowledgment, a star of the first magnitude. With the name of ROBERT LEIGHTON [1] there is no other that will pair. His history and his character, notwithstanding the brilliant qualities that marked him, still retain an air of mystery. In the fundamental features of his theology and his religious life, he was at one with his covenanting brethren. His theology was Calvinistic to the very core. Jesus Christ was as precious to him as He was to Samuel Rutherfurd. The Word of God was as thoroughly his standard of divine truth as it was to David Dickson or Robert Blair. It is simply ridiculous in Dean Stanley to claim him, either in theology, life, or preaching, as having any affinity to the "Moderate" school. His only point of connection with them was his complacency to the powers that be.

At one time Leighton seemed to have the same views as his brethren on public policy as on other matters. He swore the Covenant himself, and even so late as the time when he was Principal of the University of Edinburgh (1653-1662) he assisted in imposing the obligations of the Covenant on the students. But there is reason to fear that Leighton took part with the Covenanters through weakness, and against his deeper convictions. The set of his mind was against their ways. In his first charge, as minister of Newbattle, he had begun to absent himself

---

[1] *Life*, by Rev. John Norman Pearson; *Life*, by James Aikman, Esq.; *Life*, by Rev. Erasmus Middleton; *Life*, by George Jerment, D.D.; Bp. Burnet's *Hist. of my own Time;* Baillie's *Letters* , odrow's *Hist.* and *Analecta*, etc., etc.

from Church courts, and to shun the society of his brethren. He appears to have had an intense constitutional dislike to controversy, and a very strong conviction that the spirit of controversy was not a good neighbour to the spirit of Christ. Leighton was one of those men who have a strong preference for the gentler aspects of Christianity. In the work of the great preachers and champions of the Church, he saw Christianity in its more warlike mood, and with comparatively few of those gentler features in which he delighted. Following the guidance of his feelings rather than his judgment, he first began to shun the society of such men, and then he thought of them as persons who were not taking the best steps for advancing the Kingdom of our Lord Jesus Christ.

And in this mood he yielded to the temptation which was brought to him, when on the restoration of Charles II. he was asked to take a bishopric. We call this a temptation because Leighton had sworn the Covenant, which bound him to resist prelacy to the death. His father, too, had suffered shameful wrong and indignity at the hands of prelacy. He seemed to fancy that episcopacy might restore peace, and Scotland might become a garden of the Lord. What further motives he may have had for this step it is hard to say. It has been common to speak of him as above all human infirmity, but probably he had his share of infirmity, of human ambition, and of human resentment. In the Lauderdale Papers, recently published, it has been remarked that he seems never to have shown much concern about the atrocities against which Richard Baxter wrote to Lauderdale in earnest remonstrance. There are many letters from Leighton to Lauderdale, but none in the strain of Baxter's. How foolish it was to imagine that the opposition of the ablest and best men in the Church might be overcome, based as it was on so intense convictions ; how foolish, also, to imagine that God's blessing would rest on the schemes of the men to whom he joined himself—open enemies, many of them, of all real godliness— Leighton did not need many years to discover. His confession to Bishop Burnet that in the whole progress of that affair there appeared " cross characters of an angry Providence, showing that God was against them," was a complete and decisive confession of error and folly ; nor can we wonder that, after coming to such a conclusion, Leighton should have resigned his bishopric, and buried himself in his sister's country house far off in the county of Sussex.

But we have to speak of Leighton as a preacher. Having a somewhat feeble voice and shrinking manner, he was not fitted to be very popular. But, according to Bishop Burnet, " his preaching had a sublimity both of thought and expression in it. The grace and gravity of his pronunciation was such that few heard him without a very sensible emotion ; I am sure," he adds, " I never did. His style was rather too fine ; but there was a majesty and beauty in it that left so deep an impression that I cannot yet forget the sermons I heard him preach thirty years ago ; and yet with this he seemed to look on himself as so ordinary a preacher, that while he had the cure he was ready to employ all others ; and when he was a bishop he chose to preach to small audiences, and would never give notice beforehand. He had indeed a very low voice, and so could not be heard by a great crowd. He soon," continues Burnet, " came to see the follies of the Presbyterians, and to dislike their Covenant, *particularly their imposing it*, and their fury against all who differed from them. He found they were not capable of large thoughts ; theirs were narrow as their tempers were sour, so he grew weary of mixing with them. All the opposi-

tion that he made to them was, that he preached up a
more exact rule of life than seemed to them consistent
with human nature; but his own practice did outshine
his doctrine."

This has not the look of fair criticism; it is bitter
and partisan. And whatever else the Presbyterian clergy
might say of Leighton, it is incredible that they should
have accused him of being too hard on human nature,
when the whole strain of their teaching was that human
nature must be transformed by the power of divine grace.
Burnet seems to miss the whole drift of Puritan theology when he ascribes this sentiment to the opponents of
Leighton; just as Sir Walter Scott has done in *Old
Mortality* when he makes Macbriar, the Covenanting
minister, speak of a course of life that will "*deserve* eternal happiness in the life to come." The only objections
that Leighton's Scotch brethren took to his preaching
were these two : first, that, like Hugh Binning and others,
he discarded the old method of arrangement by observations, doctrines, and uses; and second, that he did not
preach to the times. The former objection we smile at ;
the other is more important. Leighton broke loose from
the rule that from the Reformation downwards had been
so much regarded in the Scottish pulpit—the rule which
regarded approval of a certain public policy in Church and
State, and devotion to it, as an essential part of practical
religion, an essential obligation on all who would be loyal
to Christ. Against this rule he rebelled. He strove to
get men to regard their duty to Christ in a more private
and personal light, to withdraw their attention from the
consideration of public transactions, and concentrate it on
each man's personal condition and life. That there was
some ground for Leighton's view we readily allow. That
the religious feeling of many went out mainly in vehement
political and polemical feeling, and that comparatively

little heed was given to faith, hope, and charity, and the other personal graces of the followers of Christ; in other words, that the element of fiery zeal was too conspicuous, and the element of gentle love too much neglected, can hardly be denied. Yet, on the other hand, these zealous Covenanters, beyond all reasonable doubt, loved and valued the Gospel of Christ above life itself, and their supreme desire was to secure its safety and success. The noisy elements that accompanied their movement were like the rattle of wheels on a stony road, and were not much to be wondered at on the part of a people like the Scots, who had never attained to much polish of manners, and who had been exposed to most unjust and exasperating treatment. Even if Leighton was repelled by this spirit he might have borne with it, and tried to temper it; the worst turn he could have done to the cause of Christ was to ally himself with its enemies, who, under shelter of his high character, broke into furious persecution of the true-hearted servants of the Lord Jesus Christ. Leighton's was one of many instances of a good man helping Christ's enemies out of apparent zeal for Christ, on grounds of theory that seemed to him quite sound, but miscalculating the necessary effect of his actions.

It is now time for us to grapple with a very momentous question : What was the effect of all this preaching on the character of the people? Was it preaching that promoted the interests of Christian truth, of Christian life, and of social and moral integrity? or was it an unwholesome declamation promoting, not intelligence but superstition, not sanctity but sanctimoniousness, hypocrisy rather than honesty, violence rather than virtue, ferocity rather than faith?

If we try to answer these questions from the opinions of historians and critics, we shall find ourselves involved in a labyrinth of contradiction. No passage has been more frequently quoted than that in which Kirkton,[1] himself one of the outed ministers, testifies to the admirable efficiency of the Reformed Church just before it was overthrown. "Every parish had a minister, every village had a school, every family almost had a Bible; yea, in most of the country, all the children at school could read the Scriptures, and were provided with Bibles either by their parents or ministers. Every minister was a very full professor of the Reformed religion, according to the large Confession of Faith framed at Westminster. None of them might be scandalous in their conversation, or negligent in their office, so long as a presbytery stood. I have lived many years in a parish where I never heard an oath; and you might have ridden many miles before you heard any. Also you could not, for a great part of the country, have lodged in a family where the Lord was not worshipped by reading, singing, and public prayer. Nobody complained more of our church-government than our taverners, whose ordinary lamentation was, that their trade was broke, people were become so sober."

If we discount this testimony on the ground that Kirkton was a strong supporter of the Presbyterian cause, we must in like manner discount Bishop Burnet's, who was quite as strong in the opposite interest. Burnet speaks slightingly of the popular preachers of his time, and ascribes their influence in the country to the fact that by birth or marriage they were related to some of the best families of Scotland. The fact may be noted, although the explanation is weak. At no subsequent

[1] *The Secret and True History of the Church of Scotland, from the Restoration to the year* 1678, by the Rev. Mr. James Kirkton. [The edition of Charles Kirkpatrick Sharpe, Esq. (1817), is garnished with notes that seem only designed to impugn the accuracy of the historian!]

time in the Church of Scotland have so many of the
leading ministers been connected with the landed class.
But to make this the ground of their popularity and
influence as preachers is simply absurd. When Presbytery was restored at the Revolution, Burnet uses the most
violent language to denote the treatment received by the
Episcopalian clergy, and would have us believe that the
spirit engendered by the covenants was not the spirit of
Christ, but the selfish violence of unholy zealots. But
Burnet himself was not in the country, and the vexation
connected with the collapse of Episcopacy in Scotland,
after all the efforts, *per fas et per nefas*, to keep it up,
may explain the bitterness and the exaggeration with
which he speaks of its opponents. It may serve to clearness in discussing the question, if we briefly consider the
bearing of the Covenanter pulpit and struggle generally,
up to this time, 1st, on the interests of Christian doctrine ; 2d, on the interests of spiritual life ; and 3d, on
the interests of ordinary morality.

1. The answer to the first question admits of little
doubt. The people for the most part were well instructed
in Christian truth, and what they accepted as such was
thoroughly evangelical. There was, indeed, no diversity
in the country of theological views. And if it should be
said that this was owing to the narrow intolerance of
the leading clergy, who would not endure so much as a
whisper against Calvinistic doctrine, the conclusive answer
is, that in point of doctrine there was as yet but little
apparent difference between Presbyterians and Episcopalians. The Westminster Confession was the statutory
authority in the Church even during the Episcopalian
period, and though it be true that a nominal adherence to
the same confession is no security for identity of views,
yet in point of fact there was little avowed departure
from the letter of its teaching. If we go back as far as

1616, we find that there was submitted then to the General Assembly a new Confession designed to supersede the Confessions formerly in use. This Assembly was wholly under the influence of the king, the prelates, and those who sympathised with them. The Confession was compiled by John Hall and John Adamson, both ministers of Edinburgh, and before it was printed it was revised by the Bishop of Galloway and four other leading members of the Episcopalian party. In point of doctrine, it is decidedly Calvinistic. It affirms that only those who are elected before all time are saved; that the Lord Jesus Christ fulfilled the whole law in our behalf, both doing all that the law requireth of us, and suffering the punishment due to our disobedience, even to the curse of the law and death of the cross; that God justifies sinners by remitting of their sins, and by imputing to them the righteousness and obedience of Christ; that we are justified by faith; that the meritorious cause of our justification is not in the faith which apprehendeth, but in the righteousness of Christ which faith does apprehend; that the sacraments are aids to faith, and have no efficacy *ex opere operato*, but only by the powerful application of the Holy Ghost.[1] In conformity with this fact that even the Episcopalians at this time were guilty of no divergence from Calvinistic theology, is the very pronounced Calvinism of such Episcopalian writers of the time as Archbishop Leighton[2] and Professor Henry Scougal,[3] son of the Bishop of Aberdeen.

Not only did sound evangelical views prevail, but the

[1] Calderwood's *Hist.*, vii. 233-242.

[2] See Lecture on Leighton, by the present writer, in the *Evangeli cal Succession* Series, vol. ii. p. 202, in connection with Coleridge's remarks in his *Aids to Reflection.*

[3] Author of *The Life of God in the Soul of Man.* Scougal holds that the particular sins committed by us were laid on Christ, and brought on Him the particular forms of punishment He endured.

people apprehended them clearly. Bishop Hall records with great satisfaction that there was hardly a congregation in Scotland that had not a preaching pastor, and that "as for the learning and supremacy of the preachers, whether prelates or presbyters, our ears were for some of them sufficient witnesses, for though their maintenance hath been small, yet their pains have been great and their success answerable."

Notwithstanding these facts and testimonies, it is at the same time true that even before the era of active persecution began, tendencies towards a departure from strictly evangelical preaching had shown themselves. "We find the Commission of the General Assembly in 1645 and 1650, in their causes of fasting, lamenting over many ministers 'who labour not to set forth the excellency of Christ in His person, offices, and the unsearchable riches of His grace; the new covenant, and the way of living by faith in Him; not making this the main and chief theme of their preaching, as did the Apostles (1 Cor. ii. 2), not preaching other things with a relation to Christ, and pressing duties in a more legal way; not urging them as by the authority of God's commands, so from the love of God, and the grace of the Gospel; not pointing and directing people to their furniture for them in Jesus Christ; oftentimes craving hard, but giving nothing wherewith to pay.'" [1]

Here was the little cloud like a man's hand that next century darkened the horizon. It was the beginning of a style of preaching which afterwards allied itself more formally with the doctrines of Pelagianism and Arminianism, and ultimately developed into deism and indifferentism. Such preachers thought to take a broader hold of the soul, to meet a larger number of its needs, and to promote a wider culture. It turned out that they only lost that

[1] See Brown of Whitburn's *Gospel Truth*, p. 3.

mighty grip which the Gospel takes of the soul; like the
dog in the fable, they dropped their piece of bread into
the water, in favour of a shadow; and having no Gospel
to preach which was worth the taking, their people
became listless and sleepy, careless of their feeble moral-
isings, indifferent to what only mocked the appetite of
their souls. History sometimes repeats itself; and if it
be here that the lifeless moderatism of the eighteenth
century had its origin, it becomes all young preachers to beware lest they be enticed to the region of
danger.

2. How was it with the Scottish people at this time
in respect of spiritual life? There is no reasonable
ground to doubt that very many throughout the country,
and especially in the south and the west, had undergone
the great change which in Scripture is called a turning
"from darkness to light and from the power of Satan
unto God." From among the highest and the lowest
alike, from the Marquis of Argyll to John Brown the
carrier, a great multitude professed to prize their Lord and
Saviour above all other treasure, and by their readiness to
suffer death in His cause, and the triumphant demeanour
of so many of them in the age of persecution, on the
very eve of execution, showed how true their profession
was. What proportion of the people were under the
influence of saving faith, it is quite impossible to determine; but there is every reason to believe that it was
large. For beyond the circle of those who were personally under the vital influence of the truth, there was a
certain sympathy with it on the part of the community
at large. The evangelical conception of the Gospel was
the prevalent conception of it. Salvation by grace was
the acknowledged way of life; and few would have
denied the doctrine, "Neither is there salvation in any
other."

3. But probably it would not be denied by any that the people were religious after a sort; it would rather be contended that it was a feverish, excited, unwholesome religion; and that it was particularly deficient in the spirit that makes men open, straightforward, generous, self-controlled, and faithful in all the relations of life.

Now, if the testimony of Kirkton be worth anything, it proves the opposite of this. But we are willing to grant that the testimony of Kirkton is too sweeping; all Scotland was not the moral garden that he pictures; human nature was not altogether transformed; even in the best men original sin had not died out. The truth seems to be this : in some of the best-served parishes there had been a great blessing and a beautiful transformation ; this was regarded by all the earnest ministers and people as the true ideal of the Church, the real standard to be regarded, the consummation at which all were to aim. The public sentiment of the Church was guided and stimulated by the happy results in not a few such parishes, and the current of hope and expectation moved strongly in that direction. But many parts of the country were yet wild and unregenerate. Many people even in the best parishes had not turned to the Lord. And the best people in the best parishes had still some marks of old Adam in their hearts.

In spite of all that has been said by Mr. Buckle, and reiterated on his sole authority by Mr. Cotter Morison, we believe that the moral tone of the country was greatly raised under the influence of the preachers. As for Mr. Buckle, the value of his historical judgment may be sufficiently tested by the extraordinary blindness that led him to couple Scotland and Spain as the two countries that had been most degraded by superstition and priest-craft ! Hardly less monstrous is his proposition that the same clerical tyranny which destroyed every vestige of religious liberty, conferred on the people, beyond every other country, a political freedom which was the glory of the nation! As for the array of well-authenticated facts with which Mr. Buckle supports his charge of demoralisation, and which Mr. Cotter Morison retails at second-hand, they remind us of what would take place if one were to give a moral picture of England from the *Police News*. The genius of a true historian lies in discovering representative facts—facts that give a faithful portrait of the time. No one pretends that Mr. Buckle has done anything of the kind.

It would be a most unreasonable thing to expect that a country like Scotland, which before the Reformation was sunk in debauchery, and torn with wild and bitter strife, should, after a century of the Reformed Church— a century of almost constant conflict with the civil power, of imperfect arrangements, of a half-starved ministry, and of incessant intrigue and change—have become a garden of the Lord. The old spirit of the people had not altogether passed away; and a good share of that stern old spirit showed itself even in the religious contendings of the time. Still, as Wordsworth has said, the hand which the Scottish Church held on her people was "the strong hand of her purity." The conscience of the nation was undergoing a magnificent discipline. The struggles of the Church and the lessons of the pulpit alike were proclaiming to men that there is a Power above all earthly power, and a duty to that Power paramount to every consideration of interest, comfort, or earthly good. Wherever the human soul has come into this attitude to that Power, you have the essence of all morality.

Note.

"*Presbyterian Eloquence Displayed.*"

We have not deemed it necessary to introduce in the body of this chapter any notice of the book bearing this title. But as it has been lately republished in a cheap form, and as some may be misled as to the authority due to it, it may be well briefly to refer to it here. In the early part of the century, it was brought prominently forward in a High Church journal, *The British Critic*, in a review of Sir Walter Scott's *Tales of my Landlord*, as proving incontestably that the novelist had presented a true picture of the Covenanters and their preachers. For a sober, careful, and accurate estimate of the character of the preachers of the time, and refutation of the statements in *Presbyterian Eloquence Displayed*, it may be sufficient to refer to Dr. M'Crie's *Review of Tales of my Landlord*, pp. 78 *et seq.* (Collected Works of Dr. M'Crie, vol. iv.) [This work is referred to more particularly in our next chapter.] *Presbyterian Eloquence Displayed* was the production of a curate, it is not even a contemporary book, for it was not published till 1719. The grossly indecent stories which it contains ought to warn any respectable writer against committing himself to its authority. An anonymous answer was issued to it in three parts—(1.) A catalogue of the cruel and bloody laws, with instances of the numerous murders and other barbarities inflicted by the prelatists against the Scotch Presbyterians. (2.) An exposure of the self-contradictions, lies, blasphemies, and disloyalty of the obscene scurrilous pamphlet called the *Scotch Presbyterian Eloquence*. (3.) A collection of their ridiculous expressions in sermons, and instances of the vicious lives of their bishops and clergy. This last is a foul and horrible record, and very unsavoury reading. That there was much immorality on the part of some of the Episcopalian clergy, cannot be denied. Burnet bears a strong testimony. "They were the worst preachers I ever heard ; they were ignorant to a reproach, and many of them were openly vicious. They were a disgrace to their order and to the sacred functions ; and were indeed the dregs and refuse of the northern parts" (*History of his Own Time*, i. 229). See also Wodrow's *History of the Sufferings of the Church of Scotland*, i. 333. Sir Robert Murray, who was in the Government soon after, having made a tour through the west, declared on his return, that "the clergy were such a set of men, so ignorant and so scandalous, that it was not possible to support them unless the greater part of them could be turned out, and better men found to be put in their places, but that it was not easy to know how this could be done" (Dodds's *Fifty Years' Struggle of the Covenanters*, p. 129).

CHAPTER VII.

THE FIELD-PREACHERS.

It is one of the saddest epochs of the history of the Church of Scotland that begins with the Restoration of King Charles II.

Both internally and externally the Church was under a cloud. In the first place, the bitter strife within the Church itself between Resolutioners and Protesters, which had been raging with great virulence for some years, was still bearing its fruits; and though the immediate occasion of it died away when the Act of 1662 was passed, throwing all who resisted it into a common furnace, new occasions of division and strife arose, when the successive indulgences were offered ; and still another towards the end of the persecution in connection with the proceedings of the Cameronians, and their renunciation of the authority of the king.

In the next place, the flower of the clergy were driven from their charges. Very many of the 400 that were ejected from their livings in 1662 [1] were young men, who had been trained under David Dickson and Samuel Rutherfurd, most of them of the Protester party, the most thorough and earnest champions of Presbyterian policy and evangelical doctrine. It was but few and scattered opportunities they got after 1662 of exercising their preaching gift, and only among such of the people

[1] The number at first seems to have been about 300; Wodrow's list of about 400 contains those who afterwards joined them. See Wodrow's *Hist.* vol. i. pp. 324-329.

as no threat of fine and imprisonment, of torture or of death, could turn away from the services which they loved.

In the third place, the Church did not enjoy long the benefit of the counsel and guidance of the veterans who shared, or would have shared, the afflictions now so abundantly measured out. There was a remarkable mortality of the older men about the time of the restoration of King Charles. James Durham died in 1658; Samuel Rutherfurd died, and James Guthrie was executed in 1661; David Dickson died in 1663; William Guthrie in 1665; Robert Blair in 1666; John Livingstone (in Holland) in 1672; and Robert Douglas, who, however, did not come out,[1] died in 1674.

In the fourth place, the storm of persecution that burst on the Church, and raged with few intervals till the Revolution in 1688, was extremely fierce. Occasional lulls there were, and to those who could accept indulgence, there was a measure of peace; but the more resolute spirits would have nothing to do with indulgence, and on this very account they became all the more vehement in denouncing defection, and were exposed to all the more violent forms of persecution.

At the very beginning of the period, the shameful execution of the Marquis of Argyll and of James Guthrie of Stirling was designed, by its very audacity and outrageousness, to strike terror into all who might have any sympathy with their views. The wildest efforts were made by the bishops and their friends to put down conventicles; grievous fines were imposed on men of property who might attend them, amounting, in all, according to Wodrow's computation, to upwards of a million pounds Scots;[2]

---

[1] His wife seems to have been more staunch, for Wodrow mentions her as having been proceeded against for attending conventicles. —*Hist.* ii. 238.

[2] See a full list of them in his *History*, vol. i. pp. 271-279.

to harbour a preacher, or to help him in any way, exposed
one either to a heavy fine, or to imprisonment, perchance
with the boot and thumbkins, possibly even to death; the
preacher, with a great price on his head, had no certain
dwelling-place, and where there was no friendly cottage
to shelter him, had to wander about in wild lonely places,
sleeping in woods and caves, often cold and wet and
hungry; racked by rheumatism or prostrated by dysentery;
glad if he could succeed in keeping his pocket-Bible dry,
and not so much as dreaming of the luxury of books, or
of a quiet room for study.

These conditions were not unfavourable to good preaching of a kind; but it was not the preaching that depends
on wide research, or calm thought, or breadth of view, or
that expresses itself in correct and careful language. It
was the preaching that seizes as with the grip of a drown-
ing man what is most vital, and precious, and reassuring
in the whole sphere of religious truth; seizes the truths
that bring courage and hope to souls on the verge of
distraction; that bring to the wandering, homeless outlaw
compensation for the loss of all earthly things; that raise
men above the fiercest storms, and enable them to defy
the gates of hell.

It is this that, to one investigating the elements of
effective preaching, gives such interest to the field-
preachers and their work during that dreary time of persecution between 1663 and 1688, and more especially the
last few years of that term. If ever circumstances compelled the Lord's servants to preach " as dying men to dying
men," it was then. Neither preacher nor hearer could
ever be sure that the dragoons would not burst on them
before the sermon was ended, or that before nightfall their
life-blood would not be staining the ground. As a well-
known writer of the times says, preachers seemed at times
to feel the bloody rope round their neck, or the bullet in

their brain ; the word came from their hearts and went to the hearts of their hearers, and stuck there for their conversion, confirmation, and comfort.   Persecution, like the deathbed, has a wonderful sifting power.   It tears away all disguises, shams, falsehoods, and formalities ; it compels men to look the stern realities of life and death right in the face ; it sweeps away the refuges of lies, and leaves only those truths to cling to which will sustain them in the agony of conflict.

It is interesting to inquire what were the truths which stood this test in the times of the field-preachers, and in what manner were they accustomed to serve them up to their hearers ?   The answer to the first question is, they were the great saving truths of the Gospel.   It is extraordinary that any historian should have missed this fact. It is ridiculous to fancy that men and women looking out for the dragoons, with but a step between them and death, could be fed with the subtleties of scholasticism, or the ravings of fanaticism, or the denunciations of sectarian spite ; yet how often have they been caricatured as if unable to rise to anything higher !   The topics for such scenes could be no other than the incomparable grace of the Saviour, the infallible certainty of His salvation, the magnificent sweep of His promises, the poverty of this world as a portion, and the unfading glory of the inheritance which He has provided and prepared for His own. If these topics were sometimes interspersed with lamentations over defections, and with denunciations of divine wrath upon the persecutors, such outbursts derived all their point from the vital centre of truth ; for it was because Jesus Christ was so glorious a King and so gracious a Saviour that it was so mean to compromise His cause, and so wicked to fight against it.

It was no ordinary bracing that men's minds needed in those days to make them steadfast and unmoveable in the cause of Christ. And that which alone, and beyond all comparison, was fitted for this purpose was the message of free forgiveness and full salvation through the blood of God's Son; through Him who was made, by the suffering of death, a little lower than the angels, but was now crowned with glory and honour; who was indeed subjecting the fidelity of His people to a dreadful trial, but at the same time cheering them by His promises, and holding over their heads the glorious crown of life. And the lesson that comes to us all from this painful chapter of our history is, that whether men are suffering persecution, or are sitting under their vine and their fig-tree; whether they are in the article of death, or in the full play and vigour of life, it is the great saving truths that will prove the true food and support of their souls. What is proved by the tried fitness of these truths for the night of persecution and the hour of death, is, their inherent divinity and glorious vitality; without them souls cannot be nourished even for ordinary duties and trials; they are the life-blood of spiritual existence, and the pith and marrow of all the preaching that maintains the life of God in the soul of man.

Whatever amount of human infirmity may have shown itself in these field-preachers, and whatever importance they may have attached in their preaching, or in their dying testimonies, to points that to us seem of minor importance, it was a sublime witness they bore to the supremacy of conscience and the paramount claim of the Unseen Lord of all. Their active enemies, of course, looked on them as but obstinate miscreants who would not obey the law, and who were therefore to be crushed and extirpated like vermin; others might think of them as misguided men, strangely blind to their solid interests, wrong-headed, and fit only for lunatic asylums; but a more fair and thoughtful part of the nation could not but be

struck with the overwhelming sense they manifested of
unseen realities, and with their profound regard for God
and His will. Even though such persons did not throw
in their lot with them, they must have been greatly impressed by their marvellous faith in God and in Christ,
and their confidence in a glorious and speedy recompence
of reward. It was a splendid chapter in the education of
the nation, set over-against that neglect of God, and un-
concern for the retributions of eternity into which, in
quiet times, men are so apt to fall. No man can estimate
the influence of these sufferers in keeping alive in future
generations that fear of GOD which is the beginning of
wisdom, as well as securing that honour for the Lord Jesus
Christ, which is due to the King of kings and Lord of
lords.

But let us get among the men, and learn something
more specific of their character and their ways. One of
the most picturesque and notable of the field-preachers of
the earlier period was ALEXANDER PEDEN.[1] In any walk
of life Peden would have been a " character," saying his
sayings and doing his work in a way of his own. It was
like him, when leaving the church of Glenluce, after his
three years' ministry, to knock with his Bible three times
on the pulpit door, and three times utter the words, " I
charge thee in my Master's name, that no man ever enter
thee but such as come in by the door as I have done."
It was like him to express himself so quaintly and so
strongly respecting the destiny of persecutors on the one
hand and faithful men on the other, that his words seemed
prophecies, and he became known for that, and for his
prayerful spirit, as " Peden the prophet." Peter Walker's
Life of him is just the counterpart of Adamnan's *Life of
Columba.* Ten years of the period of persecution he

[1] See *Biographia Presbyteriana*, vol. i., *Life of the Rev. Alexander
Peden*, by Peter Walker ; *Scots Worthies ;* Wodrow's *History ;
The Bass Rock, its Civil and Ecclesiastical History*, etc., etc.

spent as an outlaw and a field-preacher, eluding the dragoons with marvellous adroitness, aided at times by the forces of nature, as when, with exhausted strength and the dragoons close in pursuit, he asked God " to cast the lap of his cloak over him," and a thick mist sprang up to cover him.

In 1673 he was apprehended and sent to the Bass. Five years of misery were spent in that desolate prison —misery of body but not of spirit ; " constrained to silence as to men, he spoke the more to God." Often would he remark the beautiful seafowl of the island careering in mid-air, the very symbols of freedom, or dashing into the sea in the full consciousness of strength, and wonder why God allowed them to be so free, but kept him and his brethren in such distressing bonds. Released from the Bass, he was sentenced to perpetual banishment, but by a singular accident he regained his freedom. Then followed five years of roaming again over the south of Scotland, years of daring ventures and hairbreadth escapes. He was very earnest in maintaining close communion with God in this time of knocking about, and he pressed the duty earnestly on his hearers too. In one of his sermons preached in 1682, shortly before his death, he pleads on this behalf with his usual quaintness and earnestness :—" O sirs, you must pray ploughing, harrowing, reaping, and at all your other labours ; when you are going out and coming in, eating and drinking, and at all your other employments. O that noble life we must have of communion with God ! It is He that makes heaven pleasant ; it is communion with God that makes heaven. Do you long to be there, O people of God ?" Then he assures them of God's wonderful condescension and readiness to come near them and bless them *in common things.* " Will ye trust God and give Him credit ? I will tell you what He would do to you. He would

plough your land, sow your corn, reap your corn, sell
your corn, and bring home your money. He would even,
as it were, rock the cradle, if it were necessary, for you.
He would condescend as low as ye desire Him ; only
once close with Him, and that upon His own terms, and
make a surrender of your hearts unto Him." Here was
religion in common life, that aspect of religion which is
usually considered to be the furthest remove from fanaticism.   This venerable preacher, with his storm-tossed
and weather-beaten face, standing with his audience in
some bleak and lonely moor, beseeches them to carry on
all their secular work in communion with God, and put
Him to the test whether He will not be their daily companion, and establish upon them the work of their hands.

    There is a dash of genius in Peden's preaching, some-
times of a homely kind, and sometimes burning with
emotion.   The chiefest aim of all is to bring sinners to
Christ, and he never forgets that even in an audience
gathered in defiance of the powers of this world, there
may be some who in heart are yet afar off.   But most
of the audience were more in sympathy with him, and
his desire towards them is to commend Christ, and urge
a faithful adherence to Him and to His cause, let the
cost be what it may.   And don't let them fancy that
their troubles are proofs of the anger of their Lord.   " A
poor believer never gets a more beautiful blink of Christ
than when the cross lies heaviest betwixt his shoulders ;
for suffering is the ready way to glory, and this is the
experience of all the crowd of witnesses that have
suffered with Christ." They are not to judge of their
inheritance by what they have in hand ; it is not always
wise to give a young man possession at once of all his
property.   " Many of you people of God, like fools, would
have your stock in your hand. But if ye held it, you
would soon squander it away, as our old father Adam

did. Adam got the stock in his own hand, but he soon played it off. In a morning, at two or three throws of the game, he lost all his property. But now our blessed second Adam hath all our stock a-guiding, and He will manage better. He will give you but as you need it, people of God, in fourpences, sixpences, and shillings, but if He bring any of you to a gibbet for Him, He will give you, as it were, dollars in your hands."

Many is the plea he urges to encourage steadfastness in suffering. And never do his words glow with warmer enthusiasm than when he depicts the restoration of all things. Hear what he says to the young men and young women of Scotland with reference to those who had followed Christ through all the stormy blast, and laid down their lives for him : " Your eyes shall yet see them on thrones, and crowns on their heads, clothed with robes of glory, having harps and palms in their hands. And ye that are young folk in this country-side, if He call you to it, if ye will venture to follow Him in this storm and abide by His back, and stick by His persecuted truths in Scotland this day—He shall set you on thrones, and ye shall give in your judgment and sentence with Him." Not less effective, probably, was the anecdote he told of a poor widow whom he met with in his wanderings, when he asked her how she came on in these evil times. " I do very well," she said ; " I get more good of one verse of the Bible now than I did of it all lang syne. He hath cast me the keys of the pantry door and bidden me take my fill." Or what he told of another woman whose husband fell at Bothwell Brig, when the soldiers came to plunder her house. They threatened to take all she had, to leave her nothing to put in her or on her. " You can't," she said ; " you can't take God from me, and He is the portion of mine inheritance." And this was the man whom the dragoons strained every nerve,

but in vain, to apprehend; and when they were balked
of their living prey, wreaked their impotent vengeance on
him when dead, rifled his grave, and hung his body in
chains.

JOHN WELCH of Irongray in Dumfriesshire was one of
the boldest and most popular of the field-preachers. He
had a splendid clerical ancestry; he was the son of
Josiah Welch, who had done much noble work in times
of danger, especially in Ireland; the grandson of John
Welch, of Ayr, the man of prayer, who had been sentenced
to death for his fidelity, confined in Blackness Castle, and
who had behaved so valiantly at the siege of St. Jean
d'Angely in France; and the great-grandson of John
Knox. And he was worthy of them all. At Irongray it
is said that he had the greatest spiritual success of any
minister of the country. When he was compelled to leave,
the distress of his people was overwhelming,[1] and it may
well be believed that those whom he had trained were in
no humour to listen to a hireling curate. For taking part
in the rising at Pentland, he was declared a traitor. He
was a special object of pursuit to the dragoons, for no
preacher drew such crowds, and there were four hundred
pounds upon his head. Through the country he went, all
the same, encompassed, as it were, by the angel of the
Lord, now in Lanarkshire, now in Fife, now in Perthshire,
with audiences at times of eight or ten thousand souls.
Memorable conversions sometimes took place; that of
Lady Lindsay, afterwards Countess of Crawford, among
many others.[2] Sometimes it seemed impossible that he
should escape the soldiers, yet they never were able to lay
a hand upon him. As a mere record of danger, of enterprise, of hairbreadth escapes and providential deliverances,

[1] See Crichton's *Memoirs of Rev. John Blackader*, p. 89.
[2] *Ibid.* p. 167.

his history would be more wonderful than any romance. At open-air communions, the services often lasted for several days, yet were never interrupted. It is a proof how utterly out of sympathy with the dragoons the mass of the people were, that no one gave them information where the gatherings were to be. Usually, they were utterly at sea as to where the people were to assemble.

Welch was a most spiritual and rousing preacher. The one theme of his discourses was the grace and glory of the Lord Jesus Christ. At communions he urged very earnestly the greatness of the feast. What made it so great? " You have heard of great persons that when they made a feast to great men that invited them much, they have taken their bonds and obligations after dinner, and cast them into the fire, and so have given them besides their dinner a free discharge of all their debts. Well, this is what our Lord Jesus Christ is doing. He is calling you to-morrow to eat His flesh and drink His blood, and besides all that, He is to cast all your bonds into the fire, and give you a free discharge of all your debts. He will draw a score through all the accounts that stand between Him and you."

Yet Welch was very keen in his rebuke of those who, by forsaking the covenant, had lifted up the heel against Christ. For he regarded that as the reason why the shower of blessing was withheld, especially at communion times. " It is because of the many affronts He hath met with in Scotland, and the little resenting of the wrongs that have been done Him. It is because we are not touched with the injuries done Him in His office of Prophet, Priest, and King ; because there are so few that are concerned for the breaches made in His house, and for the breaking down of the walls thereof, and for all other affronts, and for the shedding of His servants' blood. How few are concerned for these things ! There are few

whose spikenard is sending forth a pleasant smell.   Few
of us have any lively exercises ; yea, few have any distinct
knowledge of their necessity."   And then he urges that
if they would have His presence, they must be ready to
prove their love to Him, by abandoning all their idols,
and " preferring Jerusalem above their chief joy."

After a life of extraordinary exposure and labour,
Welch died in his own house, which was situated on the
English bank of the Tweed, 9th January 1681.

The name of GABRIEL SEMPLE [1] is often associated
with that of Welch as one of the earliest, most intrepid,
and most successful of the field-preachers.   But for want
of space, we must pass him over in favour of another, not
less estimable, who is well entitled to a brief notice.
JOHN BLACKADER,[2] now best known, perhaps, as having
died in captivity on the Bass Rock, the representative of
an ancient and honourable family,[3] was minister of
Troquheer in Galloway before his ejection, and in that
sphere exerted himself so energetically in pastoral work
as to remind us in some degree of Baxter's wonderful
labours at Kidderminster.   After his ejection in 1662,
Blackader, under deep family trial, was silent for a time.
But in a few months he entered on the work of field
preaching, continuing at it from time to time, under
extraordinary risks and escapes, till at length he was
apprehended in 1681, and committed to the prison of
the Bass.

We may gather the tenor of his preaching during this
long period from some of his texts.   " Necessity is laid
upon me ; yea, woe is unto me if I preach not the gospel."
" Oh that I knew where I might find Him !"   " In those
days the house of Judah shall walk with the house of

---

[1] See Wodrow's *History*, etc.
[2] See Wodrow's *Hist.*, Crichton's *Life*, *The Bass Rock*, etc., etc.
[3] Blackader of Tulliallan.   He had succeeded to the baronetcy,
but did not take up the title.

Israel, and they shall come together out of the land of the north to the land that I have given for an inheritance unto your fathers." It was to the richest Gospel pastures that these preachers led their flocks. It often happened that word was carried to the Government of the persons who had attended them, and forthwith an order came down to these to pay enormous fines, or lie in prison till the uttermost farthing was paid. When such temporal losses hung over their heads the preachers strove to give them the best spiritual food, and wrestled mightily in prayer for God's presence and blessing. And it was experience of that blessing that in spite of fine and imprisonment made the meetings so popular and so precious. Once, when Blackader was residing in a house near Bo'ness, being in poor health, he had not intended to preach; but in the morning of the Sabbath, such a number of people had assembled, many from Linlithgow, a place noted for opposition to covenants and conventicles, that he agreed to give an address in a room. But when the gates were opened, hundreds poured in, filling the house, while many were standing in the court outside. And there was present an honest woman from Linlithgow, who had fallen from her horse on the way and broken her arm; but so eager was she to hear the sermon that she came forward, and sat all the forenoon composedly, without fainting, and would have stayed the afternoon too, if Mr. Blackader had not ordered her husband to take her home. And it was observed, that when men were fined for being at a conventicle one day, they and their neighbours were present in greater numbers the next.

There were occasional intervals called the "blinks" where the keenness of persecution abated, and the conventicles then were extraordinary. On one day in Fife it was calculated that three conventicles were attended by 16,000 persons. Many instances might be given of

spiritual success.   Once, when Blackader had come very
close in his appeals, and was protesting against any who
would not take Christ, a woman exclaimed, " Hold your
hand, sir, I give my consent."   On another occasion, one
of the wickedest men of the place was so overcome by a
representation of the miseries of those who had lost God
for evermore, that after falling and writhing on the
ground, he started up exclaiming, " Let me till [to] him, for
the Lord's sake, let me till him" (meaning Mr. Blackader);
when alone with him, he confessed his sins, and was
directed to the blood of sprinkling that cleanseth from all
sin.   Mr. Blackader's son, in narrating this case, remarks :
" Such instances of the power and irresistible grace of
God, he used to say, rejoiced his heart, and did him more
good than twenty years' stipend."

We must pass over the thousand interesting incidents
of Blackader's life, spread over the nineteen years from
1662 to 1681, during which, at continual hazard, he
preached the Gospel all over the south and east of Scotland, till at last he was apprehended and committed to
the Bass.   In this dreary prison he spent the last four
years of his life.   His brutal jailers refused him even a
temporary liberty after the hand of sore disease was on
him ; in 1685 he died in prison, still thanking his Lord
for much spiritual blessing, and longing for that rest in
glory, the vision of which had cheered him, as it cheered
John in Patmos, amid the hardness and loneliness of his
banishment.

We come now to the men who represented the last
and most excited period of the covenanting struggle, when
in addition to the old testimony for the covenants, and
against the indulged ministers, a blow was aimed at the
authority of the king himself ; when it was boldly proclaimed by a few of the field men that Charles II. had

forfeited all claim to the allegiance of his people, and was no longer to be regarded as their king. It was a step of extraordinary boldness, and drew upon its authors the severest anathemas. It was a singular step to be taken by a handful of preachers, wanderers on the face of the earth, the forlorn hope of a cause that to all appearance was on the very verge of extinction. But it was a step of as great insight as boldness. What was sedition, anarchy, and madness in 1680 became constitutional patriotism in 1688 ; and James II. was deposed by the deliberate voice of the nation for offences of the very same kind as those for which his brother Charles had been arraigned in Cameron's Sanquhar Declaration, and Cargill's Torwood excommunication.

DONALD CARGILL [1] is often spoken of as the very ideal of a fanatic ; an impression which has been fostered by some reckless assertions of Bishop Burnet, who fathers on him certain excesses committed by a man named Gibb, whom Cargill utterly repudiated. Certainly there was one quality for which Cargill was marked, which is not usual in fanatics,—the shortness of his sermons and his prayers. When he was reproached for not giving an ample meal to hungry souls, who greatly prized the bread of life, his answer was one most worthy to be pondered by every preacher : " When my heart is not affected, and comes not up with my mouth, I always think it time to quit. What comes not from the heart, I have little hope it will go to the hearts of others." From 1662 to 1680, Cargill had gone up and down the country, preaching a rich and blessed Gospel, unfolding much of the fulness of Christ ; sometimes arrested yet set free ; sometimes discovered but not arrested ; sometimes wounded but never fatally. His sermons made a great impression, and Peter

[1] *Scots Worthies;* Peter Walker's *Life;* Wodrow's *History,* etc., etc.

Walker, who heard some of the last of them, tells us that the printed sermon could give no idea of the sermon delivered.   Here is his account of the last sermon Cargill ever preached.   It was in Dunsyre Common, betwixt Clydesdale and Lothian, where he lectured on the 1st chapter of Jeremiah, and preached upon that soul-refreshing text, Isa. xxvi., last two verses : " Come, my people, enter into your chambers," etc., " Wherein he was short, marrowy, and sententious, as his ordinary was in all his public sermons and prayers, with the greatest evidences of concernedness, exceeding all that ever I heard open a mouth, or saw open a Bible to preach the Gospel, with the greatest indignation at the unconcernedness of hearers. . . . It came from his heart and went to the heart; as I have heard some of our common hearers say, that he spake as never man spake, for *his words went through them.* . . .   He exhorted us all earnestly to dwell in the clefts of the rock, to hide ourselves in the wounds of Christ, and to wrap ourselves in the believing application of the promises flowing therefrom ; and to make our refuge under the shadow of His wings, until these sad calamities should pass over, and the dove come back with the olive leaf in her mouth.   These were the last words of his last sermon." Some one said to him that he preached and prayed best when he was in the greatest danger.   " He said it was so ; that the more that enemies and all others did thrust that he might fall, the more sensibly had the Lord helped him ; and then as if to himself he repeated the words, ' The Lord is my strength and my song, and is become my salvation.'   The 118th psalm was the last he sung on earth.   He sung it on the scaffold."

To the personal virtues of Cargill his friends bore the most glowing testimony ; he was abstemious, self-denied, tender-hearted, generous to the poor, and most sympathetic, as well as full of devotion and faith.   The excommunica-

tion of Torwood, in which, all by himself, he excommuni-
cated the king, the Duke of York, and others whom he
considered to be ruining the kingdom, can only be
accounted for on the principle that in dead earnest he
believed it to be a right step, and when no one would join
him, he did it alone. It brought him furious retribution.
A price of 5000 marks was set on his head, and when he
was arrested one morning, the brutal soldier who found
him broke into ecstasies at the thought of his prize.
Rumour had it that he was to be put into a barrel pierced
by spikes and rolled down a hill; or roasted in an iron
frame that was to be gradually heated; but the enemy
was satisfied with hanging him with four others at the
cross of Edinburgh; after which the hangman "hashed
and hagged his head off," to fasten it to the Nether Bow.
He died in the most perfect peace of mind, full of delight
in the thought that he was just entering into glory, and
that the Lord was waiting to welcome him.

With the name of Cargill we usually associate that of
one who died before him, less than half his age, but left
even a deeper mark on the more resolute Presbýterians
of the day—RICHARD CAMERON.[1]

Cameron was a born preacher. He had had no theological course; but Semple, Welch, and other field-
preachers, struck with his wonderful vein of natural
eloquence, called him to the office of preacher, and some
time after, he was ordained in Holland. He had been an
episcopalian, but was converted, apparently under the
ministry of a field-preacher of the name of Mair. Of this
Mr. Mair, Peter Walker says (and the remark is true of
many more) that when he went north to preach he never
touched the sin of prelacy, nor any other national defec-

---

[1] *Biographia Presbyteriana;* Wodrow's *Scots Worthies;* Grub's
History; Dodds's *Fifty Years' Struggle of the Scottish Covenanters.*

tion ; for he felt that if any were convinced and converted under his ministry, they would come right on these questions as a matter of course. It may be well to say here, that Donald Cargill was in the habit of insisting that it was dangerous and ruinous to place much if not all religion in the outward parts of it, "as prayers, fastings, and mournings, and contendings for the testimony ; " and in the same spirit, another famous preacher, with the same extreme views, Walter Smith, in drawing out rules for the " Societies," into which their adherents were formed, strongly urged " that nothing be done that might occasion needless animosities, contentions, and debates, which tended to the marring of love and edification ; but let the questions proposed be only practical questions, about the ordering of the conversation, so as that the same might be holy and inoffensive, and whatever might tend most to the stirring up of God's grace, mortifying their corruptions, and preserving them and others from snares and temptations."[1]

When Cameron was converted to Christ, he carried out his presbyterian principles to the utmost, so that he could not refrain from denouncing all those ministers who had accepted the indulgence, and even went so far as to call on their people to leave them. Ultimately he joined with Cargill,—though in this the great body of the Presbyterians repudiated his action,—in declaring that the king had forfeited his throne, and in justifying the taking up of arms against him. Of a singularly open, fervent, and perhaps narrow nature, he was one of those men who know nothing of the wisdom of the serpent, and who rush at their object with unfaltering ardour, scorning all who refuse to accompany them.

A better estimate of him than that of Dodds, in his *Fifty Years' Struggle of the Scottish Covenanters*, could not

[1] *Biographia Presbyteriana*, ii. 78.

be found. "Although Cameron was a remarkable and 'representative man,' I do not claim for him any of the higher attributes of intellect. I do not mean that he was an original or profound thinker, or a man of literary attainment. On the contrary, his scholarship, considering his opportunities, must have been of as humble an order as a public teacher could well have. . . . His whole modes of thought were drawn from two very old sources, the Bible, and the standards of the Scottish Kirk. But he had an honest mind that insisted on carrying out its convictions to their full legitimate consequences. . . . He had the firm front of the confessor, the strong nerve of the soldier, the unflinching spirit of the polemic, and—rarest, grandest, most heavenly gift!—he had the calm willingness to die for the cause which his conscience taught him to be of God. The people always love and follow the man who goes straight like an arrow to his mark, and is not eaten up of doubts and difficulties. . . . Hence the intense and life-like power of that eloquence (rustic and primitive, no doubt, so far as regards artistic form) which he thundered forth in the moors and mountain-recesses of Scotland. It was not talk; it was not the perfume of the breath, the honey of the lip. In [his discourses] we see a brave, truthful, elevated soul, living and communicating kindred life to others. The function of the preacher is not to dig down in search of obscure and hidden dogmas; not to weave fine and intricate webs of argument; not to play off the legerdemain of style and unmeaning rhetoric; but seizing the great and necessary truths where all spiritual and eternal reality lies, so to flash them upon the hearts and consciences of men, that they shall be forced to exclaim, like the multitudes on the day of Pentecost, What shall we do? what shall we do? In this sense, Richard Cameron was a mighty preacher.

"Picture to yourselves this noble and majestic youth, with blooming countenance and eagle eye, standing on some huge rock uplifted in the wilderness. Ten thousand people are grouped around him : the aged, with the women and children, seated near this pulpit of nature's handiwork ; the men of middle age and the stalwart youths of the surrounding hamlets composing the outer circle, many of them with their hands on their swords, or their trusty guns slung by their side ; and on each neighbouring height may be seen the solitary figure of the watchman, intently gazing in all directions for the approach of the troopers. . . . It is a Sabbath in May . . . How sublime and peaceful the moment! even in this age of violence and oppression—of the dungeon, the rack, and the scaffold, and murder in cold blood in the fields. Heaven smiles on the 'remnant.' All is hushed and reverent attention. The word is precious. . . . The psalm has been sung, and the echoes of the myriad voices have died on the moorland breeze. The prayer has been offered, the earnest wrestlings with Heaven of men who before sunset may themselves be an offering for their religion. The preacher rises. . . . There is in his manner more than the usual solemnity. . . . Yes, he knows that his days are numbered ; and but a few more suns the heather sod shall be his bed of death. A strange, almost unearthly sympathy is visible, stirring those assembled thousands to the very depths of their being. Rousing himself from the reverie which had passed over him, the preacher announces his text—' Ye will not come to me that ye might have life.' "

It would occupy too much space to give an account of this sermon. It is a most fervent pleading for Christ in every part of it. When he comes to close quarters with his audience it seems impossible that any can escape. " Will ye take Him, yea or nay ? Will ye take

Him home with you? It is a great wonder that any one in Scotland is getting such an offer this day. About this time twelvemonth it would have been thought strange to have heard it said that field-preachings would have come under such disdain. But take Him, and change your mind; give up with banning, cursing, and swearing; give up with cess-paying; give up with the indulgence, and give up with all the ministers that take not up the cross of Christ which we are bearing at this day. Take the glorious Person who has occasioned our coming together here this day into this wild place. What! shall I say that any of you were not content to take Him? I would fain think that some will take Him. And if, from the bottom of your heart, ye have a mind to take Him, ye shall get the earnest of the Spirit, He will in no wise cast you out. Poor, vile drunkard, take Him. Swearer, adulterer, liar, be what you will, we give you the call and warning to come and take Him. Upsitten professor, it is such as you He is seeking after. Our Lord cannot get entertainment among the scribes and pharisees. Well, poor thing that hast neither skill nor religion, are ye content to take him? He speaks peace to you. Go, sin no more. Let us not return again to folly. Let us redeem the time because the days are evil." . . .

"My Master hath been crying unto you in the parishes of Muirkirk, and Crawfordjohn, and Douglas, 'Ye will not come unto me that ye might have life.' What say ye? Shall I go away and tell my Master that ye will not come unto Him? . . . I take instruments before these hills and mountains around us that I have offered Him unto you this day. Angels are wondering at the offer. They stand beholding with admiration that our Lord is giving you such an offer this day. Look over to the Shawhead and all these hills—look at them! They are all witnesses now, and when you are dying they shall come before your face."

" Here," says an old chronicler, "both minister and
people fell into a state of calm weeping."

One hardly expects this in these stern Covenanters
among the hills. "A state of calm weeping"! How
unlike the mood of fiery, ferocious fanatics! How unlike
the mood that many associate with our stern nature, and
our hard theology! Yet it is a certain fact that many of
the preachers of Scotland have excelled in the tender
vein, have been great masters of pathos, and, under God,
have melted their hearers into the most gentle and tender
of moods. The first John Welch was such a preacher;
such also were Samuel Rutherfurd and John Livingstone.
In our own time the faculty reappeared in Robert
M'Cheyne, whose tender tone seemed a new thing in our
pulpit, and was wonderfully efficacious; yet it had been
shown long before in another preacher, equally youthful,
who could thunder God's judgments like another Elijah
against the sinner great in power, and yet join in calm
weeping with his poor, bleeding, persecuted countrymen.

After all, some may think, this was but a sentimental
rush of feeling, with no deeper roots. Listen again. In
a sermon from the text, " O Israel, thou hast destroyed
thyself, but in me is thy help," he dwells on the prevailing carelessness as to sin, and especially swearing and
lying. There was one form of lying too prevalent even
among professors. When soldiers came to the house and
asked if such a man is there, what answer was to be
given them? Were they to be told the truth, or were
they to be told a lie? The truth, says Cameron, and
never a lie! You may play with them a little to gain
time; but on no account are you to lie. " Rather tell them
that he *is* there, though you and your house should be
ruined by it, though it should tend to the prejudice of
the best ministers in the land. But why so? Because
God, the God of truth, will never thank you for saving

any man's life by a lie. Let us be strict and ingenuous both with God and man." Was this a man to play loose with the obligations of conscience? Was this a man to teach others to break one of God's least commandments? Cameron could not separate the two sides of the Lord's seal: "The Lord knoweth them that are His." And, "Let every one that nameth the name of Christ depart from iniquity."

Before the battle of Ayrsmoss, fought a few days after Cameron had preached the sermon on coming to Christ, he prayed, "Lord, spare the green and take the ripe." It was one of those prayers that were not answered in the letter. The aged Cargill escaped wounded, the youthful Cameron fell. His body, falling into the hands of the enemy, was brutally mutilated, and the head and hands carried to Edinburgh. There, they were shown to his father, who was lying in prison for the same cause, as if for the very purpose of lacerating his heart. The old man recognised them with intense emotion; but at once suppressed his personal feeling, and resigned himself to the Lord, who doeth all things well. The head and the hands were then fixed to the Nether-Bow Gate. It is a proof of his remarkable influence that the name "Cameronian" has stuck for 200 years to some who agreed in certain of his views, notwithstanding their repudiation of it. It has been perpetuated, too, in another connection. Our famous Cameronian regiment was composed of followers of Richard Cameron. Its colonel was John Blackader, son of the field-preacher. It has always been a name of honour in its military connection; and it is a standing witness that Cameron's principles, in their true influence, were not calculated to produce rebels and fanatics, but faithful, valiant men, that feared God and honoured the king.

M

There is another young minister who deserves cordial
recognition in this very imperfect sketch, the last of all
the Scottish martyrs, but one for whom the furnace was
made hotter than for many before him. The proceedings of
Cargill, Cameron, and the rest had irritated the Government
intensely, and their measures of coercion were now so hot
and furious that our fathers called this "the killing-time."
At the Cross of Edinburgh on 27th July 1681, as Donald
Cargill was endeavouring, amid much interruption from
the drums, to deliver to the spectators his last testimony,
and assure them of the joy and peace that filled his heart,
there stood at the foot of the gallows gazing on him with
awe-struck face, and drinking in every word of his dying
testimony, a young man of eighteen, JAMES RENWICK,[1] on
whom his mantle was destined to fall.   It was not, however, as a preacher that Renwick was most eminent.
True, indeed, as Mr. Dodds has said, the little fragments
that remain of his sermons prove that he preached only
Jesus Christ and Him crucified ; and that with a fulness,
earnestness, and success that might have put to shame
his accusers.   Renwick was ordained in Holland, and
when he returned to Scotland in 1683, the special work
with which he charged himself was to testify against the
defections of the Presbyterians, and especially of those who
had accepted the indulgence. The remarkable feature of
his career was that, during the hottest years of the persecution, when the whole resources of the Government were
let loose against the party formed by Cargill and Cameron,
and when he was the only field-preacher left, he guided
their affairs with consummate wisdom, tact, and success ;
restrained their tendency to extremes ; helped "the
Societies" which were formed for worship and mutual
protection ; wrote most of the public documents that

[1] Shield's *Life and Death of Mr. James Renwick ;* Wodrow; *Cloud
of Witnesses ;* Walker's *Theology and Theologians of Scotland.*

were issued; conducted a large correspondence with foreign churches; preached constantly, visited the sick, and wrote letters of advice, condolence, and encouragement to all in suffering, in bonds, or in banishment. And all the time he was a poor outlaw, the severest penalties hanging over any one that gave him so much as a cup of cold water; obliged to hide from innumerable enemies; to spend miserable winter nights in wretched cattle-sheds, high among the hills, ill off for food, which was sometimes brought from far distances by children without knowledge of their parents; and compelled to make his many journeys by the obscurest roads and in the darkest hours of the night. After more than four years of this life, when all the resources of the country were in operation against him, he was at last caught, tried, and condemned. When he appeared in court, his enemies could hardly believe that the boyish-looking youth, little in stature, with his pretty face and red cheeks, was the monster whom they had been hunting for years, and who had sustained the cause of the Covenant on his single shield. They would fain have spared him, but he would not yield. His marriage-day had come; the bridegroom was ready, and he would not delay. On the 17th February 1688, so near the hour of national deliverance, he died at Edinburgh on the gallows. In a lull of the noise and interruption, his voice was heard in a glow of triumph—" I shall soon be above these clouds—I shall soon be above these clouds—then shall I enjoy Thee and glorify Thee, O my Father, without interruption and without intermission for ever !"

We have had to pass over the names of many who were eminent field-preachers in their day—Welwood, M'Ward, Arnot, Walter Smith, Hugh M'Kail, some of whom too won the martyr's crown. But had we gone

into their history, we should have found the same
results—the same emphasis in their sermons on the
grace and glory of Jesus Christ; the same testimony to
the need of personal union to Him, and transformation
through His Spirit; the same conviction that dishonour
was done to Christ in the recent ecclesiastical proceedings; the same endeavour to comfort and cheer His
suffering people by the assurance of a coming retribution,
and the same warning to persecuting kings and bloody
counsellors to kiss the Son lest he be angry, and they
perish from the way. But we have seen enough to enable
us to answer a question to which we now proceed. Was
it a historical picture of the field-preachers, even of the
last years of the struggle, that Sir Walter Scott gave to
his readers in the Gabriel Kettledrummles, the Ephraim
Macbriars, and the Habakkuk Mucklewraths of *Old Mortality*? Who among the heroes we have sketched can
fairly sit for the portrait of any one of them? To represent such raving fanatics as types of the men whose
movement led to the same result as regards the sovereign
of the country as was achieved by the Revolution of
1688; or to represent sermons full of blustering rage and
spite as what stirred the souls of the men and women
who forsook all for the sake of their faith, is not only a
falsifying of history, but indicates a singular blindness to
human nature. It is strange indeed how often secular
writers, in accounting for religious movements, can do so
only by a wholesale theory of madness, unwilling to
ascribe the conduct of the men to divine influence, and
finding no other available cause but wholesale insanity.
Any feasible explanation of Covenanting history, while
allowing a full share of error and infirmity, of violence
and intolerance to its preachers, under the influence of
the fiery trials to which they were exposed, ought surely
to admit that they were human beings, men of like

passions with ourselves, and to explain their conduct on that supposition.

Dr. M'Crie's review of Sir Walter's story was one of the most complete and destructive pieces of criticism ever written. It was with a bad grace that Sir Walter defended himself in the *Quarterly Review*, anonymously reviewing his own books; but even there he had to admit that his picture represented only some of the wildest and most violent preachers. At an after period he showed a franker spirit, and a disposition to make the *amende honorable*, in his *Tales of a Grandfather*. Speaking of the clergy of the Reformed Church of Scotland at large he says:—" They were endeared to the people by the purity of their lives, by the depth of learning possessed by some, and the powerful talents exhibited by others; above all, by the willingness with which they submitted to poverty, penalties, and banishment rather than betray the cause which they considered as sacred. . . . In throwing away the external pomp and ceremonial of worship, they had inculcated in its place the most severe observation of morality. . . . No one who considers their works and their history can deny to these respectable men the merit of practising in the most rigid extent the strict doctrines of morality which they taught. They despised wealth, shunned even harmless pleasures, and often endangered their own lives in attempting to put a stop to the feuds and forays which daily occurred in their bounds. . . . There is no doubt that these good men and the Christianity which they taught were one of the principal means of correcting the furious character and revengeful habits of the Scottish nation, in whose eyes bloodshed and deadly vengeance had been till then a virtue."

In regard to the Covenanting struggle, Sir Walter thinks that the clergy became too much mixed up with political interests to allow their lessons on religion to

have their due weight with the people.   He utters an
indignant protest against the vile laws on " intercom-
muning ; " denounces the drunken Parliament of Middleton, which brought about the overthrow of Presbyterianism
and the deprivation of 400 ministers ; thinks the instances
of violence used by the Covenanters towards their enemies
and persecutors fewer than might have been expected ;
and while characterising the murder of Archbishop Sharp
as a violent and wicked deed, shields the body of the
Presbyterians from the reproach it brought on them, inasmuch as they cordially disowned it, although they might
be of opinion that one who had unjustly inflicted death
on so many deserved himself a similar retribution.   This
was so far satisfactory ; but the representations of *Old
Mortality* continue to fly to all parts of the world like
thistle-down, while the corrections of them probably do
not reach more than one in a hundred of those who read
the story.

One word here on the portrait of the religious character
we often find in novels.   Sir Walter vindicated his Kettledrummles, Macbriars, and Mucklewraths, on the plea
that there were such men among the Covenanters, only
they were exceptional and extreme.   The same vindica-
tion may be made for the evangelical monsters of Dickens,
of Thackeray, of Kingsley, of Mrs. Oliphant, and of George
Macdonald.   But is it a fair way of delineating a species
to introduce only its dwarfs or its ogres ?   If writers of
fiction are to take the responsibility of tracing the connection of cause and effect in the theological world, ought
they not, with profound conscientiousness, to make a
separation between what is normal and what is abnormal?
Would not every honest naturalist be most careful to do
so in botany or in zoology ?   And when men are dealing
with divine truth and human character, are they warranted
to be less conscientious than the naturalist ?   We make

no quarrel with them for delineating offensive religious characters. We are all the better, every one of us, of seeing ourselves as others see us. What we object to is, representing these as types of the species. And in the case of the Covenanters, representing them as leaders of a great world-conquering religious movement. Here, as in so many other instances, let us mark the lesson we derive from honest John Bunyan. Who would blame him for his portraits of Worldly Wiseman, and By-ends, and Formality, and Hypocrisy, and Obstinate, and Pliable? But then we see at once that these are the abortions of the race; in Christian and Faithful, Hopeful and Honest, Watchful and Valiant-for-the-truth, we see the genuine samples of the stock; by their human frailties, manifestly our brethren; but by their noble efforts to conquer sin and bless mankind, true children of God.

The view of the Covenanters expressed by another popular writer, the late Dean Stanley, is substantially this—they were splendid fellows, they fought most brilliantly; but what was it all about? It was too small a matter to fight over. The Scotch Church has always been fighting about small points. As the Frenchman said of the charge of the Light Brigade at Balaclava, "c'est magnifique; mais ce n'est pas la guerre." It is doubtless true that many ecclesiastical contests in Scotland have been about little points; but that does not prove that they have been petty struggles. The contest at Thermopylæ was for a little pass; the fight of Horatius was for a bridge; the struggle at Waterloo for the château of Hougomont. But who would measure the importance of the battle by the size of the places attacked or defended? It will be found that in Scottish conflicts, the little points have been held, at least on one side, to represent very vital truths. Whether this has always been a correct view may be doubted; that it was a correct view in the

Covenanter struggle, facts, we think, abundantly prove. Survey the parties in the field; trace their genealogies; mark what they have learned to regard as the most vital of interests; and you will have little hesitation in concluding that in the main the Covenanters' struggle was a struggle for the Gospel of Salvation, and that it was this profound conviction that gave to them their faith, their enthusiasm, their perseverance, their contempt of loss, suffering, and death, and their invincible assurance that the Lord was on their side.

At the same time, it is to be noticed that in great religious movements there is a class of men who become singularly zealous for all the outer distinctions of their party, who are singularly precise in carrying out all the logical conclusions of their principles, but who, at the same time, are conspicuously deficient in the soul of the movement, in all that gives it its real importance and weight. Often fussy, forward, and conceited, they represent the worst features of the cause; in their hands it is stript of all its heavenliness and nobility, and brought down to the level of a common carnal conflict. It seems inseparable from this imperfect world, that some such men always hang on the skirts of noble movements. They afford a ready handle to enemies to scoff at the cause with which they are connected. That there were enough and to spare of such men in the Covenanter movement we cannot doubt. But as little can we doubt that the real leaders of the cause were strong men of God, whose conversation was in heaven, and who gained their influence over their fellows because they were enabled to minister very richly to the deepest needs of their nature, and because they were themselves manifestly treading that path of self-denial which they declared to be the way of God.

CHAPTER VIII.

IT had often been the confident testimony of dying martyrs on the scaffold, that a glorious day would yet dawn on the reformed and covenanted Church of Scotland. It cannot be said that this prediction was conspicuously verified in the age that followed the Revolution. Though it was the reformed, it was not the covenanted Church that was then restored, much to the disappointment and distress of the Society-men or Cameronians, who could not conceal their indignation at the unworthy compromise they held to have been come to. But apart altogether from the question of the covenants, it must be confessed that there was a great contrast between the Church of the Revolution-settlement and the Church of the preceding half century. From a Church of heroes and martyrs, full of noble daring and sublime endurance, conspicuous for fearless resistance to human might, and for blazing testimonies quenched in blood, it became a Church of homely ministries, of respectable but not very distinguished preachers, a Church to a large extent, doubtless, faithful and laborious, but by no means brilliant; and, moreover, blemished by the presence in it of a considerable proportion of clergy who were neither in sympathy with the theology of the standards, nor with the aims of an evangelical ministry.

It was in 1690 that the first General Assembly under

the Revolution-settlement met. Of the four hundred ministers ejected from their livings in 1662, only ninety now survived, and the hardships and troubles through which they had passed made them look much older than they were. "On glancing round this new Assembly," says the younger Dr. M'Crie,[1] "one is struck with the number of grey heads and furrowed cheeks that present themselves. It is literally 'an assembly of the elders.' It looks as if the bodies of those old saints had come out of their graves into the holy city to witness and attest the resurrection of their beloved Church. . . . There are men there who were at the battles of Pentland and Bothwell Bridge; who fled from mountain to morass, and hid themselves, with their Bibles clasped to their bosoms in the dens and caves of the earth; men who bear on their bodies the marks of the rack and the thumbscrew, and can tell of the horrors of Dunottar Castle and the Bass Rock."

Besides the ninety ejected ministers now restored to their former charges, the Church consisted of those Presbyterians who had accepted the indulgence, and of the Episcopalian clergy, or rather that part of them who owned William and Mary as the rightful sovereigns of the country. A hundred and seventy-nine of the Episcopalian clergy refused to comply with this condition, and were for that reason deprived of their benefices.

The ninety restored men were by far the most resolute and daring portion of the reconstructed Church. The other Presbyterians were men who, by accepting the indulgence, had more or less acted on the principle of accommodating themselves to the necessities of the time. Such men could not be very happy in the reconstructed Church. They could not forget that their more enduring brethren had counted them to have acted an unworthy

[1] *British and Foreign Evangelical Review*, vol. ii. p. 513. See also his admirable volume, *The Story of the Scottish Church*, p. 423.

part, and that the Cameronians had openly denounced
them as traitors, with whom earnest Christian people
ought to have no communion. Even supposing them
able to justify themselves to their own consciences, they
must have felt that depression of soul which comes of
preferring the way of worldly peace and profit to the way
of self-denial and courageous suffering. All this tended
to subdue the enthusiasm and chill the ardour of the restored Presbyterian Church. Add to this, that for the first
time in the history of the Reformed Church of Scotland
there was no visible opponent, no organised opposition to
rouse her energies by antagonism; and, on the other
hand, no National Covenant or Solemn League to rally
them in her defence. The Romish cause was reeling
under the Revolution; the Episcopal cause was disposed
of by the new settlement of the Church; the extreme
Covenanters, comparatively a small body, refused to come
within its pale; so that, while there was great need of
vigilance lest old enemies should revive, and of care lest
the existing settlement should be disturbed, there was
nothing to stir the blood of the Church or rouse the
energies of the preachers as in the days when the Covenant was signed in the Greyfriars Churchyard, and the
dying testimonies of faithful men were sounding forth at
the Grassmarket or the Cross of Edinburgh.

There were still some of the older preachers who had
gone through the persecutions, and who continued to lift
up their voice with strength; but they did not represent
the prevailing spirit. There were a few men like old
Gabriel Semple, of whom Thomas Boston says, that once
when he heard him give an address from the reader's
desk, "I was in a manner amazed, for his words went out
through me and in through me, so that I said in my
heart, Happy are those that hear thy wisdom!" Semple,
who was a man of ancient family, son of Sir Bryce Semple,

and descended from the Lord Semple who fell at Flodden, had always been a singularly powerful preacher, both in Scotland and in Ireland; and the blessing continued to rest on his work after the Revolution, when he was minister of Jedburgh. It is said that when it was proposed in 1696 by a Committee of Assembly to give, among the reasons for a Fast, the restraint of the Spirit in ordinances, Semple would not hear of it. " I was witness," he said, " to the old times before the Restoration, and to the times under persecution, and I never saw so much of the Spirit poured out as I have seen since the Revolution."[1]   There was Henry Erskine, a most spiritual preacher, the father of Ralph and Ebenezer, afterwards the leaders of the Secession, the spiritual father, too, of Thomas Boston, and of many more in the days of persecution ; such were the straits to which he had often been reduced, that when there was no bread to give his hungry children he would try to sooth them by a tune on his zither, and comfort their mother by words of prayer,—playing and praying in turn. There was Thomas Hog of Kiltearn, a Highland minister of remarkable godliness, who, when a prisoner on the Bass, having petitioned Archbishop Sharp during an attack of illness for a temporary release, was ordered to the lowest cell of the prison, but, through the good hand of his God upon him, recovered, and was spared to carry on that great and good work in the Highlands in which he has had so many distinguished successors.

But the majority of the ministers were of a much less pronounced and demonstrative type. There is no reason to doubt the Christian excellence or the Presbyterian loyalty of William Carstairs, who had so large a share in guiding the policy of the Church ; but Carstairs was a courtier and a diplomatist, and the great aim of his policy was to keep things quiet, to avoid commotion, and main-

[1] Wodrow's *Analecta*, i. 344.

tain the *status quo*.   Dean Stanley has tried to make out
that Carstairs was a forerunner of the moderate party,
represented by Robertson and Blair in the following century.   But this is only an imagination of the Dean's,
founded on the circumstance that Carstairs was remarkable for prudence, and for successful diplomacy.   On the
other hand, Wodrow speaks of him in his *History* as a man
of shining piety, who left behind him a most savoury
remembrance of constant service for Christ, for souls, and
for the good of the Church;[1] and in his *Analecta* he tells
of the remarkable serenity of his deathbed, and his testimony that he had "peace with God through our Lord Jesus
Christ."[2]   It resulted that while the Church might now
make herself more acceptable to the world, while she
might give less offence than her thorough-going spirit in
religion had given in former days, she had at the same
time less of spiritual power, and acted a feebler part in the
great battle with the world, the devil, and the flesh.   The
passing of the Act of 1712, restoring lay patronage, was
another damaging blow, fitted to weaken the Church's
spirituality and bring her more under the influence of the
god of this world.

In harmony with this condition of things, the old
theology of the Church began to be discredited, and a
theology more in harmony with the natural feelings of
men began to show its horns.   It was not, however, so
much that the old Calvinistic creed was formally attacked,
as that the doctrines of grace were discredited, and in some
degree neutralised by the introduction of a spirit of legality.
In one notorious case indeed, that of Professor Simson, a
charge had been brought of doing away with the divinity
of our Lord, and with the doctrines that stand in vital
connection with it.   Simson was acquitted in 1717, but
to many his acquittal was an act of most heinous unfaith-

---

[1] *History*, iv. 96.   [2] *Analecta*, ii. 311.

fulness on the part of the Church to the great truths of which she was the guardian.

We can trace the process that was going on more clearly in connection with what was known as the "Marrow" controversy. This controversy derived its name from a book termed *The Marrow of Modern Divinity*, which had turned up in Scotland in a remarkable way. In the early years of the ministry of Thomas Boston, he had found an old book with this title in the window-sill of a cottage in the little parish of Simprin in the Merse. The master of the house had been a soldier in England in the time of the civil wars, and was understood to have brought it home with him. "The treatise," says the younger Dr. M'Crie, "is in the form of dialogue, the interlocutors being Evangelista, a minister of the Gospel, Nomista, a legalist, Antinomista, an Antinomian, and Neophytus, a young Christian. It is in fact a compilation from the writings of the Reformed divines, including such foreigners as Luther, Calvin, and Beza, and such Englishmen as Ainsworth, Ames, Bolton, Caryl, Hall, Hooker, Perkins, Lightfoot, Reynolds, and others, all of whom in 1646 were considered of modern or recent date, and hence the title of the book, though by the time of its republication in Scotland, it had outlived the fitness of that title. The dialogue is conducted with great spirit, and considerable tact is shown in keeping up the different characters; though, of course, Evangelista has the most of the conversation and the best of the argument to himself. The design of the whole is to elucidate and establish the perfect freeness of the Gospel salvation; to throw wide open the gates of righteousness; to lead up the sinner straight to the Saviour; to introduce him as guilty, perishing, and undone; and persuade him to grasp, without a moment's hesitation, the outstretched hand of God's mercy." [1]   Boston got great personal benefit from this

<hr>

[1] *British and Foreign Evangelical Review*, ii. 427.

book, of which he says that by the year 1700, he had
digested the substance, and began to preach accordingly.

It is generally admitted that there were some para-
doxical positions in the book, but what mainly impressed
the Seceders and other brethren who stood up for it was,
the ground it supplied for a free and universal offer of the
Gospel, in harmony with Calvinistic doctrine, especially on
personal election and particular redemption. The Marrow
controversy was a controversy as to whether Calvinism
allowed one to make, or furnished one with any grounds
for making, so free and universal an offer. The ground
which the Marrow men held to warrant such an offer was
expressed by them in the terms that God had made a
"deed of gift"—a gift of Christ to mankind-sinners, and
that every sinner of mankind was warranted and welcome
to accept that gift. They made a distinction between the
gift of the elect by the Father to Christ to be redeemed,
and the gift of Christ by the Father in offer to mankind-
sinners. "All that the Father giveth me shall come to me,"
—there was the gift of the elect to Christ; "God so loved
the world—the whole world of mankind—that He gave
His only-begotten Son," . . .—there was the gift of Christ
to the world. They were dealing, as so many have dealt,
with a problem which in its vastness is beyond the grasp
of our faculties, how to reconcile personal election with the
universal offer of salvation. All that can be said for them
is that they brought the two things a step nearer to
harmony, and that having done so, they laid more stress
than ever on the fact that the Gospel was good news for
every sinner. There is no reason to say that before this
time the offer of Christ had not been made very freely to
all; we saw in a former chapter how gloriously Richard
Cameron flung it round among his ten thousand moorland
hearers, and how earnestly he called every hill and mountain to bear witness that every one of them had had the

offer and the opportunity of eternal life. What the
Seceders and other Marrow men seem to have felt was, that,
on the basis which has been mentioned, they had found
a Scriptural ground justifying the universal offer; at any
rate, they threw an intense fervour and enthusiasm into
this department of their preaching, and the warmth with
which they pressed it constitutes one of its brightest
features. Perhaps we may say too, that from this time
the person of Christ came more prominently out than
before in connection with the proclamation of the Gospel.
Men were invited not so much to believe a doctrine of
salvation as to intrust themselves to an all-sufficient
Saviour. Union to Christ, to a personal Saviour, acquired
a new prominence; and one of the things which the
Erskines did, with a richness and power which has
never been surpassed, was to set forth the incomparable
blessedness of this union.

When the book came under the notice of Mr. Hog
of Carnock, an earnest minister of the old school, it was
so much appreciated that he republished it with a recom-
mendatory preface. On the other hand, Principal Haddow
of St. Andrews was greatly dissatisfied with it, and began
to preach against it, and against those who agreed with it.
In the recent prosecution of Professor Simson the Evangelical men had said very hard things not only against
him, but against those who exonerated him; and now,
by way of reprisals, the "Marrow" was brought in 1720
under the notice of the Assembly; five propositions said
to be extracted from it were condemned, and all ministers
were strictly prohibited from doing anything, either by
preaching, writing, or printing, to recommend the said
book, and required wherever they might find it, to warn
their people of its dangerous contents, and exhort them
not to read the same.

Against this condemnation twelve ministers of the

Church in 1722 made a representation, which brought for them the name of Representers. In the further proceedings twelve queries were addressed to these brethren, to which they were required to furnish answers; the answers were very carefully drawn up, and formed an able and important theological document. The Assembly of 1722 condemned the answers, and rebuked the twelve ministers, one of whom, in name of the whole, gave in a protest, which the Assembly refused to receive. Here ended the formal proceedings of the Church against the Marrow men.

But the Church had now come to the parting of the ways, and henceforward two very different schools of teachers were found in its pale—the formally orthodox, and the spiritually earnest. Among the points in which the General Assembly differed from the Marrow men were the following: The Assembly bogled at an unconditional offer of the Gospel to all men, being disposed to limit the offer to those fulfilling the conditions of faith and repentance; while their opponents held true repentance to be a part of salvation, and itself the gift of the Lord Jesus Christ. The Assembly laid stress on the obligation of obedience to the moral law, as revealed under the covenant of works, and to the fear of punishment and hope of reward as being still considerations that ought to influence believers in their life; while the others held the believer to be free from the obligation, of the law as a covenant, and maintained that, under the new covenant of grace, gratitude, filial love, and delight in God were the true motives to obedience. There were other important points of divergence; but the effect of the whole was that one school of preachers in the Church of Scotland made the obligation to obey God's law the main subject of their preaching, while the other urged faith in Jesus Christ, not only as the way to salvation, but as the entrance upon that relation to Him whereby alone obedience was pos-

sible.   It is interesting to observe that the doctrine of
atonement did not enter into the area of debate.   No
attempt was made to dispute the position that our salvation is due to the substitution of Jesus Christ in our
room, and His endurance of the penalty in our stead.
Neither was there any dispute on the subject of election
or final restoration.   Indeed, on some of these points the
Assembly professed itself more careful than their opponents, expressing dislike to the doctrine that God had
made a free gift and grant of Christ to all mankind as
savouring of universal redemption.   Strange to say, the
more "moderate" section of the Assembly posed as higher
Calvinists than the other.   But the real drift of
things in the one school was to approach nearer to the
position to which the human mind has always shown
such a proclivity, that eternal happiness depends on our
own obedience, and that the benefit of the Gospel is,
that God now accepts a modified in place of a perfect
obedience.   The drift of things in the other school was
to maintain and magnify the glorious grace of God, and
sometimes, through fear of an undue place being given
to personal obedience, to speak of it somewhat disparag-
ingly.   Not that the evangelical school failed to maintain the necessity of obedience; not that they failed to
urge that a faith that was not followed by works was no
living faith, but only a dead pretender; but somehow
they did not feel called to expend their strength on this
department of truth ; they regarded it as something that
in a large degree might take care of itself; if they were
successful in procuring the right kind of faith, good works
would certainly follow; but to preach good works before
faith was to try to reap a harvest where no right seed
had yet been sown.

These remarks may enable us better to appreciate the
work of the outstanding preachers of the first half of the

eighteenth century. The most prominent of the evangelical school were Thomas Boston, and Ebenezer and Ralph Erskine; others followed both in the Establishment and out of it, and thus kept up the evangelical succession.

THOMAS BOSTON was born in the town of Dunse in 1676, and through his father, a staunch presbyterian, his sympathies were early enlisted on the side of the persecuted; his father was sentenced to imprisonment for his presbyterian tendencies, and to keep him company his little son, six or seven years of age, lay with him in the prison of Dunse. Till his twelfth year, he had been accustomed to attend the episcopal church at Dunse; but one day his father having taken him to hear Mr. Henry Erskine preach, at a meeting-house in the parish of Whitsome, the boy's heart was touched, and a memorable change took place. Mr. Erskine's texts were, " Behold the Lamb of God, that taketh away the sin of the world! " and " O generation of vipers, who hath warned you to flee from the wrath to come ?" " I was touched quickly," says Boston in his remarkable autobiography,[1] " after the first heading, wherein I was like one amazed with some new and strange thing." In his soliloquy on the art of man-fishing, he exclaims, " Little wast thou thinking, O my soul, on Christ's heaven, or thyself, when thou wentest to the Newton of Whitsome to hear a preaching, where Christ first dealt with thee, where thou gottest an unexpected cast! . . . Thou wast going on the way to hell, as blind as a mole ; at last Christ opened thine eyes and let thee see thy hazard, by a preacher that was none of the unconcerned Gallios, who spared neither his body nor his credit nor his reputation to gather thee and the like of thee."

[1] *Memoirs of the Life, Times, and Writings of Thomas Boston*, written by himself, and addressed to his children.

"After that," says Boston, "I went back to the kirk no more till the Episcopalians were turned out, and it was the common observation in these days that whenever one turned serious about his soul's state and case, he left them." It is very certain that it is always to preachers of the type of Henry Erskine and Thomas Boston that men turn, when they come to be in earnest about the state of their souls. Boston gratefully records that among those who received saving impressions in the year when the Presbyterian Church was restored was his own mother, on whom he could now remark a very manifest change.

With considerable difficulty Boston contrived to obtain a University education at Edinburgh, the whole cost of which, for three sessions, including fees and maintenance, was a hundred and twenty-eight pounds, fifteen and eightpence, Scots money, or about fourteen pounds sterling. After a somewhat painful but very useful experience as a tutor in the family of Bruce of Kennet, he became minister of Simprin in 1699, a small parish in the Merse, now united to Swinton, whose adult population was but ninety souls. Here it was (as we have said) that he came to be acquainted with the *Marrow of Modern Divinity*, and identified himself with those who, for recommending that book, were subjected to the rebuke of the General Assembly. After eight years' service at Simprin, he was translated to the parish of Ettrick, in Selkirkshire, where he spent the remainder of his life.

His great learning, his powerful gifts as a preacher, and the force and sanctity of his character, would have marked him out as eminently adapted for a higher sphere ; but the days had now come when the other party manœuvred to prevent the promotion of such "high-flyers," as they were called, and the result in this case was, to use his own expression, that he was " staked in Ettrick."

During the last years of his life he was grievously

tortured by a most distressing ailment, while his comfort was further impaired by the long illness and final prostration of his wife, a woman of high gifts and great excellence. He succumbed to his ailment in 1732, in the 57th year of his life.

For many years in his early ministry Boston underwent great trials in his parish, his faithful, searching preaching and discipline exposing him to the bitter opposition of some of the heritors and other parishioners. But in the end he outlived the opposition and gained from high and low a place of most remarkable esteem. No more striking testimony could be conceived to the purity and consistency, and therefore power, of his Christian character. To this very day, as has been lately testified by a writer in the *Edinburgh Review*, his memory is cherished with veneration in Ettrick. The testimony bears alike on the power of his preaching and the power of his character. In vain we shall search for an instance of the same kind in the case of those who have preached only the philosophy or the ethics of the Gospel; the enduring veneration in his own region for the name of Boston is a proof that the truths which penetrate deepest in the soul of man, which move it most powerfully, which transform it most thoroughly, and which are cherished most gratefully, are those which form the warp and the woof of the *Crook in the Lot* and the *Fourfold State*.

The elaborate autobiography of Thomas Boston is a writing almost unique among works of the kind. It is based on a faith in the particular providence of God, in the intimacy of His fellowship with His children, and in the closeness of the connection between their spiritual and their natural life, the like of which perhaps no man of equal intellectual power ever attained. No man ever carried out more fully and minutely the doctrine that not a sparrow falls to the ground without the Father, and that the hairs of our head are all numbered. The whole practical life of Boston turned on these two principles : first, that it was his duty to try to ascertain, and his privilege to know if he tried properly, what the will of God was in reference to every matter, great or small, with which he was concerned; and second, that things both external and spiritual fell out with him well or ill just as he followed or failed to follow the divine will. Whether or not he should preach at such and such a sacrament, and whether he should stay all night or return home; whether Catherine Brown was the woman who should be his wife, and whether he ought to propose to her; whether the view which he took on that learned question, Hebrew accentuation, to which he devoted a world of study, was the right view, and whether he should give it to the world—were all questions on which God had a definite mind, on which it was his duty to try to ascertain that mind, and in accordance with which, when ascertained, it was his duty to act, on pain of God's most serious displeasure.

He was perpetually on the watch to see how things turned out with him; ascribing it to God's gracious favour whenever anything succeeded; but when it went wrong, blaming himself, and trying to discover wherein he had failed, either in his endeavours to learn God's will, or in his actings with regard to it. The scrutiny extended even to his frame of mind. If he was cold, straitened or dull especially in prayer, praise, and preaching, he believed that in some way he had grieved the Holy Spirit, and the straitening was due to His having left him. And then what pains he took to get things put right again ; what seasons he had of fasting, and of intense self-scrutiny, and tearing down of idols, and passionate crying and tears—" Restore unto me the joy of thy salvation, and uphold me with thy free spirit." We may believe that Boston was often too hard on himself; we may believe that the languor he

sometimes felt in duty was not due to God's forsaking
him, but was the natural reaction from a strain too intense and protracted, unrelieved by due rest and relaxation; we may believe that the habit of so frequent
introspection was not a very healthy one, unless it was
accompanied by a not less constant habit of looking out
from self to Him in whom alone we have righteousness
and strength; but he must be a poor creature who can
make sport of the sublime spectacle of a child of humanity
thus making himself of no reputation, and striving to
bring his every act and thought and feeling into line
with the glorious pattern sketched for his guidance in the
highest heavens. And he would be a very blind observer
who did not connect this intensity of inward discipline
with his great spiritual power. It has sometimes been
represented by those who understand absolutely nothing
of the spiritual life, that holding the views which Boston
did respecting sin and its doom, and stating them as he
did with unflinching boldness, he must have been a
fanatic, hard-hearted and cruel. There could not be a
greater error. Certainly he dwells very terribly on the
misery of lost souls; he delineates with a minuteness,
not warranted by the reserve of Scripture, the agonies of
the damned, but he is as far as possible from doing this
in a hard-hearted spirit; he does it in the agony of his
desire to save careless souls who like himself, as he says,
before his conversion, were posting on, utterly heedless,
to the place of woe. But for himself he was gentle,
unobtrusive, affectionate, domestic. An express messenger once arrived at far-away Ettrick, to say that his
little daughter, fourteen years of age, then paying a visit
in Edinburgh, was dangerously ill of fever and in high
delirium. The good man was tortured with the thought
that her illness was a chastisement on him for having
yielded to some inward temptation, some besetting sin

that should have been resisted. At five o'clock in the evening, he says, "I took my horse and journeyed all night. Many thoughts about her went through my heart like arrows, while I was by the way ; but still I held on by this, that whatever the Lord should do in her case it would be done well, it would be done best, and my soul would approve it as such. And the faith of this was my anchor. I considered all of my children, and if any of them was to be removed by death, I was satisfied it would be her, though she has had a very particular room in my affection ; for I looked on her as the fittest for that change. At Peebles, the passage of Peter's wife's mother coming before me in prayer, I was helped to pray that God would rebuke the fever. Betwixt eight and nine next morning I arrived in Edinburgh, and having asked if she was alive, my trembling heart was eased with the answer that she was better." What a ride that was, in the dark night, between Ettrick and Edinburgh ! What a tender heart that during the long hours thought so wistfully of her, schooling itself into submission, and anchoring itself on the indefeasible rightness of God's doings !—experiencing a hundred times the bitterness of death, yet ever clinging to the hope of life ! He rides, we may say, slightly altering well-known words—

" O'er moor and fen, o'er crag and torrent, till
    The night was gone ;
  And with the morn a maiden face did smile,
    Which he had ever loved, but lost a while."

We proceed to inquire what was specially characteristic of Boston's preaching, enabling him to subdue that wild pastoral parish, and inscribing his name among those which never die.

Very obviously, it owed little to mere outside qualities. Boston was not a born orator. He had no dash, no rhetoric, no poetic colouring, like Bunyan or Rutherfurd ; no great store even of popular illustration. What he did in the way of illustration was done in a very homely, prosaic style. Sometimes there is considerable force and originality in his homely comparisons. The sudden work of death laying low the strongest body is like a spark lighting on gunpowder, and blowing up the strongest house. The mystery of the divine power raising up the human body from the grave is not greater than the mystery, as it first appeared to the Indians, of Europeans with their guns producing thunder and lightning, and killing men afar off at their pleasure. The fairest rose wants not prickles, and the heaviest cross is sometimes wrapt up in the greatest earthly comfort. " As when a man, by a violent stroke on the head, loses his sight, there arises to him a kind of false light whereby he seems to see a thousand airy nothings ; so man, being struck blind to all that is truly good for his eternal interest, has a light of another sort brought into his mind."

But such illustrations are far too rare in Boston's sermons to constitute any considerable source of their power ; we must look elsewhere for their attraction. In regard to the subject of his preaching, the dominant element is grace. Like almost all the great preachers of Scotland, he is of the school of Paul. " By grace are ye saved through faith," is his watchword as much as it was the apostle's. In opposition to the views that were now predominant in some parts of the Church, mixing up law and gospel, and recognising in man a certain native ability to do right, or to co-operate with God in doing right, he enforced pure grace as the source of salvation. Grace in its sovereignty, "not of him that willeth, or of him that runneth, but of God that showeth mercy :" grace in its freeness, offered to all without money and without price ; grace in its fulness, pardoning, adopting, sanctifying, glorifying ; grace in its simplicity, without works of law; grace in its security, ratified by an everlasting covenant; grace in its appointed channels, coming mainly through word and ordinance; grace in its practical fruit, teaching men that "denying ungodliness and worldly lusts, they should live soberly, righteously, and godly in this present evil world." All experience shows that this is the message which most deeply stirs the soul of man, and which furnishes the best foundation for a serious, earnest, holy life.

It was the gift of Boston, as of many of his contemporaries, to be able to set forth this and all related subjects with a fulness and variety that left on the minds of their hearers a very copious and deep impression. He was never satisfied to spin a single thread of truth. If he was dealing with a truth analytically, he would split it up into all its filaments, and hold up each to his audience. If he was dealing with it practically, he would not merely note its principal use, but dwell fully upon all. When a truth has to be commended to his hearers, there is quite a multitude of recommendations. Is he describing vital union to Christ? It is (1.) a spiritual union; (2.) a real union; (3.) a close and intimate union; (4.) though not a mere legal union, it is yet a union supported by law; (5.) it is an indissoluble union; (6.) it is a mysterious union. Does he dwell on the wrath of God? After showing that it is a wrath not in the *affections* of God but in respect of the *effects* caused by it, he remarks (1.) there is wrath in the *heart* of God against the sinner; (2.) in the *Word* of God; (3.) in the *hand* of God. And this wrath falls (1.) on the sinner's body; (2.) on his soul; (3.) on his enjoyments; (4.) it places him under the power of Satan; (5.) it gives him not a moment's peace. Does he describe regeneration? (1.) It is a change of qualities or dispositions; (2.) a supernatural change; (3.) a change into the likeness of God; (4.) universal—covering the whole man ; (5.) yet imperfect ; (6.) nevertheless lasting. One of the items is, that the mind is enlightened (1.) in the knowledge of God ; (2.) in the knowledge of sin ; (3.) of the sinner himself ; (4.) of Jesus Christ ; (5.) of the world's vanity ; (6.) generally, of spiritual things. It was a mode of treatment suitable to a leisurely, deliberate age, that was not satisfied with a thin glimpse of a truth, but desired to see it in all its aspects. It had all the effect of repetition without its monotony, it had the interest of unity in diversity, and diversity in unity. The hearer could not fail to have a full view of the subject. Add to this, that every position was supported by proofs from Scripture ; that all was expressed in plain language, in short sentences, compact and antithetic ; that the attention was often quickened by the putting of questions ; that the discourse was not read, but spoken in an earnest business tone to the men and women that were sitting before the preacher, and that it was mingled, as it were, with his prayers ; and you will be at no loss to understand how it came to be as instructive and penetrating as any message that ever fell from a Scottish pulpit.

The element in which it was deficient was joyousness. Sin was such an awful thing,—in one, around one, ever active, ever spreading its blight, ever offending God, ever ruining man,—that Boston could not get over it. As he looked into eternity and thought of lost sinners, the gloom gathered, his awe deepened. But this did not prevent him from preaching a free and full salvation for all ; it rather impelled him to increased earnestness in the proclamation.

From Boston we pass by an easy step to the two brothers so influential in founding the Secession Church —Ebenezer and Ralph Erskine.

EBENEZER ERSKINE,[1] the son of Henry Erskine, already adverted to, was born at Dryburgh in 1680, four years after Boston. The family was an offshoot of the Erskines, Earls of Mar, and had some standing in the neighbourhood. In 1703 he was ordained minister of Portmoak in Fife, and in 1731 translated to Stirling, where he died in 1756. His brother, Ralph Erskine, was born in 1685, being five years younger, and ordained minister of Dunfermline in 1711, where he remained till his death in 1752. Though younger in years, Ralph was earlier in the kingdom of God, or at least he was further advanced in grace. The story goes that one day while sitting in his room with the window open, Ebenezer Erskine overheard a religious conversation between his wife and his brother Ralph, who were sitting on a seat outside. He was struck with the simplicity and firmness of the ground on which they were evidently resting. It gave him a new view of God's grace, and the way to His favour. From that day he was a new man. The whole style and character of his pastoral work changed. He became a great preacher, and a laborious and most successful pastor. In the pulpit he devoted himself to the exposition and application of the doctrine of grace. He became so popular that many flocked to his ministry, and the communion seasons at Portmoak were festivals attended by a multitude. When he removed to Stirling, he was in a more conspicuous position. He was one of the twelve "Marrow men" who upheld the doctrines of grace, as substantially contained in *The Marrow*, in opposition to the General Assembly. In 1732 he came further into collision with the Assembly

---

[1] *Life and Diary of Ebenezer Erskine*, by Donald Fraser, D.D., Kennoway; M'Kerrow's *History of the Secession Church; Historical Sketch of Origin of Secession Church*, by Andrew Thomson, D.D.; *Life of Ebenezer Erskine*, by James Harper, D.D.

in connection with the Patronage Act. In that year he was suspended and loosed from his charge. The proceedings against him were prolonged to 1740, when he was finally expelled from the Church and deposed from the ministry. This was some years after Mr. Erskine, along with Mr. Wilson of Perth, Mr. Moncrieff of Abernethy, and Mr. Fisher of Kinclaven had formed themselves into the "Associate Presbytery." During the last period of his life, his fortunes were wholly linked with the Secession.

RALPH ERSKINE'S [1] public life was very similar to his brother's. He was a diligent student and a devoted pastor. He had not the same intellectual power and independence as his brother, but he enjoyed great popularity as a preacher. Voice, matter, and manner were alike attractive. "I can never forget those days" (said John Brown of Haddington) "when I travelled over the hills of Cleish to hear that great man of God, whose sermons I thought were brought home by the Spirit of God to my heart. At those times I thought I met with the God of Israel, and saw Him face to face." [2] The communion seasons at Dunfermline were like those at Portmoak and Stirling. But it was not till 1737, four years later than his brother, that Ralph Erskine joined the Secession. He was induced to do so from hopelessness of obtaining a speedy reform of abuses in the Church of Scotland, or a return to the old principles of the Church. Boston, while sympathising with the Erskines and their friends, died in the pale of the Established Church. But his death occurred in 1732, the year before the formation of the Associate Presbytery. Boston's son, who was like-minded with his father, and who succeeded him as

---

[1] Same authorities as for Life of Ebenezer Erskine; *Life and Diary of Rev. Ralph Erskine of Dunfermline*, by Donald Fraser, D.D., Kennoway. [2] M'Kerrow's *History*, p. 856.

minister of Ettrick, left the Church in 1757, became
minister of a church in Jedburgh, and one of the three
founders of the Relief Presbytery.

The preaching of Ebenezer and Ralph Erskine, while
subject to numberless faults in exegesis, style, and taste,
was remarkably fitted to rally and edify earnest souls, at
a time when the fashion of the age was bearing away in
the opposite direction.   Neither of them had the intellectual grip and compass of Boston, but they were one with
him in his purpose to know nothing in the pulpit but
Jesus Christ and Him crucified, and in making it their
one object to explain, commend, and apply the great
doctrines of grace.   They were always conscious, and
they made their hearers to feel, that they had a grand
and glorious theme ; they handled it in the spirit of Paul
in his Epistle to the Ephesians, like men called to exhibit
unsearchable riches, and invite all to partake of them
freely.   Their theme was the Gospel—the good news of
the kingdom, and they made it good news.   Their sermons
were festival sermons ; in their hands the bread of heaven
was always a banquet; and men feasted under their
ministry.   Their preaching had more of gladness in it than
Boston's.   Not that they differed from him as to sin and
its awfulness, but simply that their minds dwelt more on
the remedy than on the disease; their habit was to contemplate the victory more than the enemy, the blessing more
than the curse.   The texts they chose were usually such
as naturally introduced the richest aspects of the grace of
God.   If you count their texts, you will find that con-
siderably the larger portion of them were from the Old
Testament ; [1] but chiefly from the Messianic portions of

---

[1] Of fifty-one sermons of Ebenezer Erskine, thirty texts are from
the Old Testament and twenty-one from the New ; of seventy-eight
sermons of Ralph Erskine, forty-one are from the Old and thirty-six
from the New.

it, the Psalms, the Song of Solomon, and Isaiah. Nor were they hampered by any hard rules of exegesis, as to the application of the Old Testament; if a passage seemed to fit Christ, it was at once applied to Him. They followed the old plan of doctrines and uses, and the old division into innumerable heads and particulars; like Boston they heaped up features and qualities, they turned their subject round and round, as in a kaleidoscope, bringing out something fresh at every turn. In our days of careful exegesis and more rigid intellectual discipline, their sermons often appear wild and over-luxuriant, but if there be a barbaric profusion about them, it is a profusion of "pearl and gold." Often they give us the finest of the wheat; souls are satisfied as with honey from the rock.

It needs hardly to be remarked that their sermons are full of Scripture, and contain hardly so much as an allusion to any other book. They are especially fond of Bible figures and analogies. It is their delight to set forth a mass of particulars in which a Bible figure wraps up spiritual truth. Differing entirely from the modern method of interpreting the parables and other analogical passages of Scripture—that is, to limit the analogy to the one point indicated by the context—they believe that the more points of analogy they can find the better. The Erskines had an element of poetry which Boston wanted, and in their working of it, we mark a singular combination of licence and restraint. There is almost unbounded licence as to the application of the figure or symbol, but a careful restraint in the manner of applying it. In the one they often go to fantastic extremes; but their manner, all the while, is sober, measured, prosaic. Ebenezer Erskine has a sermon from that text in the Song of Solomon: "The king is held in the galleries." What are the galleries in which the king is held? (1.) The gallery of secret meditation; (2.) of prayer; (3.) of reading the

Scriptures; (4.) of Christian converse about soul matters;
(5.) of preaching; (6.) of the sacraments. But what resemblance have these to galleries? (1.) Galleries are magnificent apartments of royal and stately buildings; (2.) they
are lightsome and pleasant apartments; (3.) they are places
to walk and converse; (4.) of public feasting and entertainment of friends. The preacher gets contradictory through
the very freedom of his imagination; how can secret meditation be a gallery if a gallery be a place of public feasting and entertainment of friends? But this real licence
of imagination is disguised by the singularly staid and
sober manner in which the subject is set forth. It cannot
be doubted that this unbridled range of imagination was
one element of their popularity. They often chose poetical
texts. The first volume of Ebenezer Erskine's sermons
contains discourses on keeping the garments clean; the
breath from the four winds in the valley of vision; the
king held in the galleries; the groans of believers; Christ
in the believer's arms; the dayspring from on high; the
rainbow round about the throne; the tree of life shaking
her fruits and leaves among the nations; the stone
rejected by the builders become the head of the corner.
The ingenuity and fancy of the speaker found ample scope
in applying the figures.

Their fervour of tone was another great element of
interest and power. Their souls went out with their
words. They did not content themselves with setting
forth the truth, and leaving their hearers to deal with it
as they pleased. They grappled with them at close
quarters. Few sermons wanted a direct appeal. And
generally, the great object of the appeal was to induce
the unbelieving hearer to accept of Christ. Considerations why he should do so, and do so at once, were pressed
upon him with the utmost vehemence. The consequences
of neglect were borne in upon him with unsparing

severity. The preacher could hardly have spoken more earnestly if the sign of the Son of Man descending to judgment were already seen in the heavens. In his earnestness to save souls he forgot himself, and poured out his appeals with much of the impassioned fervour of Richard Baxter.

It would be folly to deny that this preaching had its faults. In structure, it was formal and inelegant. In scope, it was limited—very limited as compared with the amplitude of Scripture. Except in the one aspect of atonement, it had hardly a word on the earthly life of Christ—the great field covered by the four Gospels. It scarcely recognised that there could be any difficulties in the way of faith, except in the evil hearts of men. On ethical subjects there was only generality. It expressly urged that the believer must maintain good works, but there was no systematic endeavour to train him to them. Ebenezer Erskine has a sermon entitled " The necessity and profitableness of good works asserted," but its object is to refute the objections brought by their opponents against the Marrow men, and to make clear the footing on which alone good works can be accepted. Faith and hope were amply dwelt on, but not charity. The maintenance of the Christian spirit amid secular temptations, provocations, and worries was not one of their themes. It was not long before fierce strife broke out in the Secession—a strife so bitter as to undo much of the moral influence of the noble testimony which the ministers had borne to the doctrines of grace. Alas, how much good seed has been rendered unavailing, especially in Scotland, by the tares of strife, and by that want of watchfulness against the loss of charity which seems inseparable from our Church controversies !

Yet, while the preachers of this school were doubtless subject to many defects, they had this great distinction,

o

that they kept alive the flame of evangelical truth, and
darted its rays boldly and brightly across the country, at
a time when it was in great danger of being extinguished.
They held the fort till the reinforcements came. The
truth as it was in Jesus sounded forth from Ettrick, from
Portmoak, from Dunfermline, and from Stirling, the same
in substance, if not in form, as it had sounded forth from
Jerusalem in the days of Peter, or from Antioch and
Thessalonica in the days of Paul. The communion
seasons at these places showed how even Calvinistic
sacraments might become festival seasons, dispensing joy
unspeakable and full of glory. The heroic age was not
yet past. Under such preaching, men of the type eulo-
gised by Carlyle, the peasant-nobles of Scotland, the
James Carlyles and David Hopes of the eighteenth century,
were rising up, with hearts tender as a child's, but with
an inflexible sternness of principle, that made them ready,
like their fathers, to lay down their lives for the truth.
Notwithstanding the temporary eclipse of the evangelical
cause, the Gospel continued to show itself the power of
God unto salvation. Where evangelical truth was silenced,
godliness decreased, morality fell, neglect of church-going
grew apace. Where the Gospel was still a power, the
conscience was quickened, the claims of God were honoured,
communion with the unseen was maintained, and there
were still men who could say : " Lord, I have loved the
habitation of thy house, and the place where thine honour
dwelleth."

The three ministers who were associated with the
Erskines in laying the foundations of the Secession
Church, Wilson, Moncrieff, and Fisher, were in entire
harmony with them in the matter of their preaching,
and in their several spheres did excellent work in the
pulpit, although they did not rise to equal distinction.
Dr. Fraser of Kennoway said of Mr. Fisher (who was the

author of the well-known Exposition of the Shorter Catechism) that "neither as to sentiment, composition, nor delivery, had he ever heard his superior" in the pulpit. Of Mr. Wilson, John Brown of Haddington bore his testimony : "When sitting on the Brae of Abernethy (at his open-air services) I got more insight into that marrow of the Gospel, *my God*, than ever I got before or since." Alexander Moncrieff, whose worldly position and connections might have found for him a very different sphere, devoted himself to his ministerial duties, and did admirable service both as preacher and professor of divinity. But it was not by natural gifts of eloquence that the most of the seceding clergy maintained the character of their pulpit; it was because their hearts were so thoroughly in their work; what they preached was a message they had got from heaven, a message of salvation, which they felt in the depths of their souls, and burned to make known to all. Acquainted in their own experience with the ways of the spiritual life, they were looked up to as competent guides by all who were earnest in the endeavour to serve God and walk in the footsteps of His Son. Their earnest preaching begat earnest hearing. Men said of them, as the possessed damsel at Philippi said of Paul and Silas, "These men are the servants of the most high God, which show unto us the way of salvation." A higher character or a more honourable position can hardly be conceived.

Of this order of preachers was the famous JOHN BROWN of Haddington, still well known for his Self-interpreting Bible, and honoured as a patriarch in the Church—sons,[1] grandson,[2] and great-grandson[3] having

[1] Rev. John Brown, of Whitburn, and Rev. Ebenezer Brown, of Inverkeithing.
[2] Rev. Professor John Brown, D.D., of Broughton Place Church, Edinburgh.
[3] John Brown, M.D., author of *Rab and his Friends*, etc.

been all memorable men. Rising from the humblest
rank in life, he became equally distinguished as a linguist
and a scholar, and respected as a minister of the Gospel.
His manifold labours did not prevent him from cultivating with ceaseless devotion the life that is hid with
Christ in God.   It is said of David Hume that, hearing
him preach on a certain occasion, he said : "That's the
man for me; he means what he says; he speaks as if Jesus
Christ was at his elbow."[1]   An English divine, who heard
him preach about the year 1770, stated his impression
thus : "I well remember a searching sermon he preached
from these words : 'What went ye forth into the wilderness for to see?'   Although at that time I had no
experimental acquaintance with the truth as it is in
Jesus, yet his grave appearance in the pulpit, his solemn,
weighty, and energetic manner of speaking used to affect
me very much.   His preaching was close, and his address
to the conscience pungent.   Like his Lord and Master,
he spoke with authority and hallowed pathos, having
tasted the sweetness and felt the power of what he delivered."[2]

Brown had two sons in the ministry, John Brown
of Whitburn and Ebenezer of Inverkeithing.   Of John
the elder, his grandson the author of *Rab* has a touching
picture, praying at the grave of his son's young wife
(mother of the author of Rab), and with a voice full of
pathos, amid his tears and sobs, thanking God that though
the grass had withered, and its flowers had faded, the
flowers would bloom again, never again to fade; and what
was now sown in dishonour and weakness would be raised
in glory and power, like His own glorious body.

Ebenezer Brown shone in the pulpit.   "Six days he
brooded over his message; was silent, withdrawn, self-

[1] Dr. John Brown's Letter to Dr. Cairns on the life of his father.
[2] M'Kerrow's *History of the Secession Church*, pp. 856-7.

involved; on the Sabbath, that downcast, almost timid man, who shunned men, the instant he was in the pulpit, stood up a son of thunder. Such a voice! such a piercing eye! such an inevitable forefinger, held out trembling with the terrors of the Lord! such a power of asking questions and letting them fall deep into the hearts of his hearers, and then answering them himself with an 'Ah, Sirs!' that thrilled and quivered from him to them."

The story which Dr. John Brown gives of Lord Brougham going to hear him preach, accompanied by Mr. Stuart of Dunearn, is interesting not only as showing the independence of the man, but the secret of his pulpit power. The two gentlemen arriving a little before the hour of service, Mr. Stuart sent a message that they would like to speak to him. "Mr. Brown's compliments to Mr. Stuart, *and he sees nobody before sermon.*" He spent these moments with other company. Lord Brougham was greatly impressed, and sent word to Lord Jeffrey to lose not a week in coming to hear this great natural orator. Jeffrey came next Sunday, and often afterwards declared he had never heard such words, such a sacred, untaught gift of speech.[1]

Out of the host of names which might be enumerated of men who did honour to the Secession pulpit, we notice two, not so much for extraordinary gifts as for their extraordinary diligence and perseverance. Dr. LAWSON of Selkirk was long Professor of Divinity in the Burgher section of the Secession. He devoted a large measure of attention in the pulpit to the exposition of Scripture, and performed the remarkable feat, in the course of his ministry, of having lectured through every book of the sacred volume. He left behind him no fewer than eighty volumes of manuscript sermons. In his Lectures on the

---

[1] *Horæ Subsecivæ,* ii. pp. 271, 272.

Book of Ruth, the Book of Esther, and the history of Joseph, we have samples of his work. Plain, practical and instructive, they aim simply at bringing out the lessons of the narrative and showing their application to common life.

Dr. JOHN JAMIESON, of the Antiburgher section of the Secession, has acquired a lasting fame as an antiquarian, and especially as the author of the Etymological Dictionary of the Scottish Language, in six volumes, quarto. Moreover he was a poet, a story-writer, a topographist, a philologist, and a historian (*History of the Culdees of Iona*). Such an accumulation of interests and employments was rare in the Secession ministry. But although Dr. Jamieson could not have been so exclusively bent on the objects of his ministry as if he had had no other interest, there is no reason to suppose that he failed to give to that work the chief place in his heart. A diligent and systematic use of time may enable one to achieve what seems impossible to the random worker. For a long period Dr. Jamieson ministered with much acceptance to a large congregation in Nicolson Street, Edinburgh. Not a popular preacher—at least latterly—in the usual sense of the term, he made his mark through the solidity, the Scripturalness, and the usefulness of his sermons. Two volumes of discourses on "the heart"— mostly on the disorders and failings of the heart—show that he conscientiously aimed not at popularity but at usefulness. To lay bare the plague of the heart—to show that it was deceitful above all things and desperately wicked—to detect enmity to God at its core, and thus stop every mouth and declare the whole world guilty before God, would have been strange themes for any one bent on popularity. But they served to scatter the delusion so common among men that they are "rich and increased in goods and have need of nothing;" they showed them that they were "miserable and wretched, and poor and blind and naked;" and prepared the way for a full exposition of the grace of Christ and the work of the Holy Spirit,—that Divine remedy for all the disorders of humanity, which it was the privilege and the glory of the Secession preachers to proclaim, wherever their Master sent them.

CHAPTER IX.

THE MODERATE SCHOOL.

THE "moderate" school in the Scottish Church, in all its more salient features, was very unlike anything which the Church, in the exercise of her freedom, had been, or had desired to be, either in the sixteenth or the seventeenth century. It was equally unlike that early development of the Christian life of which the old Celtic Church furnished so beautiful a type. Moderatism was unquestionably an innovation. We cannot with any reason call it a development; it was a reaction and a contrast. It was unlike the Reformed Church in theology, in life, in preaching; likewise in Church administration, in its relation to the people, and in its relation to the world. It is difficult to explain with precision the causes of the rise and predominance of this school, because what in one aspect was a cause, was in another aspect an effect, and *vice versâ.* One person would say that it began with doctrinal degeneracy, out of which sprang change of spirit, change of life, and change of preaching. Another would say it began with decline of spiritual life; this inclined the Church to loose theology, to conformity to the world, and to cold, passionless preaching. Very frequently its origin has been ascribed to the mixed elements that constituted the ministry under the comprehensive Revolution-settlement. From a very different point of view we should be told by others that moderatism was a reaction from the fanaticism, the violence, the

narrowness, and the coarseness of the earlier Church. It
would probably be admitted even by its defenders that it
was a recoil to the opposite extreme, and that it would
have been desirable to retain somewhat more of the
elements which it displaced. As we enter on this field,
let it be borne in mind, that in this book our subject
is the history of preaching, and not the history of the
Church at large. It is not our part to discuss this
question exhaustively, but only to refer to it in order to
find some explanation of the very singular change which
appeared now in the preaching of the Church.

Whatever, then, may have been the cause, the fact is
certain, that from the beginning of the eighteenth century,
there set in a decline of the evangelical spirit, which had
reached its zenith under Samuel Rutherfurd, William
Guthrie, John Livingstone, and men of their stamp.
There came to be less of spiritual earnestness in the
Church. Men who were still conspicuous for that quality
were less thought of, and had even begun to be looked on
by some as troublesome, uncomfortable neighbours, of
whom the Church would be well to be rid.

Ere long, there began to appear a recoil from evangelical doctrine, and a disposition to modify the message
of grace. Men who have never felt the burden of sin in
their own hearts, cannot be expected to appreciate the
doctrine of atonement or the doctrine of regeneration; not
feeling the need of atonement or regeneration, they cannot
see the importance of a divine Saviour to atone, and a divine
Spirit to renew. Of necessity, Jesus Christ must come
down from the place of supremacy and vital influence
which He holds in the teaching and preaching of those to
whom the sense of sin is the most awful experience of
life. The supernatural features of the Gospel must pass
away, as things do pass away that are not needed, and
that which remains can be little other than an intensified

naturalism—natural religion brightened up by the reflection of Christianity. Men cannot help in these circumstances inclining to Deism or Socinianism. And not believing in the change of heart and change of taste which regeneration implies, they cannot but regard earnest religion as something of a sham, nor can they be expected to call on men very earnestly to renounce the world in order to follow Christ. They consider that in point of fact your high-flying men do injustice to the world—it is not such a bad world after all : it can be made a very tolerable world; there are many pleasures in life which are perfectly harmless, but which your fanatics condemn ; and so it becomes one of their objects as preachers to recover back for enjoyment as much of the world as they can decently reconcile with a Christian profession.

This seems to have been the chief cause of the great change which the eighteenth century witnessed in the Scottish Church. The natural man recovered himself, and asserted himself, and strove hard to bring the Church into harmony with his tastes and interests; and the force of evangelical life around him was not strong enough to keep him down.

But to give a fair view of the position of those who brought about this change, we must offer two qualifying remarks. The first is, that there was no open repudiation of evangelical doctrine by the moderate school; certainly not in its earlier days. It was one of the marvellous achievements of the Reformed and Covenanting divines that they had placed Calvinistic doctrine on a pedestal that almost defied assault. Moreover, in the Confession of Faith, that doctrine was bound into the very constitution of the Church, and no John Henry Newman had then arisen to proclaim that honest men might warrantably declare their assent to articles of faith which they did not believe as they stood to be true. It was not by open assault, but by a process of sapping and mining that the old faith came to suffer. Men like Leishman and Simson were upheld in office, while Erskine and Gillespie were deposed. Even in the sermons of advanced Moderates, the fault is not so much that evangelical truth is opposed, as that it is ignored. In all Moderate literature we shall probably find no such repudiation of the old theology as we have in one page of the *Scotch Sermons*.[1] There can be no doubt that during last century many ministers whose hearts were in the world preached fairly orthodox sermons. But they preached without life or power. In some cases, it would have been difficult to draw the line between preachers of the Moderate and preachers of the Evangelical parties. Just as in England, in connection with the Deistical controversy in the eighteenth century, we find the sap and spirit of the Gospel as thoroughly wanting in many of the apologetical works of the period as in those of the Deists, so the spirit of the Gospel, the fire and fervour of men in dead earnest for the good of their hearers, is as wanting in some of the orthodox as in the Moderate preachers. Yet the bare bones of Calvinism may be found in both. We have already seen that in the Marrow controversy the opponents of that doctrine affected to be more consistent Calvinists than the Marrow men, and found fault with Boston and others for departing from the Calvinistic tenets. This was not true; but while the one side retained only the dry orthodoxy of Calvinism, the other exemplified its life and power.

The other qualifying consideration to be borne in mind is, that the evangelical pulpit of the preceding age did afford some grounds for dissatisfaction. If it was earnest, Scriptural, faithful, it was somewhat rough, controversial, dogmatic. In the excited period of the

[1] The page we refer to is 200, *Scotch Sermons*, 1880.

persecution it could not well have been otherwise. And it was not well adapted to meet the new social features and forces which rapidly developed after the Union with England. For after that event the social manners, especially of the educated classes, underwent a material change in the way of refinement. The educated intellect of the country became more active, and looked about in this direction and in that both for material on which to feed, and for work to which to direct its energies. The conviction first expressed by the Cambridge Platonists, that reason had been unduly cramped, and that there was more scope for its exercise in religion than Protestantism had been willing to allow, spread widely in Scotland. A feeling arose that preaching directed solely to produce and nourish spiritual faith and experience was one-sided, and that far more attention should be given to ethical culture, to the production and exercise in secular life of the practical virtues of Christianity. The unprecedented popularity of the sermons of Tillotson cannot be accounted for except on the ground that they filled this void in England, and in a very attractive form. This was a state of things which the old style of preaching did not meet. There was therefore scope, in some important points, for a new departure in the pulpit. The preaching of the Seceders, precious and rich though it was in the highest elements of Gospel truth, did not take note of these new conditions. The evangelical preachers in the Established Church were not much alive to them, and even if they had been, they wanted the commanding force needed to guide the current into safe and orthodox channels. What was the result ? For the best part of a century the evangelical cause was in a state of collapse and defeat, and incapable of more than incidental and occasional efforts to proclaim the old message, and summon the people to the old banner.

And the lesson to after-generations is one that we shall do well to lay to heart. It will not do for the Church to disregard those changes in the taste and cravings of the people which arise under new social and intellectual conditions. The policy of some excellent and conscientious men to cling to everything that is old, and resist everything that is new, is a dangerous policy. Recommending itself as safe, it is really most hazardous. Hating change, it fosters revolution. God give us preachers with divine skill to draw the line; to recognise the distinction between the vital and the transitory; to leave the transitory to the influences that assail and shake off so many human adjuncts even in divine institutions, in order that in this way " those things that cannot be shaken may remain."

Under the influence of such causes as these, and greatly aided by the treacherous Act of Queen Anne restoring patronage, the Established Church of Scotland drifted along quietly till past the middle of the century, when a policy was deliberately entered upon having for its design to deliver her, out and out, from evangelical restraints, and make her such a Church as the most thorough-going Moderate could desire. This was the policy of Principal Robertson. As leader of the Church, he bent himself with all his energy to give full, uniform, constant effect to the Patronage Act, as a means of purging the Church from the evil influence of fanaticism. His policy was a policy of " Thorough." With Robertson were associated, but with different degrees of resolution, men like Dr. Blair and Dr. Carlyle of Inveresk. What grieved them above all things was that the Church was not in sympathy with, or at least was not alongside of, the culture of the age. Many of its ministers were not capable of associating with scholars, philosophers, artists, actors. If they were not up to the intellectual level of such persons, how could they be their guides from the pulpit? Many ministers were boorish in manners, ignorant of the ways of good society, with no powers of conversation, incapable of taking their place at the dinner-tables of the lords and lairds of their parishes. Evangelicalism was fanaticism. It was the most narrow-minded of all the *isms*. It was made up of bigotry, pretence, and sourness of temper. It looked with horror on a Papist or an Episcopalian. It saw no good save in its own narrow system. It frowned on everything pleasant and joyous in social life. Novels were the devil's books. When Dr. Blair borrowed a novel, he had to pretend that it was for the use of a member of his family. The door of the theatre was the door to perdition. This world was the kingdom of the devil. All this sort of thing should be cleared away if the Church of Scotland was to retain the respect of the rational part of the community. The ministrations of the pulpit should no longer be marked by the severe and repulsive dogmatism of which Boston's *Fourfold State* was a sample, but should aim at cultivating an upright, generous, kindly type of character, in harmony with the true Christian spirit. Was not charity the queen of Christian graces? And was it not the very spirit of charity to be good-natured, indulgent, ready to promote the amusement of one's friends, forbearing towards their faults, charitable to their opinions? Would not mild discourses advocating these virtues produce far more of real Christianity than the wild, high-flown, irrational appeals that were constantly issuing from evangelical pulpits?

In the carrying out of their scheme, the three men we have named, Robertson, Carlyle, and Blair, had a wonderful measure of success. Robertson worked the Patronage Act; Carlyle held him to his position, when his feelings might have caused him to hesitate; and Blair wrote model sermons on the new plan. Robertson was a splendid leader, not brilliant, but capable of forming large schemes, and working them steadily out; always able to make the best of his case, with a plausible and popular eloquence that turned to the best account whatever could contribute to success. Since the patronage law had been enacted in 1712, excuses had often been found for not carrying it into effect. Where a presentee was unpopular, the Church had remonstrated with the patron, or had delayed the settlement for years, or had even enjoined the presentee to withdraw. It was this dilly-dallying to which Robertson resolved to put an end. The law of patronage must be made absolute, and complete effect must uniformly be given to it. The opposition of the people must be disregarded, and "the call," which was still nominally requisite for a settlement, must be reduced to a nonentity. The practice of the General Assembly to petition Parliament every year for the repeal of the Patronage Act must be stopped. Even "riding commissions," designed to supersede reluctant presbyteries in effecting unpopular settlements, must be discontinued, and the strictest orders given to presbyteries to carry out unpopular settlements regardless of the voice of the people. And whenever a minister should refuse to obey these orders, albeit he might plead that his conscience forbade him, he was to be remorselessly deposed.

Such was Robertson's policy as to the law of patronage, designed to secure for the Church the active favour and support of that class of society on which he believed that her prosperity mainly depended. It is remarkable that in our own day the Established Church somewhat abruptly reversed this policy. At her instigation, the old law of patronage, which had been the sheet-anchor of Robertson's policy, was suddenly repealed, and the voice of the people, which Robertson had laboured to stifle, was made predominant in the appointment of ministers. No stronger impulse could have been given to the cause of democracy and the ascendency of the people. Certainly Robertson would have stood aghast at the change.

But Principal Robertson was not the strong man to carry out all this policy by himself. It required an iron will and an iron hand to stand to all that it involved; to stop one's ears to the piteous cry of congregations that would not have a hireling for a shepherd; to witness masses of devout people passing over to the Seceders; or to depose from the holy ministry, in the name of the Lord Jesus, holy men like Ebenezer Erskine, or Thomas Gillespie of Carnock, who had ever been among His most faithful and exemplary servants. What was lacking of these qualities in Robertson himself, was supplied by his friend and coadjutor, Dr. Alexander Carlyle of Inveresk. Appearing far less prominently on the ecclesiastical arena, the hand of Carlyle did much of the work. He was noted for an audacity which never shrank from uttering the boldest sentiments, or from enforcing the extremest measures. His autobiography, given to the public only within the last twenty-five years, paints him in worse colours than even his opponents would have dreamt of. It is probably the only autobiography of a minister of the Gospel which contains no solitary word of sympathy with the great spiritual ends of the Christian ministry—hardly even an allusion to Him whose love and grace that ministry is designed to proclaim. The writer is purely and simply a man of the world. His book is a picture of worldly manners, and a recommendation of the better forms of worldly life. He avows that it was only to please others that he chose the profession of the ministry; when he preached his first sermon he was inwardly pleased that he had chosen the ministry, because a young lady told him that she was charmed with his oratory. His great merit in his own view was that he had delivered the Church of Scotland from fanaticism. Of his specific services to that Church, the most meritorious and the most useful in his judgment was, that he had vindicated the right of ministers to go to the theatre, and checked a spirit "that would have prevented young men of good birth and ingenious (*sic*) minds from entering into the ministry."[1] At Newcastle, he is bored with disagreeable society, but, "two or three of the clergy could be endured, for they played well at cards, and were not pedantic." When he supports a proposal for augmenting the incomes of the clergy, his chief ground is, that "there are few branches of literature in which the Church has not excelled."[2] Sir Walter Scott described him as the grandest demigod he ever saw, "commonly called Jupiter Carlyle, for having sat more than once to a painter for the king of gods and men; a shrewd, clever old carle, no doubt, but no more a poet than his precentor." He might have said with equal truth, no more a minister of the Gospel.

We have a characteristic glimpse of the way in which Carlyle influenced Robertson in an incident recorded with perfect frankness by Carlyle himself in connection with a visit paid by them together at a gentleman's house in Bute. The landlord was one of the best hosts possible for a large company, for he was loud and joyful, and made the wine flow like Bacchus himself. For four days the entertainment had gone on, the wine being excellent, and flowing with a sort of royal freedom. At last the Principal became concerned, for a young gentleman of whom he had charge was one of the company, and he asked Dr. Carlyle to second him in a request that the time for drinking might be shortened. Carlyle objected that they would be laughed at, especially as they had said nothing about it all the previous days. The Prin-

[1] *Autobiography of Alexander Carlyle*, p. 323.   [2] *Ibid.* p. 561.

cipal gave way to him, and concluded that "they would
end as they had begun."

The unscrupulous character of Carlyle, when a party
purpose had to be served, was shown in a painful incident,
also recorded by himself with the utmost *sang froid*. A
great debate had just been completed in the General
Assembly, and the vote was in the course of being taken,
when an old and intimate friend of Carlyle's, Dr. Jardine,
fell from his seat. He was immediately removed, a great
commotion took place, the calling of the roll was
interrupted, and there was some danger, if business should
be stopped, that the result would not be favourable to
the motion of Carlyle and his friends. Making his way
to the door, he found a surgeon in attendance on Jardine,
and learned from him that all was over. Returning to
the Assembly, and resuming his place, he gave out that
there were hopes of Jardine's recovery. The voting
accordingly went on, and the motion was carried by a
large majority. One hardly knows which was worst;
the moral recklessness that could utter such a lie in the
house of God, and in the presence of death; or the moral
levity that could see his friend hurried into eternity with
such awful suddenness, and at the very moment devise
a mean and lying trick to make sure of a party motion.

This was the man that acted as backbone to Robertson. For Robertson seemed at times not to be able to go
through with his own plans. His sudden retirement from
the leadership of the Church in the full maturity of his
powers was a step which has never been fully explained,
but which appears to have arisen from some misgiving
as to his being able to carry out his principles in the
complications that were likely to arise.

But our business is with the pulpit work of this
school; and we proceed to inquire what were its characteristics.

Principal ROBERTSON need not detain us long. A single sermon, preached in 1775 before the Society for Propagating Christian Knowledge in Scotland, is all he ever gave to the public. It is entitled "The situation of the world at the time of Christ's appearance," and the text is Col. i. 26, "The mystery which hath been hid from ages and from generations, but is now made manifest to his saints." In reality it is a historical survey, not a sermon. Its object is to show that God manifested the mystery of the Gospel at the time when the world stood most in need of it, and was best prepared for receiving it. In proof of this he dwells on various considerations in the state of the world, moral, political, religious, domestic, that seemed to call emphatically in Christ's time for a revelation. The sermon exhibits the same features as his historical writings. Not original, not striking, not incisive, it is clear, orderly, sensible. He has occasion to touch on the department of the Society's work for foreign missions. To this department he has no objection. He has even a word of patronage for the zealous and active spirits that have arisen in a degenerate age, and the societies formed on the generous plan of propagating the knowledge of Christ to nations far off, that never heard His fame, nor have seen His glory. But that is not *his* idea of the way to propagate Christianity. The great missionary recommendation of Christianity is the fact that it has made nations that have embraced it so prosperous and enlightened, and furnished their life with so many advantages and comforts. When heathen nations come to know of these benefits they will become very friendly to the religion under whose auspices they are to be obtained. It is a low-toned argument, unworthy of a great historian. Had he searched all Church history he would have found no case of Christianity embraced merely for its temporal benefits. The sermon concludes with a few mild reflections on the

advantage of a religious over a worldly life; but there is
no word in it commending the redemption that is in Christ
Jesus; no direct address to his hearers; no appeal to the
conscience, the feelings, or the imagination; the only
faculty which he condescends to appeal to is reason.

In no sense was Principal Robertson a great preacher.
In his *Account of his Life and Writings,* his friend Professor Dugald Stewart says of him:—" His pronunciation
and accent were strongly marked with the peculiarities
of his country; nor was this defect compensated by the
graces of his delivery. His manner, however, though deficient in ease, was interesting and impressive; . . . his
diction was rich and splendid, and abounded with the
same beauties that characterise his writings." [1] It is
worthy of remark that Robertson did not read his discourses in the pulpit. In his later years, he did not even
write them out. To quote again from Dugald Stewart:
" The facility with which he could arrange his ideas, added
to the correctness and fluency of his extemporary language
encouraged him to lay aside the practice of writing, except on extraordinary occasions, and to content himself in
general with such short notes as might recall to his memory
the principal topics on which he meant to enlarge." [2]

The fact is, that up till now the reading of sermons
in the pulpit was hardly known in Scotland. Carlyle, in
his autobiography, speaking of the year 1745, gives an
account of a visit to a minister of the name of Lawson at
Renfrew, and says, " he was almost the only person who
read in those days." [3] And Mr. Hill Burton, in his
Supplementary Chapter on Carlyle's Life, adverts to " the
habit acquired by a clergyman of the Church of Scotland
who had to preach sermons committed to memory " as
enabling him to retain finished pieces of composition in
his mind. [4] It is beyond doubt, however, that it was

[1] P. 194.   [2] P. 200.   [3] P. 78.   [4] P. 570.

under the moderate *régime* that the practice of reading sermons became general in Scotland.

With regard to Robertson, his broad Scotch accent was a matter of general observation, and was rather out of place in an apostle of culture. It is a significant fact that when Sir Walter Scott, in *Guy Mannering*, desires to introduce his readers to a characteristic Scotch preacher, it is not the portrait of Robertson that he gives, but that of his evangelical colleague, Dr. John Erskine. Sir Walter in his youth had listened to both; in his own views and feelings he was nearer to Robertson than to Erskine; yet when his object is to present a specimen of the school that had moulded the religious life of the Scottish people, it is not the moderate, but the evangelical preacher whose portrait he draws.

Of "Jupiter" Carlyle's sermons we have a few specimens in print, preached, however, on public occasions, including a Synod sermon, a funeral sermon on Lord Hailes, and a sermon before the Society for the benefit of the Sons of the Clergy. It is with pain one marks the extremely low pitch of these sermons. The Synod sermon dwells on the usefulness of the Church of Scotland to the general interests of the country, and the right of the clergy to a condition above the pitiful poverty to which they had been doomed. But though the clergy may be poor, they have higher rewards. (This is the most painful part.) The Church presents "a shining path to reputation that will answer the desires of their hearts. For admiration is the passion of young and generous minds; and the love of distinction is predominant with the youth of genius, far above the love of wealth." The sermon on Lord Hailes, besides eulogising its subject, contains a vehement and impassioned warning against the rise of those new-fangled sentiments in politics which were threatening our unrivalled constitution, and which, unless they were utterly crushed, would drive us to anarchy and barbarism. Most characteristic of all is the sermon which bears the title "Usefulness and necessity of a liberal education for clergymen." The right kind of minister must be far removed from that vulgar illiterate type, which is often the most popular with the multitude. A liberal education, especially if it be accompanied with some knowledge of the world, enables a minister to maintain his dignity and his influence; it gives him a large, disinterested heart; it commends him to the upper ranks; it is ornamental to society; it enables him to enrich the literature of the age. The preacher refers with great complacency to the memorable fruits of literary industry which had made so many of the clergy of his day illustrious, and contrasts the narrow principles and illiberal spirit of the preceding century with the culture and enlightenment of his own. On such points he enlarges in correct and forcible language, and with no little fervour. But nowhere in any of his sermons can one find so much as a hint that man by reason of sin has fallen under God's displeasure, lost communion with Him, and become liable to eternal death; not once, except in the most incidental ways, is the name of Christ to be met with; nor is there a word that could lead any one to imagine that the Christian minister is the ambassador of Christ, and that his office is to pray men in Christ's stead to be reconciled to God. David Hume on one occasion, as Carlyle himself records, gave a characteristic account of his preaching. Being on a visit to Gilmerton, Sir David Kinloch constrained Hume to go on Sunday to Athelstaneford Church, where Carlyle was to preach for John Home. On meeting before dinner, Hume said to Carlyle, "What did you mean by treating John's congregation to-day with one of Cicero's academics? I did not think such heathen immorality would have passed in East Lothian."[1]

---

[1] *Autobiography*, p. 276.

We pass now to the great ornament of the moderate
pulpit, Dr. HUGH BLAIR. He was the son of an Edinburgh
merchant, but sprung from a distinguished family, for his
great-grandfather was the Robert Blair of St. Andrews,
who, as we have seen, was one of the lights of the Scottish
Church in the early and middle part of the seventeenth
century. It is amusing to see how this good man and
fervent Covenanter is treated by Professor John Hill, in
his *Account of the Life and Writings of Dr. Hugh Blair*.
Stress is laid (very properly) on his having been a regent
in the University of Glasgow in his youth; on his ability
as a preacher, on the important missions to which he was
appointed from time to time, and on his poor opinion
of Oliver Cromwell; but of his fervid evangelism, the
revival work in which he was engaged in Ireland, and his
intense devotion to the cause of the Covenant, we have
hardly a hint. Licensed in 1741, Hugh Blair's first
charge was at Collessie in Fife, where he remained less
than a year; he was called to the Canongate, in Edinburgh,
thence to Lady Yester's, and thence to the High Church,
where he was inducted in 1758, and where he remained to
his death in 1800. Thus for the long period of fifty-
eight years Blair was a conspicuous man in the Scottish
metropolis. In 1762 he was appointed to the chair of
Rhetoric and Belles-Lettres. On the death of Principal
Robertson in 1793, though now at the age of seventy-five,
he would fain have succeeded him in the principal's chair,
but the office was conferred on Dr. Baird. He died on the
27th December 1800, within a few days of the close of
the century of which he was so remarkable a representative.

The fame of Dr. Blair was quite marvellous; though
to us, reading even his most celebrated sermons, hardly to
be accounted for. In the year of his death, 1800, the
twenty-second edition of his sermons was published in

four octavo volumes. At the present moment the book is hardly saleable at any price. Strahan, the bookseller, declined the risk of the first volume, but after one of the sermons had been highly extolled by Samuel Johnson, he gave £100 for the volume, increasing the sum to £600 each for the third and fourth volumes.

It does not appear that the discourses of Dr. Blair were set off by any great charms of delivery. Dr. Somerville of Jedburgh, in his Autobiography,[1] remarks : " His manner of delivery was not equal to the matter of his discourses. It was stiff, formal, and not altogether free from affectation." Though we have searched for information we have not been able to discover whether or not he read his sermons in the pulpit. We know that they cost him much labour ; Boswell, in his *Tour to the Hebrides*, speaks of his taking a whole week over one.

In point of thought, the sermons hardly ever rise above the level of commonplace, but they are composed in neat, careful, and pleasing language, free from all technical and vulgar expressions ; they are clear and easy to follow ; they never puzzle the head, nor startle the conscience ; they have little of the dogmatic, little of the experimental, and bear chiefly on the duties and graces of ordinary life. As Mr. Leslie Stephen has said, " they are the best examples of the sensible, if unimpassioned and rather affected style of the moderate divines of the age." [2] Blair was the Tillotson of Scotland. Perhaps we may say that some of his sermons have more of the flavour of the Gospel than the Archbishop's. He sometimes brings forward the atonement, and regeneration ; but such doctrines fall into a much more obscure place than in bold evangelical preaching, and sometimes one meets with expressions hardly consistent with them. The aim of the

[1] *My Life and Times*, p. 87.
[2] *Dictionary of National Biography*, art. " Hugh Blair."

writer, to commend religion as " a calm, sober, rational principle of conduct " is apparent throughout. There is no such thing as a death-struggle with the sinner to induce him to flee from the wrath to come—that would be too sensational and alarming. The object is to supply a gentle stimulus and guidance towards that orderly, respectable, moral life which all Christians should lead. This does not amount to a very large recognition of evangelical Christianity; and yet even this involves the preacher in difficulties. It is difficult to find his way between opposite principles of life. We are to be devotional, but we are not to be enthusiastic. Enthusiasm, as he interprets it, is a thorough indifference to the things of the world, and that, of course, would never do. But we must not be conformed to the world. The preacher can afford no clear guidance to one who would fain use the world as not abusing it. What he appears most anxious for is that his hearers should not become too spiritual, too heavenly-minded. As if that were one of the common dangers of men ! As if the danger of their being worldly were not a thousand times greater ! He actually interprets the words " here we see through a glass darkly " as if they meant, divine things are not made very clear to us in order to prevent us from being absorbed with them. Men like Blair had no right apprehension of that entire consecration to God which makes His will the rule and standard both for the life that now is and for that which is to come. They were desirous, and properly desirous, to get men to apply Christianity more to the business of daily life. But they missed the evangelical way to this habit; they knew not how " Christ is made to His people wisdom and righteousness and sanctification and redemption ; " they did not fathom St. Paul's maxim, " through Christ strengthening me I can do all things."

Dr. Blair is very vague and unsatisfactory in a region

where some non-evangelical preachers of the present day are more discriminating. His delineations of character are more ideal than real. He has no power to arrest the conscience of his hearer, or make him feel, "Thou art the man!" If he contrasts two plans of life, that which is directed by worldly wisdom, and that which is directed by conscience, the one life is uniformly bad, the other as uniformly good. All is misery in the one, all is joy and peace in the other. Neither picture is true to nature. If he speaks of the moral effects of Christianity, they are all that could be desired, everything is *couleur de rose;* no hint is given of the blemishes of Christian communities. His words do not *find* the sinner. He fails to take that grip of the real heart which some even of our greatest novelists can take, and by which they can lead their readers whithersoever they will. For want of this incisive quality, he could have disturbed no one. He must have been like one who had a pleasant voice and could play well on an instrument. His sermons were pleasant to hear, but they pointed to a region of ideal excellence, whither one had no wings to follow ; and when the service was over they were thought of no more.

And generally we may say of Dr. Blair, and of his school, as well as of all in our day who in a sense take up his *rôle*, and seek to be practical without being evangelical, that they all lack dynamic power. They proceed on the principle that if men are but impressively told what is right, if they but have an attractive picture of well-doing set before them, they will certainly, or at least probably, proceed to do right. They do not take account of the inveterate tendency to evil which is the strongest force in the human soul, and must be mastered by a stronger, before the soul will turn to God. To take hold of the human heart and turn it fairly round, needs no ordinary dynamic. It is seldom to be done by taking hold of the reason only. You must grip the conscience, and hold the feelings as well. If, by God's help, you can seize all the three together, reason, conscience, and feeling, the object may be achieved. What kind of preaching is it that lays hold of reason, conscience, and feeling together? Is it not that which claims to be a message from our offended God, which shows at once the depth of our guilt, and the depth of God's love and grace in the light of Calvary and the awful transaction there? Is it not that which reveals God's eternal Son as our propitiation, and God's eternal Spirit as our life and our strength? And is it not when the whole soul is apprehended by these truths that the new life begins? The soul becomes *dead* to sin and *alive* to righteousness.

During a few years of the time when Blair was reigning in the pulpit at Edinburgh, a man of more varied gifts and more real pulpit power was creating no little stir in the neighbouring seaport of Leith. JOHN LOGAN was indeed born much later than Blair (A.D. 1748), but he was a contemporary of his from 1773 to 1786. Logan was not only a preacher, but a poet, a historian, a philosopher, a dramatist, and a man of varied genius. Some of our paraphrases are ascribed to him. In Logan's sermons, of which two volumes were printed, there is a tone of greater earnestness than in the more polished productions of the minister of the High Church. He gets nearer to the hearts of his hearers, makes more use of the second person, seems more bent on moving them. There is more flow and glow in his sermons. But there is a great lack of the doctrines of grace. There is a very slight recognition of any supernatural power in the work of religion. When the work of Christ is referred to, it is as if all alike shared its benefit. When you contemplate infinite goodness and everlasting love, you are necessarily inspired with affection and gratitude, as really as you are moved with wonder when you behold the vastness and the magnificence of God's universe. The minds of children are untainted with actual guilt, and this virgin innocence is a sacrifice more acceptable to the Almighty than if we should come before Him with the cattle upon a thousand hills, and ten thousand rivers of oil.

Piety is not a wild blaze of religious passion that flashes out for an hour and then vanishes away. The piety of which Mr. Logan approves is something far deeper and more pervading. He draws one of those ideal pictures in which Blair delights, where everything is perfect; but it is hard to say where he ever saw it. The fervent Christian engages in God's service with the utmost alacrity and cheerfulness. "He holds nothing too dear which will procure for him that robe of holiness which is beautiful in the eyes of heaven. He feels in his heart all the devout affections and desires so passionately described by the holy psalmist, which we know not whether to admire most as beautiful strains of poetry or raptures of devotion. 'As the hart panteth after the water-brooks, so panteth my soul after thee, O God.'" It is strange to observe how perfect pictures these orators drew of an ideal holiness, while they discouraged with much earnestness the only means by which it might be approached.

Logan was one of those who defied the puritan spirit in the Church by publishing a play which was acted in the theatre. Some time before, Mr. Home of Athelstaneford had done the same thing, but, in order to escape a prosecution, he resigned his charge soon after. Logan's play was not successful either as a book or upon the stage; and it is said that the depression caused by the failure led him into the snare of strong drink. He was compelled to resign his charge while only in his thirty-eighth year; removing to London, he sought literary employment, but died soon after, about the age of forty.

Such then was the new school of preaching, designed to supersede the rugged earnestness, the uncouth fervour, the dogmatism, and the decision of the earlier preachers of Scotland. In its immediate object it was no doubt fairly successful. It commended itself to many men of cultivation; it was more acceptable to the upper classes; it stood better with the world. Carlyle, in his sermon to the Society for the Sons of the Clergy, exults in the fact that the ministry of the Scottish Church had produced quite a galaxy of literary characters—historians like Robertson, Ferguson, Watson, Henry; philosophers like Reid, Ferguson, Campbell, Gerard; writers on rhetoric like Blair; poets like Home and Wilkie; scientists like Leechman, Stewart, Playfair, Greenfield, Finlayson, Walker, Dickson. He is especially proud of the achievements of many sons of the clergy who shine as stars of the first magnitude in the constellation of genius.[1] Higher distinction than this no Church, in his opinion, could win. There can be no doubt, likewise, that in literary grace the pulpit made decided progress under the influence of this school. The publication of Blair's *Lectures on Rhetoric*, and of a much abler book, Dr. Campbell's *Philosophy of Rhetoric*, drew attention to the forms of language most suitable for composition generally, and for conveying the instructions and appeals of the pulpit in particular. The old form of the sermon, with introductions, doctrines, uses, exhortations, and what not, distributed into ever so many heads and divisions, disappeared; while at the same time the more recent method of discarding heads and divisions altogether was not yet resorted to. In Blair we have always a number of heads, and sometimes several particulars under them. Of Robertson it is

[1] *Autobiography*, pp. 34, 35.

expressly stated by Dr. Somerville that his heads or articles were arranged with logical precision.

Even the evangelical men of the time showed that they were influenced by the change. The sermons of Dr. John Erskine show much more grace and finish in plan and expression than those of his namesakes, Ebenezer and Ralph, and especially those of the seventeenth century. The moderate school are entitled to the praise of having stripped the pulpit of much that was rugged and uncouth, and made its outward form more acceptable to men of cultivated taste and literary sympathy. If this had been effected without damage to qualities of higher importance, it would have been an important service. It is the habit of inferior men to disparage qualities which they do not themselves possess. Men of rough manners and breeding are tempted to think of a refined taste and bearing as sheer affectation, and to laugh at those who attach importance to them. But surely it is a matter of no small importance to bring all the work of the Christian Church into harmony with what commends itself to the cultivated class. In so far as the moderate school succeeded in this endeavour, they are entitled to our thanks.

But there are few who will deny that this benefit was gained at the sacrifice of much more vital interests. We do not pause to inquire whether the results to religion of the more intimate alliance between the Church and the world were beneficial or no. There is certainly nothing to prove that David Hume was led either to abandon a single sceptical view through his intimacy with the Moderate divines, or to take a more favourable view of revealed religion from any reflection of it he saw in their characters and lives. His opinion already quoted, of John Brown of Haddington's preaching (page 212), and of Carlyle's (p. 228), would seem to show that he thought little of the pulpit work of his literary friends. It is painful to remark that though Hume was in constant correspondence with Robertson and Blair, neither of them seems ever to have uttered a hint to him respecting things unseen. When he was slowly dying, and knew that he was dying, and spoke freely of the fact, the only correspondent that seems to have had the faithfulness to write anything respecting what was to happen to him after death, was not a clergyman, but an honest tradesman—William Strahan, his publisher.[1]

On the other hand, there is a great deal to prove that under the moderate reign, the Church suffered greatly in her most vital interests. Some objects that she held very dear did not prosper much under her wing. Even scholarship did not make the progress that might have been expected. It is generally allowed that the life and prosperity of a university may be tested by the number of its students who take a degree. We find that under the Moderate reign the number of graduates at our universities fell off, and especially among the clergy. In the earlier periods of the Church it was the usual practice for the clergy to take a degree; in the Moderate reign comparatively few did so, at least in the University of Edinburgh, the headquarters of the Moderate school. But we lay the stress of our argument on higher considerations. What were the effects of the Moderate policy on more vital interests—the moral and the spiritual life of the Church? What kind of Church was it that at the close of the eighteenth century gave to the world the lineaments stamped on it by Robertson, Carlyle, and Blair?

The Church was no longer one. The Secession had grown rapidly in spite of internal division, and was still growing apace. It had long been one of the endeavours of the evangelical party in the General Assembly to direct attention to the growth of schism, with the view

[1] See Burton's *Life of Hume*, last chapter.

of securing within the Church some degree of regard for
the voice of the people in the election of ministers ; but
this endeavour had been strenuously resisted and finally
crushed by the Moderates. The Church affected to despise
the Seceders. Equally severe treatment was dealt out
to the Relief, though they held by the principle of an
Establishment. Having little faith either in the conscientious earnestness of the men who had left her, or in their
power to create anything better than the vulgar shadow
of a Church, they looked on their proceedings with
careless contempt. They treated the seceders as France
had treated the Huguenots—as men whom it was a
benefit to want. Little though they thought of it, the
policy of the Church to the seceders, while it increased
their number, embittered their spirit, and drove them into
a hostile attitude that prevented the Establishment from
ever again becoming the one undivided Church of Scotland.

It can hardly be denied that this policy was most
hurtful to the spiritual life of the nation. Earnestness
in religion was denounced as enthusiasm and fanaticism,
and "high-fliers" and "fanatics" were the epithets
commonly applied to all who cherished the faith that
overcomes the world. It was broadly hinted that give
them only scope and rope, these fanatics would introduce
times of frightful violence, and turn the world upside
down. Rational and moderate religion took things easily ;
and only demanded of men such a regard to the duties
of morality and religion as they could give without
difficulty, and such a following of Christ as did not
require them to take up His cross.

The great enemy of Christianity in the eighteenth
century was Deism. The moderate preaching did not
arrest its spread, even among the clergy. Hume remarked that no country was more leavened with deism

than Scotland. Dr. Carlyle gives a commentary on this, in an account of his visits when a probationer to the manses in the presbytery of Haddington, and shows how some of the ministers had accepted the arguments of deistical books. As to evangelical preaching, he tells how it was ridiculed by one of them, Simson of Pencaitland (brother of Professor Simson), who said he could give him a plan for any sermon, whatever might be its text—first, to dwell on the fall of Adam and the depravity of man ; second, on the way of recovery through Jesus Christ ; and then to conclude with observations, or uses, or reflections, or practical references tending to make us good men.

The growing indifference of the people to religion was manifested in many ways. It was under this *régime* that " lapsing " began. That grievous neglect of divine ordinances in our large cities with which Chalmers afterwards grappled so bravely, was a legacy from the indifference that had grown up in the eighteenth century. In one of his sermons, Logan says : " Would to God I could . . . add that we are more religious and devout than our ancestors were, that our zeal for the honour of God and the interests of religion shines with a brighter lustre, and burns with a purer flame ! But alas ! my brethren, I must here change my strain. Your own eyes, your own hearts will tell you the dismal truth. Is it not a deplorable fact that instead of being fervent in spirit to serve the Lord, an indifference about religion almost universally prevails ? The very face of seriousness is banished from society, and were it not for this day on which we assemble together to worship the God of our fathers, the very form of godliness would be exterminated from the earth."[1] There is a striking remark of Principal Robertson's in the same strain in his

[1] *Sermons*, vol. ii. p. 26.

Q

one sermon, when after pleading strongly that Christianity
had always proved the foe of slavery, he asks, How then
does it continue to exist in the American Colonies of Great
Britain ? His reply is, that the genius and tendency of
any religion are known by the operations of its vigorous,
not of its declining age ; adding that avarice had revived
what Christianity had abolished, and implying that there
was not vigour enough in the Christianity of the day to
snatch back the prey from the hands of the spoiler.

Neither did morality improve among clergy or laity.
Drunkenness became common among the clergy, and
it could not but be remarked that the shield of Dr.
Robertson and his party was frequently thrown over
the delinquents.   The Principal maintained that what he
was eager for was not to acquit the accused, but to see
that no man should be condemned on insufficient evidence.   His opponents contended that legal subtleties and
sophistries were employed in order to set aside proof that
was quite sufficient in the eye of every sensible man.[1]

As to the morals of the people, we know what kind of
dinner-parties prevailed among the upper classes, and what
sickening orgies of drunkenness were enacted there. " Profane swearing was equally common ; almost every sentence was garnished with an oath, and to swear roundly
and well was considered the mark of a gentleman."[2]
Among the mass of the people there was an evident
change for the worse.   A Society was instituted in Edinburgh " for promoting religious knowledge among the
poor" on the ground of " the great and growing depravity
of manners in this city, especially among those of the
lower ranks." [3]   " The discipline of the Church had relaxed
a little from its ancient severity, but still it was more
severe than it is in our day. . . . Still penitents required

---

[1] Cunningham's *History*, vol. ii. p. 531.   [2] *Ibid.* p. 593.
[3] Dr. John Erskine's *Sermons*, vol. ii. p. 101.

to stand up in the church, and bear a rebuke from the pulpit. . . . In some cases this painful penance was commuted to a fine, which went to the funds of the poor ; and in Edinburgh the increase of immorality between 1763 and 1783 was shown by the revenue from this source having risen from £154 to £600."[1] Strange that such things should have taken place in the triumph of a school which set itself to remedy the defects of its predecessors by dwelling more on the obligations of moral life ! Could there be a more striking testimony to the need of a moral dynamic far more powerful than moderatism could supply, to induce men " to live soberly, righteously, and godly in this present world " ?

We need but refer to the attitude of the moderate party to Christian missions as evinced in the celebrated debate in the General Assembly in 1796, when the over-tures in favour of foreign missions were dismissed as counselling the Church to a foolish, a dangerous, an im-practicable enterprise. Akin to this was the utter want of sympathy or encouragement for those who were now struggling, at fearful odds, in the cause of humanity. In a celebrated sermon on gentleness, Dr. Blair had spoken in terms of poetical delight on the nature and the achieve-ments of that grace—" how it delights above all things to alleviate distress, and if it cannot dry up the falling tear, to soothe at least the grieving heart." Yet was there ever a word spoken by any conspicuous member of the party to encourage Wilberforce in his noble struggle against the slave-trade, or Elizabeth Fry in her blessed effort to bring the light and purity of the Gospel within the dingy walls of our prisons ? Did any of them bear a hand in the formation of the British and Foreign Bible Society ? Was it not left to poor Nonconformist trades-

---

[1] Cunningham's *History*, vol. ii. pp. 593-4, and Stevenson's *Chronicles of Edinburgh*.

men, such as John Campbell of our Grassmarket, to begin
a movement in Scotland for the rescue of the harlot, to set
up the village Sunday-school, and to summon the aid of
the press to spread Christian literature among the poor ?

The eulogistic attitude of Dean Stanley to the
moderate school [1] is easily explained. Christianity,
according to the Dean, is not essentially a salvation for
the lost. It is a religion to encourage what is good in
us, and to repress the evil; to teach the fatherhood of
God and the brotherhood of man; to diffuse a kindly
and charitable spirit on every side, and to throw a pure
influence over the common interests and employments
of life. Dogmatic creeds and all else that lead men to
great intensity of feeling in religion are only sources of
evil. The moderates did infinite good by their latitudin-
arianism, their charity, their sympathy with freedom of
thought, their literary independence, and their genial
aspect towards all the interests of humanity. It is a
strange and distressing thing that any evil should ever
have been spoken of so excellent and useful a body of
men. This view is maintained by Dean Stanley, first of
all by keeping out of view the atrocities perpetrated by
the party in the form of forced settlements; then by
giving prominence to such points as modify their
conspicuous blemishes; but chiefly by painting in the
brightest colours the virtues they did possess. The Dean
has a wonderful faculty of making capital out of the
smallest assets. Even Sir George Mackenzie, he of whom
David Deans said, " He will be kenned by the name of
the bloody Mackenzie as long as there 's a Scotch tongue
to speak the word," has his redeeming qualities. He is
" a philosophic theologian of the largest type." Such
charity covers a multitude of sins. It must be owned
that he did most execrable things; but this was because

---

[1] In his *Lectures on the History of the Church of Scotland.*

he deemed himself bound to maintain law and order at whatever cost. After playing thus with his memory, the Dean ends by throwing him overboard, remarking that he remains a beacon to all liberal statesmen and divines, that liberality of theory does not always carry with it liberality of action.

It is hardly necessary to discuss with the Dean the secondary aspects of the case. He makes a great deal of the literary outburst that threw such lustre on the Moderate Church, and was such a contrast to its literary poverty under the stifling dogmatism of the preceding century. In reply to this it is enough to ask, whether the literary activity of last century has not been surpassed tenfold by that of the nineteenth, which, to say the least, ran parallel to the evangelical revival? The truth is, there never was a time when some of the most conspicuous of human interests were at a lower ebb than in the fourth quarter of the eighteenth century. The universities, notwithstanding the eminence of many professors, had little academic life; in some of them graduation in arts, common at an earlier period, had nearly died out; the books printed in that period are the shabbiest in all literature; the parish churches built then are generally huge barns, and the gentlemen's mansions pretentious but tasteless piles. Never were the people more held down; never were privilege and monopoly more held up; never was less encouragement given to any scheme for ameliorating the condition of suffering humanity. We say it is hardly necessary to discuss these aspects of the subject; they sink into insignificance beside the fundamental feature of the case. The great question is, Is Dean Stanley's religion Christianity? It has many of the most beautiful features of Christianity, but has it got its heart, its soul? Dean Stanley was a most estimable man, that won all hearts, and did good service by advancing the spirit of brotherhood, especially among Christian men and Christian ministers, who have proved themselves only too liable to forget it. We believe that personally he owed much more to those influences of vital Christianity under which he grew up than he was himself conscious of. But a religion which has no divine message of grace for fallen and guilty men; a religion which overlooks the demands of God's righteous law, and dispenses forgiveness and acceptance as easily as a rich man scatters his charity; a religion which thinks by mere rose-water applications to cure the desperate disease of the human heart in its alienation from God, and to restore it to order and beauty; a religion which undertakes to get rid of all the bitterness of strife, and to diffuse everywhere an atmosphere of peace and good-will; —a religion that undertakes all this without an atonement, without shedding of blood, without divine regeneration, may be very beautiful, very attractive, very delightful, but it is not the Gospel of Jesus Christ.

CHAPTER X.

EVANGELICAL preaching did not forsake the Established
Church with the Erskines. There remained a considerable number of ministers in full sympathy with them and
with Boston, though they did not leave the Church. From
the beginning of the eighteenth century to its close, an
evangelical succession may be found in the Establishment,
a chain of highly respectable men who left their mark in
their day, and whose names are still remembered. In
many ways there is a contrast between those at the
beginning of the century and those at the end : between
Thomas Halyburton, for example, and John Erskine
there is identity as to the message delivered, but a
notable change in its dress ; Halyburton carrying into
the eighteenth century much of the ruggedness of the
seventeenth, while Erskine shows the impress of a more
cultured age.

THOMAS HALYBURTON was ordained minister of Ceres
in Fife in the year 1700, and thereafter he was appointed
Professor of Divinity at St. Andrews. He was of the
same theological school as Boston, and there are interesting points of resemblance between the two. Both were
born in the persecuting era, and within a few months of
each other, Halyburton in the end of 1674, and Boston
in the beginning of 1676. Both were the children of

fathers who had been warmly attached to the Covenanting cause, and had suffered during the persecutions; but
Halyburton's experience of trouble was greater than
Boston's—his father, a minister, having been ejected from
his charge and his home in 1662. Both of them wrote
copious autobiographies, which in certain features resemble
each other. The characteristic of Halyburton's autobiography is that it is not a record of his life, but a history
of his spiritual change. Every feeling of which he was
conscious, every experience he passed through, every view
of truth or error that came into his mind, is duly
chronicled, and these records of spiritual experience form
the whole book. In his early life he had a long struggle
with unbelief, and even with atheism ; it was protracted
over several years; but in his twenty-fourth year he experienced a sudden and glorious deliverance, entering
happily into the peace of faith. It was his practice to
associate every feeling, whether good or bad, with some
text of Scripture which he duly set down; for he firmly
believed that every winding of his subtle heart, every
refuge of lies to which he had fled, every art and artifice
of Satan with which he had been plied, was mirrored in
the Word of God. One cannot but mark, however, the
little of scientific accuracy that guided him in the interpretation of Scripture; for the verses which he quotes
are often brought in for a kind of verbal fitness, rather
than for intrinsic agreement with his views. It was the
custom of Halyburton, not less than of Boston, to try to
obtain divine guidance on all the affairs of life, great and
small, temporal and spiritual ; and those who are interested in matters matrimonial will turn with interest
to the passages in which each of these grave divines
records his experience in the prospect of marriage.

Halyburton's ministry in Ceres was but short; in
1710, in his thirty-sixth year, he was appointed to the

chair of divinity at St. Andrews.   In that situation his
health unfortunately gave way ; and after a deathbed
experience brightened far above the common by gracious
experiences and the triumphant utterances of faith and
hope, he passed away in 1712, at the early age of thirty-
eight.

In his treatise on the insufficiency of natural religion,
in reply to Lord Herbert of Cherbury's " five points," he
took the line which Chalmers afterwards followed with
great effect, showing that natural theology is unable to
deal with man as a fallen being, and cannot satisfy the
cry of the awakened conscience : " What must I do to be
saved ? "   The answer to this question, as Chalmers used
to say, must come from a higher theology.

Our business with Halyburton, however, is as a
preacher.   In the pulpit he was popular and powerful,
of the same school as Boston, and dealing with the great
truths that form the warp and the woof of the *Fourfold
State*.   In his treatise entitled *The Great Concern of
Salvation* we have a threefold division :—(1.) A discovery
of man's natural state ; or the guilty sinner convicted.
(2.) Man's recovery by faith in Christ ; or the convinced
sinner's case and cure.   (3.) The Christian's duty with
respect .to personal and family religion.   Here the doctrines of sin and wrath, of man's ruin and inability, of
God's free grace in Christ, and of the renewing power
that worketh in the believer both to will and to do of
God's good pleasure, are fully and earnestly set forth.
There is the old scholastic method of treatment, the old
multiplication of heads and particulars, and the old
process of analytical ramification on the one hand, and
synthetical accumulation and application on the other.
He does not indulge in the fanciful analogies of the
Erskines ; but in fervour and power of probing the conscience, he is at least equal to any of his contemporaries.

There is no part of a preacher's duty more important,
yet more difficult, than to convince his hearers of sin.
Intellectual proof of it is but a very little matter; the
great business is to bring it home to the conscience, and
to leave the sense of sin rankling there.

Let us see how Halyburton attempts the task. He
presents eight views of sin. A modern preacher would
not have so many, but would select the two or three
that seemed to him most striking. Halyburton's division
is neither logical nor precise. He views sin (1.) in the
glass of God's law, (2.) in the nature of God, (3.) in the
threatenings of the law, (4.) in the judgments of God,
(5.) in the soul under a sense of sin, (6.) in the hideous
crimes sin commits, (7.) in the condition of the damned,
and (8.) in the sufferings of Christ. Such a miscellaneous
set of views rather scatters than concentrates or deepens
impression. But in some of these particulars he shows
no little power. Under the second view, for example, he
views " sin as contrary to the nature of the great God, the
seat of all majesty, glory, beauty, and excellency; and if
you look at it here, O how ugly will it appear ! Nothing
in all the world contrary and opposite to the nature of
God but sin ! The meanest and most apparently deformed
creature in the world, the toad, the crawling insect, carries
in its nature nothing really opposite to the nature of God;
Sin, only sin, stands in opposition to Him. This He cannot dwell with. Evil shall not dwell with Him, nor fools
stand in His sight. Such is the abhorrence God has at
sin, that when He speaks of it, His heart as it were rises
against it—' O do not this abominable thing which I
hate !' "

Any hearer taking this view of sin home, and leaving
church with a sense of having that in him which made
him more odious to God than the toad, the serpent, the
hyena, might well be troubled. And as often as the

view presented itself, he might well ask, What shall I do?

Yet with all his powerful denunciation of sin, we mark in Halyburton a defect which has usually been the defect of his school. It is for the most part only with sin in the abstract, in the general, that he deals. If we look through his book to find the actual sins of human beings detected and exposed as they appear in ordinary life, we are disappointed. One of his sections is " On the Christian's duty." It contains innumerable directions as to the spirit, purpose, means, ends, and so forth of God's service ; but when we turn to the head that proposes to show the work that God means His servants to do, it is despatched in general terms in one short page, and the particular graces, habits, and beauties of the Christian life are as little unfolded as ever.

Another celebrated evangelical preacher was JOHN WILLISON of Dundee, author of *Sacramental Meditations* and *Catechisms*, and other well-known practical books. He was born in 1680, the same year with Ebenezer Erskine; was minister of Brechin fifteen years, and thereafter of Dundee. Like Boston, the Erskines, and all other men of that stamp, he was greatly distressed at the passing of the Patronage Act in 1712, and at the symptoms of laxity in doctrine and in discipline that were appearing in the Church. Though sympathising with the Seceders, he did not think that they had sufficient reasons for seceding, and he was one of those who laboured hard to bring about the friendly resolution of the Assembly 1734, which was an invitation to them to return. He went to London, also, and made great exertions to obtain the repeal of the Patronage Act. Failing to obtain this object, and to avert the secession, he took little further part in the public business of the Church, and died in

1750, after a laborious ministry that nearly covered the half century.

Willison was perhaps more of a pastor than a preacher, but he was one of those men who made a diligent pastorate wonderfully subservient to a useful and efficient pulpit; one, too, in whom homely talents most carefully exercised were greatly improved, and contributed much to success in preaching. His catechisms still remain to show us what pains he took with the instruction of the young. Around the Lord's Supper especially, he sought to hang all the glory of the Gospel. His sacramental meditations are unsurpassed for gracious feeling and unction. One cannot but remark the extraordinary appreciation of the Lord's Supper that prevailed in those days. Amid the monotony of secular life, and the uniformity of religious service during the other weeks of the year, the communion season was hailed as a time of spiritual feasting and refreshing. Preachers gave their richest expositions of evangelical truth; they vied with each other to bring out in brightest colours the treasures of the Gospel of Salvation. But, in point of fact, the preachings that were accumulated round the Sacrament came to have a more conspicuous place in the service than the Sacrament itself. The festival character belonged fully more to the sermons than to the Sacrament. But Willison was one of those who sought to convey a high sense of the act of communicating. The opportunity of receiving by faith all the grace symbolised and conveyed in the bread and the wine was to be cherished with delight and enjoyed with holy awe. The participants were to be carefully prepared for the service, and brought into the frame that would enable them most fully and freely to enter into the spirit of the festival; and after they had received the Lord Jesus by faith, and feasted on His body and blood, they were to cherish the thought with unbounded gratitude, and to use it as the most powerful of all motives for renouncing the world and departing from iniquity.

This service of Willison's on behalf of the sacrament of the Supper is one that deserves to be recalled with gratitude, and pondered by us more than it usually is. A right attitude towards the sacraments, and especially the Lord's Supper, is of more importance to the welfare of the Protestant Church than is often thought.   The perversion of the Eucharist by the Church of Rome and kindred Churches is a fact of tremendous significance. The power implied in the creation of the body and blood, soul and divinity of the Lord Jesus Christ every time the Eucharist is celebrated, throws every other miracle utterly into the shade.   The ghostly influence of the man who is supposed to possess this power is unlimited.   That this notion of the Eucharist should be spreading in the Church of England is simply appalling.   Willison and such men taught us how to make much of the Sacraments without importing into them one particle of magical virtue.   A sacrament to Willison was simply "an holy ordinance, instituted by Christ, wherein by sensible signs, Christ and the benefits of the New Covenant are represented, sealed, and applied to believers."   On this simple footing it became a great festival.

And oftener than once in the history of the Scottish Church it has been seen how the sacraments may be highly exalted without a trace of transubstantiation. Dean Stanley fancied that he found a connecting link, in their common reverence for sacramental ordinances, between the ancient Culdee Church and the modern Presbyterian Church of the Highlands.[1]   The analogy was, that in the eleventh century the Culdee Church, under the influence of sheer dread, had ceased to observe

[1] *Lectures on the History of the Church of Scotland*, p. 34.

the Sacrament, and that the same dread prevailed under
the influence of the "Men" in the Highlands. But
neither of these practices is to be commended. Nevertheless, there has been in Scotland a remarkable reverence for the sacraments, especially the Eucharist, apart
from the idea of magic virtue. We have seen how early
the subject attracted attention in the Reformed Church,
and how good service was done by Robert Bruce in his
five sermons on the sacraments, preached in 1589, in
which with great clearness he gave the Protestant key-
note, showing their invaluable benefits as aids to faith
and means of grace.[1]

Willison writes like one who lived much in sunshine,
and who diffused a sunny influence around him. He
was an excellent middle-class preacher, plain, warm, and
homely. For all his spirituality and unction, he did not
shrink, when duty pressed, from entering the political
arena, and contending for popular rights. He published
"A Letter to an English M.P. from a gentleman in Scotland, concerning the slavish dependencies which a great
part of the nation is still kept under by superiorities,
wards, reliefs, and other remains of the feudal law; and
by clanships and tithes." He was grieved at seeing the
poorer classes of his countrymen ground down by needless burdens, and he struck a brave blow on their behalf.
Usually, however, his path lay in the common rounds of
pastoral duty, and his publications were the outcome of
his pastoral solicitude; and the singular acceptance in
which his books have been held by the devout people of
Scotland proves him to have had no ordinary share of
that gift so valuable to a preacher,—ability to reach the
heart.

Another distinguished name of this period, though in

[1] See his works (Wod. Soc.), pp. 5-157.

a very different walk, is that of JOHN MACLAURIN, whose
sermon on "Glorying in the Cross of Christ" was long
regarded as a *chef-d'œuvre*, although this estimate might
be questioned at the present day.   He was the brother
of Colin Maclaurin, the well-known professor of mathematics in the University of Glasgow.   After being for
four years minister of Luss in Dumbartonshire, he was
translated to Glasgow in 1723, and remained there till his
death in 1754.   Maclaurin was thoroughly evangelical in
theology, and in character singularly devout.   Dr. John
Gillies, who was his son-in-law, says that he presented
such a combination of shining gifts and beautiful graces
that it was difficult to say what were his faults.   He took
a special interest in the meetings for united prayer that
began to be held in Glasgow at this time, in connection
with the concert for prayer in Britain and America, which
Jonathan Edwards advocated so warmly.

In his preaching, Maclaurin broke loose from the
formal structure, so prevalent for generations, of multi-
tudinous heads and divisions, uses and applications, and
a set phraseology which had become like a shibboleth in
the evangelical school.   Instead of fashioning his sermons,
as his predecessors had done, on the plan of a tree, with
trunk and branches, running into branchlets and twigs in
bewildering profusion, he constructed them on the plan
of a river, flowing in one continuous channel, and gathering momentum from every rill and streamlet added to its
volume.   His plan was to take a single line of thought,
to throw upon it all the light which it required, and to
direct it to the great practical objects which it was fitted
to enforce.   The instrument of the Erskines and other
popular preachers had been like a kaleidoscope, in which
truth was presented in every variety of form and colour
of which it was capable ; that of Maclaurin was like a
lens, by which the truth in its simplicity was made more

clear, and thereby more impressive.   Maclaurin was much
more of an intellectual preacher.   And his intellect was
disciplined somewhat rigidly ; on principle he avoided the
practice, of which many of his contemporaries were so
fond, of finding a multitude of analogies in scriptural
symbols.   There is not much play of imagination in his
sermons.   The greater part of them is addressed to the
reason.

As to his mode of delivery, or the effect produced by
his sermons, we have little information.   Judging from
their qualities, we should say that they were more adapted
to men of disciplined intellect than to the mass of hearers.
Two of his sermons have obtained unusual renown ; one
entitled "The sins of men not chargeable to God," and
the other the discourse already adverted to, on glorying in
the Cross of Christ.   With regard to the latter, we are not
disposed to rate it so high as some.   It is rather a treatise
than a sermon.   Its clear, cogent, intellectual exposition,
rising at times to the heights of eloquence, must delight
every intellectual reader whose sympathies are with
evangelical truth ; but, as a sermon, it wants many important qualities.   It runs too much on the same groove,
wants freedom and ease of language, as well as closeness
of application.   If the form of the seventeenth century
was set aside with its characteristic technicalities, a
certain formality of the eighteenth century was assumed
in its stead.   There is a want of touch with the living
soul.   The preacher stands at a distance, and discourses
powerfully but not thrillingly.   In laying aside the
homeliness of the older preachers, he has lost somewhat
of their stirring power.

But this can hardly be said of the preachers concerned
in that remarkable religious movement which began in
1742, known as the "Cambuslang Revival."   There could

be no lack of close dealing and rousing appeal in connection with a work where such a multitude were led to
ask in the most intense earnestness, " What must we do to
be saved ? "   The train was laid by two ministers of the
old school, Mr. Robe of Kilsyth and Mr. M'Culloch of
Cambuslang ; and it is remarkable that it was the full
presentation of the doctrine of regeneration that prepared
the way, Mr. Robe having preached two years on the
new birth and the work of the Spirit; while Mr. M'Culloch, who held many prayer-meetings, and kept his
people well acquainted with the work of Whitefield,
had preached nearly a year on regeneration.   The whole
neighbourhood soon appeared to be wrapt in a flame of
spiritual influence.   Distress for sin fell on great numbers,
who sometimes manifested their emotion in convulsive
sobbings and protestations most difficult to subdue.
When they apprehended the grace of God in Christ, their
distress was followed by a peace and joy in believing of
almost rapturous intensity, and a marvellous relish for
the word and ordinances of God.   And according to the
testimony of those most cognisant of the movement, the
change effected on the subjects of the awakening was
highly beneficial, not only in its religious but in its
moral and social aspects.   Where vice had prevailed, it
was abandoned, injuries were forgiven, estranged families
reconciled, restoration made of property that had been
unjustly appropriated, and a new conscientiousness manifested in matters where before there had been much
remissness.   The movement reached its climax when
Whitefield came to the communion at Cambuslang.
His power not only of arresting the multitude but impressing the individual was marvellously manifested, and
the results were like those of the day of Pentecost at
Jerusalem.   The direct presentation and free offer of
all the blessings of redemption through the blood of

R

Christ fell like the bread of heaven on many a heart that had been made sore and hungry under the searching and soul-emptying preaching of the ministers on the nature and need of regeneration. The work at Cambuslang and Kilsyth was very similar to the revival at Shotts, to that in the Stewarton valley, and to that in the north of Ireland during the preceding century. Exactly a hundred years afterwards a similar work appeared at Kilsyth; before that, it had appeared in various parts of the Scottish Highlands; and since that time it has been more or less exemplified in many other parts of the country.

The movement at Cambuslang in 1742 was viewed with very different feelings by the various sections or parties of the Presbyterian Church. In the first place, it was denounced by the Seceders. The ministers of the Secession had made an earnest endeavour to limit the services of Whitefield to their congregations when he visited Scotland, but Whitefield refused to be so bound. He had not come to Scotland to testify, he had come to seek the lost. The Seceders could not believe that the Holy Ghost would work in connection with a Church which had whitewashed heretics, and driven faithful men from its pale. Fastening attention on the bodily contortions and other strange features of the movement, they ascribed it to the influence of the devil. It was a lamentable error both of head and heart, and did more to weaken the influence of the Secession than anything else they had done.

Within the Church, the moderate party looked on the movement as a strange manifestation of enthusiasm and folly. To ascribe it to the supernatural influence of the Holy Spirit seemed to them most objectionable, first, because they wished to do away as much as possible with the supernatural in religion, and to fall back on influences natural and rational; and second, because they had little faith in the Holy Ghost as a separate Person, and an active agent in the soul of man. They found it difficult to account for the remarkable effects in the work at Cambuslang, but they did their best. Mechanical movements, they said, might be accounted for by mechanical means ; example had a wonderful effect in drawing others to follow ; excitable natures were easily roused for a time. But plainly, nothing could have been more opposed to the spirit and methods of the moderate party, whose desire was that all the services of religion should be conducted with perfect order and propriety ; who were horrified with all ebullitions of vehement feeling, and who deemed most pernicious any such concern for the realities of hell and heaven as might withdraw men from a due regard for the interests and enjoyments of this earthly scene.

Most but not all of the evangelical clergy of the Church were cordial supporters of the work at Cambuslang. But for this it might have met with the denunciation of the Assembly, and its promoters might have been deposed as disorderly and fanatical. *Primâ facie*, there was much more to be objected to in the Cambuslang movement than there had been in the *Marrow of Modern Divinity*. But the then leader of the evangelical party, Dr. Webster of the Tolbooth Church, threw his shield over it, and wrote most warmly in its defence. Dr. Webster was a man of singular character, but powerful influence, and his support counted for not a little. And it was a good thing for the Established Church that the evangelical party took this course. It retained within the Church a most important element,—those of her ministers and people who mourned over valleys full of dry bones, and longed for a breath of the Spirit to quicken them into armies of living men. It secured for ministers of revival spirit in after times a manifest right to be in the Established Church, and to preach in the revival spirit in Established pulpits. It kept within the enclosure of the Establishment a section of godly people who would otherwise have been likely to join the Secession. It was to a large extent an expansion and intensification of this revival spirit that prepared the way for the Disruption of 1843. Thus the movement at Cambuslang a century before influenced in a marked degree the future history of the Church.

Mention has been made of Dr. ALEXANDER WEBSTER of the Tolbooth Church, Edinburgh, as a leader of the popular party in Edinburgh and the Church generally at this period. His father, who, like the fathers of Boston and Halyburton, had been imprisoned and had suffered keenly in the time of the persecutions, had likewise been minister of the Tolbooth Church, and was an able and popular preacher. Webster, the son, seems to have been one of those men that try deliberately to make the best of both worlds. He was gifted with remarkably popular talents, had a tall, impressive figure, an affable and attractive manner, a glowing eloquence, and a very popular delivery. It was said that he shone especially in prayer, and in the administration of the Lord's Supper. On the other hand, he was a man of the world. He delighted in convivial company, and conspicuously in the company of members of the moderate party; he was a man who could keep the table in a roar, and was as far as possible from being a teetotaller. He was active and public-spirited; he was the founder of the Ministers' Widows' Fund, he helped to form the Society for Propagating Christian Knowledge, he drew up the first census of Scotland, he helped to lay out the new town of Edinburgh, and he was an active friend of the House of Hanover. A very bad character of him is given by Dr. Carlyle of Inveresk, who, however, is not to be implicitly trusted. He speaks of him as a five-bottle man; as remaining untouched by the influence of drink after all the company were under the table; but as a sheer drunkard in old age; as shifty in his policy, and easily influenced by others; and he sums up by pronouncing him a hypocrite in religion. On the other hand, Dr. Somerville of Jedburgh, while owning that his convivial habits occasioned doubts to some of his friends respecting the sincerity of his public conduct, expresses his own confidence in his sincerity. Without ascribing to Dr. Webster all that Carlyle has written against him, we cannot but regard it as having been a calamity to the evangelical cause and the evangelical pulpit that he should for many years have been the leading man of his party. Some special attraction he must have had as a preacher, for we have heard a tradition of a man who was in the habit of walking from the neighbourhood of Carnwath, some five-and-twenty miles off, to attend his church. But his conviviality was carried to a pernicious extreme, and if it did not suggest to every one the view of his religion which it suggested to Dr. Carlyle, it must have weakened his influence greatly, and conveyed a wrong conception of the life of faith.

Certainly it was no loss to the evangelical party when Webster passed away, and the leading man who followed him in Edinburgh was Dr. JOHN ERSKINE, of Old Greyfriars.

The more that the character, gifts, and services of this man are considered, the more estimable does he appear. Unfortunately the materials for a personal acquaintance with him are small. No doubt we have a good-sized biography of him by Sir Henry Moncreiff Wellwood; but it is little more than a record of public work, and is singularly deficient in those touches which give the inner likeness of a man. Dr. Erskine was a singular godsend to the evangelical party of his day. His family connections were unusually high; the office of a Scotch minister seemed far beneath him; but his soul was deep in the work of the ministry; and as often happens in similar cases, he devoted himself more thoroughly to spiritual work and renounced the pleasures of the world more completely than many a minister does of lower social standing. He was no reverend squire, who would don his red coat to follow the hounds, or eagerly cultivate the society of his worldly compeers; but an earnest, studious, painstaking minister, whose one interest was the advancement of the kingdom of God.

He was the eldest son of John Erskine of Carnock, the well-known author of *An Institute of the Law of Scotland.* He was heir to a good estate, was connected personally and by marriage with several noble families, and might quite warrantably have aspired to the highest position in the profession of law, or in any other department of secular life. Before he got a charge he showed on what side his sympathies lay by publishing a work on the deistical controversy in opposition to Dr. Campbell of St. Andrews. Dr. Campbell's book was in reply to Tindal's *Christianity as old as the Creation ;* it was written in the "moderate" spirit, and went to show that natural reason could not guide us to the knowledge of God, a position which Erskine very strongly controverts. Hardly had he entered the ministry when he espoused the cause of Mr. Whitefield, defending him both in the press and in Church courts. After holding in succession the charges of Kirkintilloch and Culross he was brought to Edinburgh in 1758; and in 1767 he became joint-minister of Old Greyfriars along with Principal Robertson, with whom he acted as colleague, and always most amicably, for many years.

The father and mother of Sir Walter Scott were

members of his congregation, and it is of his appearance in the pulpit that Sir Walter has given so vivid a picture in *Guy Mannering.*   An Edinburgh lawyer takes an English stranger who has never been in a Scotch church to the Greyfriars.   "The colleague of Dr. Robertson ascended the pulpit.   His external appearance was not prepossessing.   A remarkably fair complexion strangely contrasted with a black wig without a grain of powder; a narrow chest and stooping posture; hands which, placed like props on either side of the pulpit, seemed necessary rather to support the person than to assist the gesticulation of the preacher;—no gown, not even that of Geneva, a tumbled band, and a gesture which seemed hardly voluntary, were the first circumstances which struck a stranger.

"'The preacher seems a very ungainly person,' whispered Mannering.   'Never fear,' replied Pleydell; 'he is the son of an excellent Scottish lawyer; he'll show blood, I'll warrant him.'

"A lecture was delivered, fraught with new, striking, and entertaining views of Scripture history, and a sermon in which the Calvinism of the Kirk of Scotland was ably supported, yet made the basis of a sound system of practical morals, which should neither shelter the sinner under the cloak of speculative faith or of peculiarity of opinion, nor leave him loose to the waves of unbelief and schism.   Something there was of an antiquated tone of argument and metaphor, but it only served to give zest and peculiarity to the style of elocution.   The sermon was not read; a scrap of paper containing the heads of the discourse was occasionally referred to, and the enunciation, which at first seemed imperfect and embarrassed, became, as the preacher warmed in his progress, animated and distinct; and although the discourse could not be quoted as a correct specimen of pulpit eloquence, yet

Mannering had seldom heard so much learning, metaphysical acuteness, and energy of argument brought into the service of Christianity. 'Such,' he said, going out of the church, 'must have been the preachers to whose unfearing minds, and acute, though sometimes rudely exercised talents, we owe the Reformation.' 'And yet that reverend gentleman,' said Pleydell, 'whom I love for his father's sake and his own, has none of the sour and pharisaical pride which has been imputed to some of the early fathers of the Calvinistic Kirk of Scotland.'"

It is remarkable (as we have already observed) that in presenting to an English stranger a sample of a Scottish minister, Sir Walter did not bring under his notice either Principal Robertson, who was Erskine's colleague, or Dr. Hugh Blair, who was charming the High Church congregation with his mellifluous elegance. The reason for this is obvious. He desired to bring before the Englishman a characteristic Scotsman, one of the class that had formed the religious character of the nation, that had brought about the Reformation and other great changes, that had exercised the moving and moulding influence under which Scotland had become what it was. Robertson and Blair were not in the true Apostolical succession. They belonged to a more modern school—a school more acceptable to Sir Walter personally, but not the real fathers of the Scottish Church. The evangelical Erskine was a more true representative of the deep faith and earnest Biblical preaching of the country.

Dr. Erskine was a scholarly man, not in a mere dilettante sense, but one who worked hard for studious ends. At sixty, he studied Dutch and German, that he might be able to read theological works in these languages, and he turned his knowledge of them to good account. He was a man of catholic heart, a warm admirer of Jonathan Edwards, a correspondent of Bishop Warburton and

Bishop Hurd; one who believed that Scotchmen might learn much from theologians of different countries, and from the different lights in which truth presented itself to them.   His personal character was consistent and irreproachable; even Dr. Carlyle, when comparing him with Dr. Webster, pays a high compliment to his "upright and honourable" character.   He died in the year 1803, having spent forty-five years as a minister of Edinburgh, and during all that time, besides his discourses from the pulpit, preached day by day and year after year that most impressive of all sermons—a life and conversation in harmony with his profession.

Sir Walter's account of his preaching gives considerable prominence to his unprepossessing appearance, awkward manner, and not very good delivery.   But it emphasises, at the same time, the substantial excellence of his discourses.   Nor would it be easy to find, in the sermon literature of Scotland in the eighteenth century, any volumes equal to his for solidity of matter, excellence of style, and directness of application.   They want the vivacity and brilliance of the orator, but they have the best qualities of the teacher.   In the first place, they have always an evangelical basis, and when they touch practical or ethical subjects it is in their true relation to the doctrines of grace.   In the next place, their mode of handling truth is full and varied, without being tedious.   In the third place, the language is clear, scholarly, exact.   And further, there is a constant recognition of the audience with whose hearts and consciences the truth must be in vital contact.   Then, with regard to subject.   The topics, for the most part, are neither elementary nor rousing.   They are not like the subjects of Whitefield's sermons, not formally directed to enforce the first principles of the doctrine of Christ.   They are designed to edify, rather than to arrest.

And in this point of view their scope is considerable. They do not shirk moral or practical questions. They embrace topics like public spirit, fidelity in personal duties, and self-denial. So far from substituting attention to spiritual exercises for the whole duty of man, they go on the principle that God is as truly served by those who do the most common secular work in His name, as by meditation, and fasting, and prayer. The sermon on "Fidelity in Personal Duties"[1] embraces everything that is valuable in Principal Caird's sermon on "Religion in Common Life." And yet Dr. Caird's sermon sounded to Prince Albert like a new revelation. Erskine is at more pains than Caird to show that it is the doing of our secular work *as the work to which God has appointed us* that constitutes it a religious service. Apart from this, doing our secular work well is no more an act of religion than eating and drinking when we are hungry and thirsty.

Perhaps it may be asked, If this was the character of Dr. Erskine's discourses, did he bear a sufficiently distinctive testimony to the evangelical cause? Did he lift up his voice with sufficient distinctness against his colleague and other men who were drawing the Church so much into a secular channel, and away from the Gospel? Dr. Erskine could speak out when the occasion required. He could administer a scathing rebuke to those who accommodated to the prevailing taste their manner of professing the Gospel. He could express his horror at the performance of plays in which conversion, the new birth, and the influences of the Holy Spirit were jeered at and derided on the stage, and his distress that many clergymen, both of the episcopal and presbyterian denomination, had given the sanction of their presence to the impious exhibition, as if the existence or the influence of the Holy Ghost were no article in their creed, and as if

[1] Vol. ii. p. 302.

regeneration were in their eyes unnecessary, nay, ridiculous.[1] What Dr. Erskine felt was, that while all duty should rest on the foundation of grace, a narrow application of Christian obligation was most unwholesome. The elevating and purifying influence of the Gospel must be applied in every direction; all duty, every habit of goodness and charity, must be right carefully inculcated in order that the man of God might be perfect, thoroughly furnished unto all good works.

Dr. Erskine was supported by able men of the same views both in Edinburgh and throughout the country. Sir Henry Moncreiff Wellwood, Dr. Walker, Dr. Davidson, Dr. Jones, Dr. Balfour, and others, ably maintained the evangelical cause, both by their pulpit labours and by their high character and consistent lives. Though their united efforts did not carry their cause to victory, they helped to secure victory in the end. They held the fort till reinforcements came. They maintained the continuity of the old Scotch pulpit, so that no gap was allowed to sever the past from the future. In certain respects the moderate school was not without its influence upon them. The structure and the language of their discourses were more correct and careful. Perhaps, also, a touch of formality might be seen in them which had not marked the early pulpit. A stage of progress was yet required, in which, while himself abreast of the age, the preacher should give forth the old message with all the fire and freedom of former days, yet with an adaptation to existing moods and cravings that would cause it to be welcomed by all classes as " glad tidings of great joy."

[1] Vol. ii. pp. 204-5.

CHAPTER XI.

THE EVANGELICAL REVIVAL.

THE star of Moderate ascendency in the Church of Scotland passed its zenith about the close of the eighteenth century. The determined effort of the party to put down high-flying in the Church, and to secure all appointments, especially those which were conspicuous or lucrative, for men of their own set, men devoid of all enthusiasm and fervour, began to be relaxed. Dissent was growing apace. Moderatism was unpopular among the people. The French Revolution had shown that there was a danger of pushing authority too far against the popular will. The spirit of liberty was rousing itself both in Church and State. Besides this, spiritual life was reviving. In England, Wesley and Whitefield had rekindled the evangelical lamp, and their movement had spread rapidly, and become powerful and conspicuous. The gospel of moderatism, such as it was, never remarkable for depth or fulness, had now run dry, and a thirst was springing up for the water of life. By the Seceders and the evangelical preachers of the Established Church the old Gospel continued to be proclaimed, and a vague feeling began to haunt the rest of the community that it was there, after all, that the elixir of life was to be found.

Among the specific agencies that served to bring about a change, the earliest in point of date was the evangelistic enterprise of Robert and James Haldane.

The fact of two gentlemen of family and high connection devoting themselves to the work of itinerant preachers could not but excite attention. Of course it was said they were mad, but there was a strange method in their madness. They could not be said to be great preachers, but the crowds that flocked to hear them were remarkable, and the message they delivered was simple and earnest. When Rowland Hill joined them, and preached on a beautiful summer evening of 1798 to 4000 earnest listeners on the Calton Hill, and again to 5000 in the cathedral churchyard of Glasgow, it seemed as if the days had returned when George Wishart preached to the 3000 in Mauchline, or Richard Cameron to the 10,000 on the moors of Lanarkshire.

But this was a movement outside the lines both of the Church and the Secession. Within both of these enclosures, however, about the beginning of the present century, not a few men of great gifts and full of the Spirit began to raise their voices, and to attract in a remarkable degree the interest of the community.

The appearance of a man like THOMAS M'CRIE at such a time was remarkable, in view of the claim which the moderate party had long made to a monopoly of literary culture and historical research. That a great historical work should come from a minister of one of the small Secession bodies was about as far from general expectation as that an oratorio should be composed by a navvy. Yet when M'Crie's *Life of Knox* appeared, it was at once acknowledged to belong to an order of historical literature higher than that which Principal Robertson himself had attained. It was a history of deeper research, based on a profounder appreciation of events, showing a better faculty of sifting evidence, and commending itself more by its inward evidence of truthfulness. It contained no such palpable blunder as that

defence of Queen Mary which made David Hume ask
sarcastically whether Robertson had ever heard that
Mary married the reputed murderer of her husband
within three months of his death. It proved that a
" high-flier " might be a man of calm intellect and
literary culture, and that the ways and tendencies gen-
dered by ministering to a plain dissenting congregation
were compatible with a high standard of literary work.
Moreover, the *Life of Knox* redeemed the great founder
of the Scottish Church from the false estimate of him
which had become common through the malice of his
enemies and the ignorance of later generations, and thus
raised the credit both of his work and of his teaching.
The collision of Dr. M'Crie with Sir Walter Scott, occasioned by the picture of the Covenanters in *Old Mortality*
which M'Crie so ably criticised, tended to raise his reputation still higher, indicating, as Hallam said, a writer of
such power that but few living controversialists would
fail to tremble before him. The Covenanters themselves,
too, were raised from the mire ; instead of a set of canting
fanatics, they were shown to have been for the most part
worthy men who were not only zealous for the faith, but
who understood the true principles of constitutional
freedom, and the very wildest of whom enunciated at
the cost of their lives the political creed that in 1688
brought about the Revolution. No man did more than
M'Crie to clear the ancestry of E,angelical Scotland, and
turn what had been counted its disgrace into a fountain
of honour.

Of Dr. M'Crie as a preacher there is not much to be
said, for it was not chiefly in that capacity that he left his
mark on the age. He was a preacher for the thinking
few rather than for the many, but he was one of those
who raise their congregations towards their own level.
Under his preaching his people were taught to think as

well as to feel; not only were their souls fed, but their minds were enlarged, and their taste was purified. He commands our respect as a man of severe taste and scholarly precision, of a mind too well schooled by the discipline of study to imitate the somewhat luxuriant style and random exegesis of the Erskines; he was one who not only counted it a privilege to preach free grace, but would have deemed the Gospel to be no Gospel without it, and yet had a wider horizon round his pulpit than many of those who, while professing to despise narrowness of mind, were probably the narrowest after all. In a well-known work of the day, *Peter's Letters to his Kinsfolk*, the clever production of Sir Walter Scott's son-in-law, John Gibson Lockhart, we have the following portrait of Dr. M'Crie as a preacher:—" I went to hear Dr. M'Crie preach, and was not disappointed in the expectation I had formed from a perusal of his book. He is a tall, slender man, with a pale face, full of shrewdness, and a pair of black piercing eyes, a shade of deep secluded melancholy passing ever and anon across their surface and dimming their brilliancy. His voice, too, has a wild but very expressive shrillness in it at times. He prays and preaches very much in the usual style of the Presbyterian divines; but about all he says there is a certain unction of sincere, old-fashioned, haughty Puritanism, peculiar, so far as I have seen, to himself, and by no means displeasing in the historian of Knox. He speaks, too, with an air of authority, which his high talents render excusable, nay proper—but which few could venture upon with equal success."

For similar testimonies to the power of M'Crie we must content ourselves with referring to Hugh Miller[1] and Lord Cockburn.[2]

---

[1] *Schools and Schoolmasters*, ch. xvi.   [2] *Journal*, i. p. 100.

Much more conspicuous as a pulpit orator and as a public Evangelical champion was Dr. ANDREW THOMSON, who in his later years was minister of St. George's, Edinburgh, a congregation then numbering many of the most influential citizens of the metropolis.   The testimonies of contemporaries to the oratorical powers of Dr. Thomson, both in the pulpit and elsewhere, are very remarkable, and indicate one who, alike by his personality and by his gifts, exercised a rare influence over all who came into contact with him.   His namesake, the present Dr. Andrew Thomson, of Broughton Place United Presbyterian Church, Edinburgh, gives a graphic account of one of his speeches, a speech on the Apocrypha question, to which, he says, "a densely-packed multitude listened for four hours with unflagging interest ; the variety was wonderful; it had nervous argument, masculine eloquence, skilfully arranged facts, clever anecdote admirably told, playful humour, and wit that never missed fire."[1]

It is not easy for one who has such gifts for the platform to rival himself in the pulpit ; yet it would have been hard to say in which of the two spheres Thomson was most eloquent.   Sometimes the question advocated from the platform has a fuller hold of the speaker's own heart and soul than pulpit themes.   It was not so in his case.   He was profoundly interested in his pulpit work. He believed that moderatism, with its lay patronage and worldly sympathies, had done untold evil in Scotland, and he burned with the desire to bring the pulpit and the people of his country once more under that Gospel which was the power of God unto salvation.   The whole energies of his deep and vehement nature were thrown into his sermons, both because he was profoundly concerned for the welfare of each member of his congregation, and because he regarded the predominance of Evangelicalism

[1] *Life of Principal Harper.*

as the very salvation both of his Church and of his country.

Of Dr. Thomson's sermons, read in the light of the present day, it can hardly be said that they come up to the fame they acquired when preached. The thoughts are plain and obvious enough, but the language in which they are conveyed is that of a burning heart. We must remember that in those days evangelical truth was comparatively unknown, and the very freshness of it gave it uncommon interest. Moreover, there was a rare magnetism about the preacher. While an ardent evangelical, he was conspicuous for qualities in which the evangelicals had sometimes been deficient. He was honest to the point of bluntness, bold and chivalrous wherever there was error to combat, or wrong to remedy ; most kindly and sympathetic especially towards the young ; and, moreover,—what was of no small importance,—he was an enthusiast in music, a performer, a composer, one who honoured art, and believed in its place in the great temple of God. But the chief point to be noticed in connection with him is the warmth and vigour which he brought into the pulpit. It was this pre-eminently that made his preaching so telling. Lord Cockburn notes that he read his sermons from manuscript, but he threw such natural earnestness and fervour into the reading that the effect was rather increased than impaired thereby.

Of the extraordinary personal influence of Dr. Thomson, we have a remarkable evidence in the case of the late Rev. Sir Henry Moncreiff, and, we believe, more than one of the other members of the Moncreiff family. " I cannot mention his name," said Sir Henry, " without strong emotion. I believe that I personally owe more to him than to any other human being for my present principles and position. In early youth I shared the effect produced upon multitudes of young men by the union of strength

S

and tenderness in his pulpit ministrations. There was the force of argumentative clearness. There was also the touching potency of affectionate pathos. His love of music, his genial sociality, his truth and fidelity in personal attachment, his wondrous energy, his devotion of time and attention to the edification and comfort of the weakest and most destitute, as well as of the highest and strongest, and his unwearied efforts for the accomplishment of good in all quarters among both young and old, these, taken along with his extraordinary eloquence, must all be taken into account in estimating the massive comprehensiveness of his character." [1]

The nature of Dr. Thomson's service to evangelism was well brought out in the funeral sermon preached by Dr. Chalmers after his sudden and deeply-lamented death in 1832. "The previous age," said Chalmers, "was an age of cold and feeble rationality, when evangelism was derided as fanatical, and its very phraseology was deemed an ignoble and vulgar thing in the upper classes of society. A morality without godliness, a certain prettiness of sentiment, served up in tasteful and well-turned periods of composition, the ethics of philosophy or the academic chair, rather than the ethics of the Gospel—the speculations of natural theology, and perhaps an ingenious and scholar-like exposition of the credentials rather than a faithful exposition of the contents of the New Testament —these for a time dispossessed the topics of other days, and occupied that room in our pulpits which had formerly been given to the demonstrations of sin and of the Saviour. You know there has been a reflux. The tide of sentiment has been turned; and there is none who has given it a greater momentum, or borne it more triumphantly along than did the lamented pastor of this congregation. His talents and his advocacy have thrown

[1] "The Free Church Principle" (*Chalmers Lectures*), p. 222-3.

a lustre round the cause. The prejudices of thousands have given way before the might and the mastery of his resistless demonstrations. The evangelical system has of consequence risen, has risen prodigiously of late years, in the estimation of general society—connected to a great degree, we doubt not, under the blessing of God, with his powerful appeals to Scripture, and his no less powerful appeals to the consciences of men."

There was a remarkable combination of power and gentleness in Dr. Thomson—a union of a giant's strength and the tenderness of a child—which Dr. Chalmers compares " to what might be found in certain Alpine wilds, where beauty is seen embosomed in the lap of grandeur —as when, at the base of a lofty precipice, some spot of verdure or peaceful cottage-home seems to smile in more intense loveliness, because of the towering strength and magnificence which are behind it. Apply this to character, and think how precisely analogous the effect is, when, from the groundwork of a character that mainly, in its texture and general aspect, is masculine, there do effloresce the forthputtings of a softer nature, and those gentler charities of the heart which come out irradiated in tenfold beauty, when they arise from a substratum of moral strength and grandeur underneath. . . . Such, I am sure, is the touching recollection of very many who now hear me, and who can tell in their own experience that the vigour of his pulpit was only equalled by the fidelity and the tenderness of his household ministrations. They understand the whole force and significancy of the contrast I have now been speaking of—when the pastor of the church becomes the pastor of the family, and he who, in the crowded Assembly, held imperial sway over every understanding, entered some parent's lowly dwelling, and prayed and wept along with them over their infant's dying bed. It is this which furnishes the key to every

heart, and when the triumphs of charity are superadded to
the triumphs of argument, then it is that he sits enthroned
over the affections of a willing people."

These last are very significant words of Dr. Chalmers,
and they remind us of the fact that under the *régime* of
moderatism, pastoral visitation, and indeed all kinds of
pastoral work, fell into disuse. With the revival of
evangelism, there revived also all manner of pastoral
activity, reacting on the pulpit, making it more real and
more adapted to the needs of the people, and disposing
the people to listen with more attention when it was so
apparent that the pastor was deeply interested in his
flock.

While we listen to the generous encomiums of Chalmers on Thomson, and to his hearty recognition of a
ministry that had served to raise evangelicalism so high
before the people of Scotland, we cannot forget that a
service still higher, and of a more commanding character,
was rendered by CHALMERS himself. It might be too
much to say that such a preacher as Chalmers had never
before appeared in Scotland; but no one had ever before
shown in the pulpit the same combination of the highest
oratory with other gifts.

Looking at his history we cannot but remark that if ever
the hand of Providence was conspicuous in the raising up
and training of any man for a particular work, that man
was Chalmers. As in the case of Paul, Augustine, Luther,
and many others, we see the training process in operation
long before the special work began. The most marked
thing in the early life of Chalmers, apart from his exuber-
ance of animal spirits, was his enthusiastic love of science.
Before he was twenty-five he had delivered a course of
lectures on chemistry, and he had been in the field as a
candidate for two science chairs, that of Natural Philosophy at St. Andrews, and that of Mathematics at Edin-

burgh. The bent which was thus given to his mind it never lost. He retained to the end of his life a great delight in the researches of physical science, and a profound respect and affection for its votaries ; and this again drew towards him the interest and respect of scientific men. In this result we find an interesting illustration of that law of Providence, which seems to apprehend and weave into its schemes the very frailties and errors, as well as the virtues of men. Had Chalmers begun his ministry with that sense of spiritual realities which he afterwards attained, he would probably from the beginning have given himself to his pastoral work so thoroughly that he would have had no time to become an adept in science. Science would have been relegated to those dim and distant courses of the future to which busy men look for the leisure that never comes.

But Chalmers had very different views for years after he was settled in Kilmany. In a controversial pamphlet on the question of pluralities published by him soon after his settlement, he deliberately affirmed that two days in the week, one to prepare his sermon and one to deliver it, was all that the country parson needed for his duty, and that the other five were at his free disposal for science or any other pursuit. How nobly and magnanimously he afterwards recanted this opinion, owning in connection with it the change through which he had passed, can never be forgotten by those who respect his memory.

But during this early period, when it was really dominated by science, his mind acquired the scientific *set*, the scientific way of looking at things ; and it continued to retain this after he had undergone the great change. He was thus enabled to perform a service which was greatly needed by the age—to bring evangelism and science into friendly connection. Science was no longer to be ignored by the evangelical preacher as an alien that had no place in the kingdom of God. No doubt, in our day, the collision between science and revelation has been much more serious than it was in his. But whatever we may think of his views on particular points, Chalmers did the work well for his day and generation, and prepared the way for the more trying battle of our time, the issue of which, like the issue of all similar collisions, must ultimately be that each will hold its place and pursue its way without disturbance from the other.

Chalmers had also a natural turn for philosophical speculation, especially in the sphere of morals. He had not, however, enjoyed much early training in this department, and his mind never underwent the discipline that would have given to his philosophical writings the precision of thought and expression found in such writers as Reid. The line of his thinking on moral philosophy, natural theology, and even political economy, though roughly and diffusively expressed, had always the interest that belongs to the speculations of a shrewd, vigorous, independent mind, and secured the respectful attention even of specialists. With literature as such, whether ancient or modern, he had hardly any acquaintance. The realms of art, too, were entirely a *terra incognita*. As a writer, but especially as a preacher, he originated, like Carlyle, a style of his own, cumbrous, unpruned, and ungraceful, with a great luxuriance of language, not ill adapted to his oratory, gathering a wonderful momentum, and interesting to hearers from its very singularity. These qualities pointed to Chalmers as fitted to bring the pulpit of his age more into harmony than heretofore with some of the forces which were specially characteristic of his time. But these elements of pulpit force would have availed but little if the prime factor of the preacher had not appeared in him with overmastering power.

That element was spiritual conviction. In early life, evangelical religion and its friends were the objects of his strong dislike. They were disliked by him for the reason which causes dislike to so many,—as interfering with the free play of one's nature, especially one's love of ease, amusement, and natural enjoyment, and placing one, and especially a minister, under a painfully serious view of life. His worthy father had been appalled at the levity with which he had assumed the responsibilities of the ministry. In his view the cure of souls was a thing very different from what it was to his son. The death of a sister, and a long illness of his own, familiarised Chalmers, however, with more serious views, and showed him how, with his extreme levity of spirit, he had been living in a fool's paradise. Asked by the late Sir David Brewster to contribute the article on Christianity to his Encyclopædia, he found how little he knew the real import of the term. At last he comes out a firm believer in that evangelical system of truth to which he has been so much opposed. And not a mere speculative believer, but as one who has personally experienced the great change on which it rests. The Lord Jesus Christ is become to him wisdom and righteousness, and sanctification and redemption. The Bible is the authoritative record of divine truth respecting man's relation to God, and God's relation to man. Fellowship with Christ is the atmosphere he delights to breathe. Substantially, too, he has served himself heir to the old theology—he has become one in vital belief with Wishart and Knox, with Dickson and Livingstone, with Rutherfurd and Boston, with Ebenezer and Ralph Erskine, with John Erskine and Andrew Thomson. He is one, too, with them all in what was more characteristic than even their theology—in his profound apprehension of the great needs of the human spirit and of the fitness of the revelation of God's grace in Christ to meet and supply them all.

But here the resemblance ended. In the form of his preaching, he was like nobody else. That form was determined partly by his scientific habit of mind, partly by the unconscious influence of the spirit of the age, but mainly by the force of his strong native genius. Not a vestige did he borrow of traditional forms, hardly any of traditional phraseology. With the ordinary nomenclature of theology he was hardly familiar. He had a great respect for dogma, but only as something subordinate to a higher object, only as a means towards penetrating the human soul with the life of God. It was not his aim to convert men to a creed, in the belief that once that creed was adopted, it would mould their spirit and their lives aright. He flew directly at their souls. He plied them with the message of the Gospel, that he might bring them into vital contact with God, and kindle in them that life without which they were little better than lumps of clay. Never did a preacher devote himself more thoroughly to the great business of moving men. To produce movement was his passion; movement along evangelical lines, and always directed to a glorious consummation—the salvation of individuals, and the production of a happy, prosperous, regenerated community.

The scientific bent of Chalmers's mind, joined to his unhesitating acceptance of the Bible as God's message to man, had a remarkable effect on his teaching. The man of science differed from the theologian in having a different book to study and to follow. The one had got the book of nature, the other the book of Revelation. The one God's works, the other God's Word. But though the volume was different, the way to use it was the same. The question for the man of science was, What *seest* thou? the question for the theologian, What *readest* thou? Neither the one nor the other was at liberty to substitute his own fancies for the substantial verities of his book. The one was as disloyal to science as the other if he put his own ideas of what ought to be in the place of what actually was. Thus it was, that when Chalmers came to receive the Bible as God's message, his attitude towards it, instead of more loose, became more emphatic through his scientific training. The Word of God was as much the beginning and the end of his teaching as of any country minister in all Scotland; to its authority he continually bowed, while at the same time he tried to commend its message to every man's conscience in the sight of God. But while striving to awaken echoes to the truth in the human soul, Chalmers never forgot that these were but echoes; and so his preaching continued to possess that great element of power which marked the Reformers and Covenanters, but was lost by the moderates—it was the message of the living God.

Chalmers's natural gift of oratory began to show itself even in his boyhood. It appeared in some of his college exercises, and it is a remarkable fact that the peroration of one of the most powerful speeches he ever delivered, when urging his friends in 1842 not to shrink from the coming sacrifice, was taken from one of his discourses for the Divinity Hall. It was a glowing picture of enthusiasm, and its wonderful achievements. His eloquence was distinguished for its arresting and overmastering power. Like all true orators, he instinctively handled his topic so as to command the interest and the attention of his audience. And once he established his hold, he hurried the audience along with him whithersoever he would. Rushing himself, with all the impetuosity of his massive nature, he made them rush too. Chalmers was not one of those orators that have great variety of address —now instructive, now historical, at one place sarcastic, at another declamatory—his whole discourse was in the same key, a boiling, foaming current, a mingled stream of exposition, illustration, and application, directed to the one great object of moving his audience to action. His soul was so penetrated with his subject, his whole nature was so roused and electrified by it, that others could not but be roused and electrified too. He saw so vividly what he pictured that his hearers could not fail to see it likewise. The personality of the man pervaded all his preaching ; hence probably one of the reasons why his sermons are so little read now.

In a memoir of Chalmers read before the Royal Society of Edinburgh, the late Dean Ramsay gives some examples of the power of his oratory. One of these was connected with a sermon on Cruelty to Animals. " He has occasion," as the Dean remarks, "to show that suffering is often inflicted by man on the lower creatures not for the purpose of torment, but as the result of some other purpose. To illustrate this, he described the excitement and the interest of an English hunting-field, and he terms it ' this favourite pastime of glorious Old England, on which there sits a somewhat ancestral dignity and glory.' And he described the assembled jockeyship of half a province, the meeting of gallant knighthood and hearty yeomen, and he spoke of the autumnal clearness of the sky, and the high-breathed coursers and the echoing horn, and the glee and fervour of the chase, the deafening clamour of the hounds and the dying agonies of the fox, in such a strain of animation that Lord Elcho's huntsman, who was present, declared that he had difficulty in refraining himself from getting up and shouting a view-halloo."

Dean Ramsay refers also to a celebrated speech of Chalmers on Catholic Emancipation, in regard to which Lord Jeffrey remarked, that never had eloquence produced a greater result on a popular audience, and that he could not believe more had been ever done by the oratory of Demosthenes, Cicero, Burke, or Sheridan. As a sample of the man as well as of his eloquence, he gives his short reply to the charge of inconsistency brought against him in the General Assembly, in a debate on pluralities, since, after having written the pamphlet in their favour already referred to, and spoken of the ample leisure of the clergy, he now took the other side. "Alas, sir," said Chalmers; "so I thought in my ignorance and pride. I have now no reserve in saying that the sentiment was wrong, and that in the utterance of it I penned what was outrageously wrong. Strangely blinded that I was! What, sir, is the object of mathematical science? Magnitude and the proportions of magnitude. But then, sir, I had forgotten two magnitudes; I thought not of the littleness of time; I recklessly thought not of the vastness of eternity!"

In an elaborate estimate of Dr. Chalmers by Isaac Taylor in the *North British Review*, the pulpit is singled out as pre-eminently his place. "He was the man who was sent from above to revive, to restore, and to re-establish the Christianity of Scotland. He had in ample measure the natural powers and the visible aspect, he had the form, the force, the vehemence, the earnestness, the boldness, and the majesty which befits a man, who, without presumption, demands to be listened to, and who can always command the attention which he challenges. . . . He seized upon the principal objects of the Christian ministry, . . . he occupied himself with first truths, and treated them with a boldness and a force and a largeness of apprehension which were in keeping with their intrinsic importance. To be great upon small matters is bombast; to be small upon great matters is imbecility; but to be great upon the greatest themes is that sort of fitness which the human mind recognises always, and which the conscience bows to, whether willingly or unwillingly, and to which the most contumacious dare not

openly oppose themselves.   Such a preacher was Chalmers." [1]

If we were to attempt to sum up the service of
Chalmers to the pulpit of Scotland, we should say that
he was equally sagacious in apprehending what men
needed, and faithful in bringing the divine remedy to
bear upon it.   First, as regards the individual soul.   He
saw the root of all evil among the children of men to lie
in alienation from God, involving guilt that needed to be
atoned for, and a sadly disordered nature that needed to
be renewed by the same power that created it.   The
atoning sacrifice of the Son of God, and the regenerating
and sanctifying power of the Holy Ghost were accordingly
the two great pillars of his house, the foundation-stones
of all his preaching.   Next, as regards society, as regards
the relations of men to each other in civil life, the same
disorder prevailed.   The elements that ought to combine
harmoniously for the common good were out of harmony ;
the rich frowned on the poor, the poor scowled on the
rich ; employers were hard on their workmen, workmen
were hard on their employers ; profits were not equitably
distributed ; the labourer had but a scanty share of the
comforts and amenities of life.

Dr. Chalmers's prime engine for remedying the disorders of society was a great Home Mission, brimful of
the spirit of brotherly love.   It was to employ many
agents, agents from among the laity, by pressing whom
into the service, Chalmers became the father of the
modern doctrine of Christian work.   He had a profound
sense both of the fatherhood of God and the brotherhood
of humanity, and he had a profound conviction that if
the richer classes would go among the poorer in the
kindly spirit of Christian brotherhood, and try to gather
them into congregations where all would be brothers,

[1] *North British Review* (Nov. 1856), vol. xxvi. p. 31.

society would assume a new aspect, and the bitter estrangement of class from class would disappear. Not only would such a scheme bring the saving grace of the Gospel into contact with tens of thousands that were living in neglect of all that was high and holy, but it would Christianise society, it would regenerate the community. It was Chalmers who first apprehended the sad extent to which the large-city system of our modern civilisation was degrading a section of the community, and it was through the power of his eloquence and enthusiasm, brought to bear on this evil, that the churches were roused from their apathy, and set to work to overcome it. And a nobler spectacle can hardly be imagined than that of a great and eloquent man, seized from near the beginning of his ministry with an overwhelming sense of this great want of humanity and of the Christian remedy for it, and never letting his eye off it, never ceasing in his heart of hearts to cherish it and work for it; drawn out of his course from time to time by such disturbing events as the Disruption of the Church, yet advocating the Disruption on the ground that a Church in shackles was utterly unfit for this noble task; and then, as soon as the Free Church was in a manner settled, returning to his favourite scheme, and setting up the West Port, not only to do good in that degraded district, but to be a perpetual call and summons to his Church never to rest, or sleep, or slumber, till every needy district of the country was pervaded by the message of the Gospel of Salvation.

Besides all this, in many subsidiary ways, Dr. Chalmers showed how well he discerned the needs of the age and the way to meet them. We have spoken of his relation to science. It was a long time since the telescope had been invented, and since the vastness of the universe had begun to be proclaimed in men's ears. All that time a thought had been at work in many minds, slumbering in some, more active in others, that this globe, reduced now to a speck in creation, was an inadequate theatre for the stupendous sacrifice of the Son of God on its behalf. Till the days of Chalmers, no one had carefully grappled with this thought; in his Astronomical Discourses, he set himself to show, that admitting all that modern science revealed of the magnitude of the universe, and the insignificance of our planet, there were other grounds to make the arrangement reasonable; there were possible relations between this globe and the universe itself, that might make the event correspond more obviously to the magnitude of creation. We seldom hear of this objection now. The Astronomical Discourses ended their career, because they ended the objection to which they furnished a reply. It is the microscope, not the telescope, that furnishes scientists now with their grounds of opposition to revelation; it may be a long time before that instrument is brought over as effectually as the telescope was by Chalmers.

Then, again, a new source of trouble had sprung up, or rather had grown to alarming dimensions, under the great expansion of commerce in the community. Commercial morality was needing to be guarded. Commercial Christianity was needing to be stimulated. Chalmers again perceived the want. His Commercial Discourses were designed, and were admirably fitted to meet it. If evangelical preaching had been weak in ethics, Chalmers spied the weakness, and hastened to supply the remedy. Yet his ethics were essentially Christian ethics. No man could have said that his Commercial Discourses might have been preached by Cicero or Seneca. What they urged was in every respect the outcome and application of evangelical Christianity.

Once more, it appeared to Chalmers that something was needed to bring out the connection of Christianity with certain of the temporal interests of men. It had been too much the habit to make an antithesis of the temporal and the spiritual, as if they belonged to quite different spheres, and to overlook their mutual action and reaction. To Chalmers it appeared that a community, to be thoroughly prosperous, needed to have its secular interests placed on a right foundation. Hence his studies in political economy. You cannot safely leave all that to haphazard. You must have a combined regard to body and soul. Has not all that has taken place since his time made this more and more obvious?

Here, then, was one source of Chalmers's unprecedented influence on his age—he understood its cravings; he supplied them on the true basis; and he did this in a way of his own, untrammelled alike by the forms and the phraseology of a preceding epoch. He let in daylight and fresh air on our evangelical enclosures. The Gospel message assumed a new importance at his hands. It came from him supported by intellect, embellished by imagination, and warmed by emotion, while it became the ally of the science, the philosophy, the culture of the age. As he became old, his broad, statesman-like capacity developed itself, his wisdom in council, his sagacity in such matters as the Free Church Sustentation Fund, and the true way of supporting the poor. And withal, while he was thus broadening out, he was growing steadily in personal religion and spiritual experience. His fellowship with heaven became closer and closer. The culture of holiness was a growing object of concern. The effect of all was, not merely the triumph of evangelical religion in Scotland, but the communication to it of qualities it had hardly known before. It became more genial and catholic, more intellectual and refined, more wholesome and more practical. It did not cease to be Scotch, though it lost some of the old Scotch features—

much of its ruggedness, its dogmatic temper, its controversial spirit and aim. Thoroughly Calvinistic in his theology, he was yet full of humanity, and breathed only love and kindness to the race; and the bones of Calvinism were so covered with flesh and skin and lifelike colour, that, in his hands, it became a thing of beauty and a joy for ever.

When we turn from Chalmers, and name next Dr. JOHN BROWN, of the Secession Church, we find ourselves in the company of one who, though not of Chalmers's stature, still towered above his fellows. The people among whom Dr. Brown lived and laboured had always been accustomed to the Gospel; but, when he came to Edinburgh, he commanded a wider audience, and his energetic voice was a distinct and great addition to the evangelical force of the day. His son, the popular author of " Rab," has very touchingly alluded to a grievous domestic bereavement that made a marvellous change on his preaching, while he was yet at Biggar; " from being elegant, rhetorical, and ambitious, he became concentrated, urgent, moving (being himself moved), keen, searching, unswerving, authoritative to fierceness, full of the terrors of the Lord, if he could persuade men."[1] And Dr. Cairns has told us of the beginning of his Edinburgh ministry, that while he did not make much change on the character of his ministrations, there was a change in one thing, the preponderance of discourses of a stern and awakening character, addressed with passionate earnestness to the unconverted, and delivered in the highest style of physical energy. His vehemence was hardly less than that of Dr. Chalmers himself in these moments of excitement; and his appeals, seconded by the glance of the eye and the stamp of the foot, seemed to shake not only the

[1] Letter to Dr. Cairns, *Horæ Subsecivæ*, p. 205.

auditory, but the very building in which they were uttered. The elements of instruction and discussion however maintained their place, and some of his most valued discourses and lectures partook most of these qualities.[1]

But not the least important of his services to the evangelical pulpit was connected with his expository discourses. From the beginning of his ministry he had searched the Scriptures with extraordinary assiduity. Further on, he had acquainted himself, at a great cost of labour, with the researches of the scientific expositors. Bringing his own soul to bear, at the full stretch of its energy, on the true meaning of Scripture, he reached results of great value. To bring all this to bear on the exposition of Scripture from the pulpit was no common service. Many a popular preacher had been superficial and careless in his interpretation of attractive texts. It was Dr. Brown's conscientious endeavour to find out the true mind of the Spirit, and to limit himself to that one view in his expositions. The exposition might seem to lose something by the process, but it gained more than it lost; and a wholesome example was set to all preachers, of conscientious faithfulness in expounding the Word.

A great contrast in many external features to Dr. Brown in the East, was Dr. RALPH WARDLAW in the West of Scotland. For Wardlaw was mild, measured, and graceful in his delivery, the polished scholar appearing in every line, and yet the fire of the Gospel warming and intensifying the whole. A tone of quiet thoughtfulness characterised his work; but the thoughts were so interesting, and the expression so clear, and the emotion, though subdued, so real, that (controversial subjects apart) a discourse of Wardlaw's was always a treat. It filled and satisfied the mind; he reasoned so convincingly, he

---

[1] *Memoir*, pp. 101, 102.

T

surveyed the subject so comprehensively, he brought out every point so clearly, that one felt that the subject was exhausted, the treatment was complete.

From the exact and well-disciplined expositions of John Brown, and the graceful prelections of Ralph Wardlaw, we seem to make a great leap when we introduce the name of EDWARD IRVING. But on this name we will not linger. Very magnificent, beyond doubt, was his pulpit work. The crowds that rushed to his church had scarcely ever been equalled in London. His voice was said to be one of the finest ever possessed by a public speaker. It could be heard in the open air at the distance of a quarter of a mile. To hear him repeat the Lord's Prayer was like listening to an exquisite piece of music. But apart from the eccentric views which he came to hold, he had one defect as a preacher that makes him unsuitable for imitation—want of naturalness and simplicity of style. Carlyle says of him : " His voice was very fine ; melodious depth, strength, clearness, its chief characteristics. I have heard more pathetic voices, going more direct to the heart, both in the way of indignation and of pity, but recollect none that better filled the ear. He affected the Miltonic, or old English Puritan style, and strove visibly to imitate it more and more till almost the end of his career, when indeed it had become his own, and was the language he used in the utmost heat of business for expressing his meaning." [1] This is the true explanation ; to speak like an old prophet at last became natural to him ; but it would be singularly unnatural to any of us, if we were so foolish as to affect it. Yet for all that, his Orations for the Oracles of God, and his Argument for the Judgment to Come, are right noble productions, and will furnish a rare treat to those that have never yet had the pleasure of reading them.

[1] *Memorials*—Edward Irving.

One may fancy that Irving lost all his usefulness when he taught that our Lord's human nature was liable to sin, and that the miraculous gifts of the early Church might yet return to genuine faith.   Yet may it not be, that He who knoweth to bring good out of evil has, by the force of recoil, made his very errors the occasion of something salutary to the Church of our days ?   Has he not taught us to realise more vividly the true but sinless humanity of our Lord, and to value more profoundly the ordinary gifts and graces of the Holy Ghost ?

We return to the companions and successors of Chalmers.   Chalmers did not institute a school, but he exerted a strong influence, which was better.   But we have space only for the most rapid survey.

GORDON, whose sermons are somewhat heavy reading, made a wonderful impression by the force of his convictions, the fervour of his spirit, and the beauty of his character.

GUTHRIE, though not excelling in scholarship or in-tellectual power, inherited covenanting blood, and the strong broad traditions of the olden time; he had a vivid imagination, and a tender heart; he wedded the Gospel to the philanthropy of the age, and devised new channels for the spirit that seeks and saves the lost.   He charmed all classes by his genial heart, and his free outspokenness, and the glee and joyousness of a temperament which showed much of what was best in Burns and Walter Scott; he brought somewhat more of sunshine and fresh air into the Scottish pulpit, and showed, as he used to say, that the Gospel is unfriendly to nothing in human nature, except its corruptions.

Writing of his power of illustration, his colleague, Dr. Hanna, said very truly, " In listening to him scenes and images passed in almost unbroken succession before the eye, always apposite, often singularly picturesque and graphic, frequently most tenderly pathetic. . . . Almost all of them were taken from sights of Nature or incidents of common life—the sea, the storm, the shipwreck, the beacon light, the lifeboat, the family wrapped in sleep, the midnight conflagration, the child at the window above, a parent's arms held up below, and the child told to leap and trust. There was much of true poetry in the series of images so presented; but it was poetry of a kind that needed no interpreter, required no effort either to understand or appreciate, which appealed directly to the eye and heart of common humanity of which all kinds and classes of people, and that almost equally, saw the beauty and felt the power."[1]

Guthrie was one of those preachers who interest and attract all sorts and conditions of men; the Gospel from his lips got the ear of many who would not have heard any other Scotch preacher; while his intense philanthropy drew the sympathy of every class, and dispelled a lurking prejudice that no Calvinist divine could be a lover of humanity.

NORMAN MACLEOD furnished a great contrast to the old moderates, in the intense fervour, the boundless sympathy, and the missionary enthusiasm of his character. A man of genius, and of great literary and dramatic power, it was his heart that made him a preacher, and the heart would hardly submit to the guidance of the head. Not seeing a way of reconciling the doctrines of the standards with that conception of the full and ever-diffusive love of God in which he delighted, he made the standards go to the wall. Neither Chalmers nor Guthrie, whose hearts were as large as his, had had to make any such surrender. But nothing could have been more admirable than the effect he gave in his latter years to his conviction that the Gospel was good news for every

---

[1] *Sunday Magazine*, March 1872.

creature. His visit to India, and his ceaseless endeavours to rouse the home Church to a sense of missionary
obligation form one of the noblest chapters of Christian
biography, and claim the warmest admiration of every
evangelical soul.

CANDLISH, notwithstanding his absorption in Church
work, for which he had an equally strong liking and
capacity, had rare gifts for the pulpit. In him a subtle
intellect, a vigorous imagination, and a tender heart, produced results like no other man's preaching. I may refer
to a very striking critique of him that appeared in the
Catholic Presbyterian of 1881, " by a member of the Church
of England," who, I may now say, was my much esteemed
friend Miss Bird, the well-known author, now Mrs.
Bishop. " As a preacher," she said, " he stood by himself. Wealth of theological ˙material, inexhaustible fer-
tility of intellectual resource, exhaustive analysis of human
motives, a plethora of expository thought, a richness and
definiteness of intellectual conception, a rare sympathetic
comprehension of the intricacies and self-deceptions of
the human heart, and of the lines of thought on which
other minds moved ; a thorough belief in the theology
which he taught, a frank and bold assumption without
any reserve or *arrières pensées* of the dogmatic positions of
a Calvinist theologian, a remarkable subordination of a
singularly speculative intellect to the great evangelical
verities as he understood and received them, a rare and
lofty conception of Christian discipleship as it might be
and is bound to be, an unfailing return from the misty
but tempting regions of metaphysical speculation to the
central truths which concern life and godliness ; a hearty
love for the simplest forms and applications of evangelical
doctrine, a profound contempt for vague generalities, and
a genuine spirituality which restrained his intellect from
over-rash excursions, gave glow and life to his arguments,

and at times raised his style into a rugged eloquence—
these were among the characteristics of a man who for
many years was justly regarded as one of the greatest of
Scottish preachers."

JAMES HAMILTON, a Scotchman all over, though a
minister of London, showed a new faculty—the art of bringing the phenomena of nature as well as the facts of literature and life to bear on the business of the pulpit, while
the radiance of a most loving nature threw sunshine over
all that he touched. If his unconventional ways sometimes carried him beyond bounds, they enabled him to
arrest attention, and sweep away the refuges of formalism.
The poor woman from Dundee who came to the prayer-
meeting at Abernyte, warm from the revival, and found
him descanting to the people on a fig-leaf, which he held
in his hand, could not understand him—" Eh, Mr. Hamilton, to gi'e them fig-leaves, when they 're hungerin' for
the bread o' life!" Yet Hamilton was a man who in
early life had given himself in solemn covenant to God,
and never would have adopted any style of ministry if he
had not conscientiously believed it to be for the glory of
God and the true good of man.

Hamilton is a connecting link with another school in
which the names of ROBERT M'CHEYNE and WILLIAM
BURNS stand pre-eminent. M'Cheyne brought into the
pulpit all the reverence for Scripture of the Reformation
period; all the honour for the headship of Christ of the
Covenanter struggle; all the freeness of the Gospel offer
of the Marrow theology; all the bright imagery of Samuel
Rutherfurd, all the delight of the Erskines in the fulness
of Christ. In M'Cheyne the effect of a cultured taste
was apparent in the chastened beauty and simplicity
of his style, if you can call it a style—in a sense he had
no style, or rather it was the perfection of style, for it
was transparent as glass. The new element he brought

to the pulpit, or rather which he revived and used so much that it appeared new, was *winsomeness.* It was an almost feminine quality. A pity that turned many of his sermons into elegiac poems, thrilled his heart, and by the power of the Spirit imparted the thrill to many souls. How precious his example and memory have been to Scotland is shown by the continued demand for his *Life and Letters.* And how invaluable the evangelistic labours begun by him and his brethren, and still continued and often blessed throughout our country, no Scotch audience needs to be told.

There is an important class of preachers, not yet touched, represented by such men as MACDONALD of Ferintosh, and STEWART of Cromarty—the Apostles of the Highlands. Under their shadow we come back to the regions where we witnessed the early triumphs of the cross. From their lips we hear the very message of grace reverberated from the old Celtic hills that sounded among them 1200 years before. The form is different, and we miss some of the elements of the olden time. But the Spirit uses the message to kindle anew the divine flame in many hearts, and to nourish a Christian life in which, whatever its imperfections, some of the highest attainments of faith and devotion have often been found wedded to the lowliest conditions of earthly life.[1]

One general remark may conclude this survey. We cannot but be struck with the variety of gifts that distinguish the preachers of the evangelical revival. It

---

[1] Some apology is due for this fragmentary reference to the preachers of the Highlands. It is not from want of appreciation that we do not go more fully into the subject. The truth is, it is a department by itself, and would not be properly handled except by one well acquainted with the Highland language, Highland literature, and the Highland people.

would not be easy to find elsewhere such a manifestation of diversity in unity. And some of these gifts would seem to have been given of express purpose to form links of connection with human interests outside the more spiritual kingdom. M'Crie is a historical antiquary. Andrew Thomson is a brilliant musician. Chalmers loves science and philosophy, political economy, and sociology. Guthrie is a philanthropist. James Hamilton is an enthusiast in natural history. That ministers of the Gospel should have such gifts and tastes is common enough. But it is not common that they should be used in strict subordination to the work of the Gospel, and laid at the feet of Christ. It seemed to be God's purpose to show us, in this nineteenth century, through the lives of these men, that all such things have a place in the economy of His kingdom. These gifts did not carry away their possessors from their Father's house like the prodigal son to enjoy them at a distance from Him. The men brought back their talents sanctified and enlarged, to lay them at His feet. Like the kings of the earth in the Apocalypse, they brought their glory and honour into the New Jerusalem. Happy the Church and happy the country that continues not only to receive such gifts, but to turn them so nobly to account!

CHAPTER XII.

THE PULPIT OF TO-DAY.

ON a retrospect of the history of Scottish preaching since the Reformation it becomes clear that all its more earnest periods have been marked by a combination of two forces or factors,—one personal, the other public ; one having regard to the direct and proper business of the pulpit, the preaching of the Gospel; the other connected with some public cause or movement, believed to have a vital bearing on the other. From the pulpit at such times the message of the Gospel has been warmly and earnestly proclaimed ; men have been called in God's name to receive in Christ the offer of mercy ; warned that the wages of sin is death ; pressed to look to the Saviour for deliverance and renewal ; and urged, while they live in this world, to live, not after the flesh, but after the Spirit. But alongside this earnest proclamation of the message of grace, the Church as a whole, and pre-eminently the foremost of her preachers, have been the earnest and uncompromising advocates of some public, if not political, course of action, deemed by them most sacred,—demanded, in their view, by allegiance to Christ, and essential to the permanent efficiency of the Church, as guardian of the Gospel. And these two forces have acted and reacted on each other ; their connection has not been incidental, but vital. We question if there be any other country in Europe where the sword and the trowel have been in such constant alliance, and where the pulpit has taken on so much of the form and hue of the Church militant.

At the Reformation, in Scotland as in other countries of Europe, it was judged necessary to concentrate every effort on the overthrow of the Church of Rome, as a political institution as well as a spiritual force; and we have seen how this necessity coloured the preaching of Knox and his coadjutors in that great battle. Then followed the covenanting struggle, extending over more than fifty years of the seventeenth century, when, to make sure of the Gospel, it was deemed indispensable to secure the liberties of the Church, and when bonds or covenants were formed against prelatical government, against the interference of the civil power in the sacred province, and in the last stage of the struggle very emphatically against the despotism of the sovereign. Then came the Secession movement in the early part of the eighteenth century, when the conflict was not so much with the civil authority as with an alien party within the Church itself, resistance to which at first, and separation from it afterwards, were deemed essential to the preservation of the truth. By-and-by, the conflict between the two parties within the Church waxed keener and more determined. To overthrow the policy of the moderates was as definitely and as necessarily the policy of the evangelical party as to preach the Gospel of grace. As the battle began to incline to the evangelical side, the other party was reinforced by a new ally. The civil courts of the country threw all their weight into the moderate scale, and gave to that section a temporary triumph, at a cost, however, which, had it been foreseen, might well have staggered the most sanguine of its champions. Inheriting the experience of so many of their forefathers, the evangelical leaders were compelled to combine the twofold occupation of proclaiming far and wide the message of the gospel, and fighting the battle of the "Ten Years' Conflict."

This remarkable combination of preaching and struggling has impressed a peculiar character on the pulpit of Scotland. In general, the best preachers, like Knox, Henderson, and Chalmers, have been the most energetic fighters. Saintly men like John Welch, Samuel Rutherfurd, James Durham, and Robert M'Cheyne, though they may have fought less, have generally been as decided as any for the public cause with which they believed the prosperity of the Gospel to be mixed up. Exceptions like that of Robert Leighton are so rare that they can count only as exceptions. No wonder, therefore, that, as a rule, the evangelical pulpit of Scotland has presented peculiar features. Its connection with so many vehement struggles lent it force, fire, decision, uncompromising fidelity, but it deprived it of some softer and sweeter elements. While it increased its force, it impaired its beauty. The tone of the pulpit was more of thunder than of the still small voice. Preachers that were called to rebuke and contend so much, needed foreheads of adamant. And inasmuch as, in the course of their contendings, they were commonly doomed to much loss and suffering, their tempers were not sweetened by such treatment. Driven sometimes to the extremest condition of earthly misery, their spiritual vitality was absorbed in the one effort to endure. This is a law of human action in times of fierce persecution that should be taken careful note of. For as in a time of civil war the weaker party, when hard bestead, have to turn everything they possess into powder and shot and other munitions of war; as books, furniture, jewels, pictures, have all to be surrendered to the one object of keeping up the resistance; so in times of fierce contending and fiery suffering in the Church, the prayers, and the trust, and the courage, and the self-denial, that in better times would be directed to the varied purposes of the Christian life, have all to be concentrated on the one object of holding out. If the Scottish evangelical pulpit has at such times been more vehement than refined, it is easy to find the cause.

But now things are changed. We have no public conflict going on, drawing the pulpit into vital connection with it, and imparting to it its characteristic features. The pulpit stands by itself, occupies its own ground, and is left to its own resources. There is no doubt that this deprives it of a source of rough vigour possessed in other times. The stirring influence derived from great public movements, sweeping along with much national enthusiasm, comes not to-day. The force of the pulpit must now, under God, depend on the strength of the preacher's convictions, the suitableness of his matter, the felicity of his utterances, and the warmth of his emotions. The kindling power not coming from any great movement without, must be derived exclusively from forces within. We are thrown, not more than ever, but more obviously than ever, on the living power of the Holy Ghost, energising in the souls of our preachers. Unless our preachers of to-day are men of deep inward exercise,—men who know profoundly the powers of the world to come—men to whom sin stands out of all things on earth the darkest and most horrible, and redeeming grace the brightest, holiest, heavenliest—men of intrepid spirit, full of faith and of the Holy Ghost—the pulpit will not have the life and energy of other days. On the other hand, the opportunity presents itself to rid it of those rougher elements that not unnaturally attached themselves to it in days of noise and commotion. Not only so, but we are called to survey the situation with greater care, and ask whether there may not yet remain fresh land to be possessed, whether there are not fields hitherto neglected now to be taken in, whether there be not perplexities besetting the inquiring spirit demanding to be dealt with, discords in human life needing to be adjusted, crooked things that have to be made straight, and rough places plain.

This absence of collateral conflict is perhaps the most outstanding difference in the circumstances of to-day. But it is not the only difference. In considering how the pulpit may be best worked for the future, there are other conditions of the age which we must carefully note.

We must remember that Scotland is not now the isolated little country it once was. The facilities of travel have brought influences to bear on it from England, from France, from Germany, from America that are modifying the national taste, as in other things, so in the pulpit. The progress of education has made the people more critical, more independent, and more difficult to please. The periodical press has become the exponent, if not the guide of public opinion, and in its swift, clever, and fast-recurring strokes it finds opportunities for dealing with the public mind which the pulpit cannot rival. Moreover, there is the play all around of a *zeit-geist* more daring than any that has hovered about us for three hundred years. The preacher's path is crossed and his message challenged by a sturdy and unceremonious critic that for want of a better name we call " Modern Thought." Of this *zeit-geist* some eminent preachers like Mr. Spurgeon make little or no account, but go right forwards as of old, hardly noticing its existence except to denounce it. Others, at the opposite extreme, are awed by its flutter, and its seemingly irresistible sweep, and they bow down before it as if it were the great sovereign force of the age, the legitimate ruler of the spiritual world. Such facts make it of special importance to reconnoitre our position, and to consider what is to be the character, what the aims, what the scope of the Scottish pulpit of the future ?

On one point of supreme importance there ought surely to be on all sides an unflinching determination. The divine foundation-stones of the institution must on no account be interfered with. It must be true for this age, as for the ages that are past, and true for all the ages of the future, that the great work of the Christian pulpit is to proclaim the message that " God was, in Christ, reconciling the world to Himself, not imputing to men their trespasses," because " He hath made Him to be sin for us who knew no sin, that we might be made the righteousness of God in Him." It will be a poor day for the Scottish pulpit when that great message ceases to be at once its foundation and its animating spirit. It will be a feeble grip it takes of the conscience when sin becomes but a weakness or an irregularity, in regard to which the Ruler of the Universe does little more than testify his disapproval. It will be a poor salve it applies to the awakened conscience when it tries by the unsupported fatherhood of God to allay its terrors and subdue its remorse. It will be a wretched solace it supplies to the bereaved heart, peering wistfully into the future, if peradventure it may find its lost one, when it preaches that our great business is with the life that now is, to improve its tone and refine its enjoyment, and that it is an unwholsome piety that stretches forward to the unseen future. Is there the slightest reason to believe, from the retrospect of the past, that such negative preaching ever will take hold of the soul, penetrate to its depths, and recast it in a heavenly mould ? Preachers trying to charm men with such strains may seem to succeed for a time, because they trade with the capital of their fathers ; they deal with men and women who, though not sharing the faith of their ancestors, are unconsciously affected by it, retain somewhat of their reverence for divine things, and are still willing to put themselves to some trouble about religion. But what will be the effect on the next generation ? The spirit of religion must die out very rapidly in any community if it be not constantly recruited from the deep springs of a living faith. The spirit of the world is more than a match for it, and all experience shows how rapidly under worldly influences religion dries up and withers away. The man in the interpreter's house that poured buckets of water on the fire would very speedily have put i′ ⸜ut but for the other man that poured in oil. Can it be supposed that in an age of abounding worldliness, the spirit of religion will survive and triumph if it have no stronger nourishment than the influences of modern thought ? no deeper view of sin than as a pardonable weakness, an ugly blot, an unfortunate dislocation of the symmetry of the soul ? no mightier impulse to do the will of God than the desire to advance that evolution of goodness and beauty which is for ever to carry the human species onward and upward and nearer to the goal ?

If there be any lesson from the history of the Scottish pulpit for the last three hundred years, it is surely this, that the notion of sin which reaches deepest into the human conscience is that which is taught at the cross of Christ, and that it is from the same source that men derive the strongest of all impulses to a new life, a life of self-denial, and of consecration to the good of man and to the glory of God. He is surely a blind preacher who does not find himself in these times face to face with a great and serious problem : How to reach to the depth of the human heart, and how to turn its strongest energies from the idolatries of the world to the service of the living God. It is no sprinkling of rose-water on the surface that will subdue that fell disease which has fastened itself like a canker on the soul ; it is no ingenious forms of speech that will appease the con-

science in its fierce writhings of self-reproach ; it is no
fancy picture that will convert the Most High God from
an object of dread into an object of confidence and
delight. Nor will it do to bring Christ forward merely
as the brother of humanity, as one who shows us how
all the forces of disorder may be mastered, who inspires
the hope of a purer life, and affords the most glorious
example of self-sacrificing love. If the death of Jesus
Christ on the cross was not demanded as a sacrifice for
sin, it was a crowning instance of the miscarriage of
justice. People talk of the immorality of the atonement ; punishment they say is for the guilty, and rewards
only for the righteous : you never can be justified in
punishing the innocent and acquitting the guilty. Yet
according to their view, the best of all the human race
suffered a shameful and cruel death, was the victim of
most miserable injustice ; and this fact, instead of horrify-
ing men, is expected to impress them above everything
else with respect for the government of God,—it is to
make such an impression on them as will rectify all the
disorders of their moral nature. Would it not have been
infinitely better, if the purpose of Jesus Christ in visiting
our world was merely to afford a pattern of self-sacrifice,
that He should have lived through the whole term of
human life, exemplifying at its every stage the spirit
of self-denying love, and showing how even to hoar
hairs life might be made beautiful by a pure devotion to
duty, and diffuse to its very close the fragrance of myrrh
and aloes and cassia ? Why cut short a life before it was
well begun that might have been so useful? The truth
is, the Cross of Christ is an utter mystery—is more than
a mystery—without the atonement. And the preaching
which ignores the work of Christ as an atonement ignores
the central truth of Christianity, the truth which God
uses most in stirring consciences, piercing men's hearts

to the core, and turning them from the tyranny of sin to the willing service of a loving Father.

It is often said that in Evangelical Churches, congregations are now so familiar with the foundation-stones of the Gospel, with the letter of the Gospel message, that no good can come of repeating it. But it should be remembered that there are ways of making the most familiar truths fresh and telling. A man of genius is never commonplace. He has a way of presenting old truths in new settings; of throwing light on them from unexpected quarters that has all the effect of freshness and novelty. But few preachers are men of genius. True; but there is another source of freshness. Living emotion is like dew to the commonest truth ; it freshens it and gives it new interest and power. Ought not preachers themselves to live on the great fundamental truths of the Gospel? Ought not our souls to be continually fed from them, and our hearts continually thrilling with them? Ought not a fresh glow to come over our hearts every day as we think of Him who loved us, and washed us from our sins in His blood, and made us kings and priests to God and to the Father? Give us the plainest preacher that ever was ; let him preach nothing that a whole congregation do not know; but let him but preach with a thrilling heart; let him preach like one amazed at the glory of the message ; let him preach in that tone of wonder and gratitude in which it becomes sinners to realise the great work of redemption,—not only will the congregation listen with interest: they will listen with profound impression. For when God's Spirit kindles emotion in the heart of the preacher, he kindles it through him in the hearts of the hearers too; and men feel, in these circumstances, This is what we need; this is the message of Heaven; this will help to set our feet on a rock. What many among us feel that they are in want of is not

U

so much light as spiritual force, moving their souls towards the good and the true. It is miserable to them to see clearly what is right and spiritually beautiful, and yet not be in love with it; to admire heaven yet cleave to earth ; to venerate goodness, yet fall into many a way of meanness and wickedness. If preaching and public services would but touch the springs of action, would but thrill the chords of their hearts, would but bring the contradictions of their souls into harmony ! May it not be one of the most needed functions of the preacher of to-day thus to present familiar truth with its appropriate emotion, so that, by God's blessing, the thrill may pass from his heart to his hearers ? Is it not this that justifies the continuance of a living ministry in these times of books and printed sermons and forms of religious instruction without number ? Is it not this that makes it ridiculous to say that most men would do well to preach other men's sermons, or to preach anything that has not passed through their own hearts, and that does not come out with the aroma and power of a living reality ? But if we are to preach with emotion, by all that is solemn let us see to it that it is genuine emotion, the emotion of hearts truly moved; to *act* emotion is beyond contempt ; it is to make the preacher an ape, the more offensive and pernicious because the sham is perpetrated in the very holy of holies.

But the foundation-stones of a building are not all the building. There is great and widening scope for the Evangelical pulpit of to-day, that if duly appreciated will not only furnish the preacher with abundance of fresh and varied material, but make him perplexed to know how he is to use it all.

To begin with : let us glance at what has long been so much valued in Scotland—expository preaching. So many valuable aids towards correct and interesting exposition have recently been furnished that we can but glance at one or two of the most important. For expounding the more difficult parts of Scripture, how invaluable is the aid furnished by that improved exegesis which ascertains the precise meaning of words, traces the connection of thought, enables us to gather the exact impression intended to be produced on the first readers, and thus helps us to adjust the whole to the meridian of our own time. Who will say that this field is exhausted? How many a question has yet to be settled in Old Testament exegesis, to say nothing of adjustments yet requiring to be made of old beliefs arising from the fact, now so generally admitted, that God's revelation both of doctrine and duty was gradually made and gradually apprehended.

In regard to the historical and biographical parts of Scripture, we owe much to recent research, and the skill of some writers in vivifying historical scenes, and setting us in the very heart of them. Greatly though we deplore the doctrinal views maintained in Dean Stanley's writings, we cannot but acknowledge our debt to that historical genius which has so often turned the past of Hebrew history into a living present, and made the actors in it not mysterious figures belonging to some other race of beings, but men and women of like passions with ourselves. In regard to biography, modern literature has just brought us back to the Scriptural method. The dramatic form of biography is the only method now tolerated, where, instead of giving dissertations on a man's character, his life is simply made to evolve itself, and the biographer's art is to supply links of connection, and the frame that unifies the whole. Such are pre-eminently the biographies of Scripture. In expounding a book so full of biography it is of great value to follow the best method of treatment; and if, instead of the formal "Scripture characters" of former days, a preacher is enabled to present a gallery of portraits of real men, the interest and the effect of his work will be all the greater. We know that such themes are sometimes handled, and ably handled, far away from the truths and lessons of the Gospel, and so as to furnish but scanty nourishment to those who delight in Gospel pastures ; but without descending to that habit of spiritualising, which is so often the resource of puzzled interpreters, we believe that the earnest expounder will seldom fail to find good and wholesome opportunity, in connection with the great biographies of Scripture, of leading his hearers under the shadow of the Cross.

Another direction in which there seems to be almost boundless scope for fresh work in evangelical preaching concerns the various *applications* of the Gospel. If we think first of its experimental or spiritual application, we find ourselves face to face with a question of great interest and some difficulty—known commonly in our time as that of " the higher Christian life." This subject, it is true, has been made somewhat repulsive to some by the theory of a " second conversion," as if there were a second spiritual change to be undergone by all persons who have accepted Christ, as definite as the first, and hardly less important. Without accepting this extreme, we cannot but remark that there are instances, not a few, in which believers are seen to make a remarkable advance in Christian life, and to come far more under the power of the truth than in the earlier stage of their Christian history. On the other hand, when we think what it is to become a Christian—vitally one with Christ—we may well wonder how little change of character and habit it appears to produce in many. There is something in the nature of union to Christ that promises far more than is commonly performed. If some brethren are able to assure us that by an enlarged exercise of faith in Jesus their spiritual life has been wonderfully deepened, the grace that flows from Christ has poured itself more fully into their hearts, and they have been enabled to live in an atmosphere of serene peace and nearness to God unknown before, the lesson is not to be rejected, but received with thankfulness and interest. It is a poor sign of a preacher if he finds himself not at home in this region, and unable to give the best and surest directions to all who are aiming at higher holiness. It is a poor look-out for a congregation if any of the people who are aspiring to the more saintly virtues can find neither aid nor sympathy either from the minister or the elders. A true minister will surely regard the elevation of the Christian life among his people as one of the most vital and interesting matters with which he has to deal. Even if he should find little appetite for higher holiness, the clear and earnest presentation of the nature and the need of it might kindle in some souls the sense of its reality, and start them in eager pursuit of blessings which would raise them so much nearer to the gate of heaven.

Passing over with a mere reference the development of the spirit of *service* as another of the directions in which it is imperative on us to apply our Christianity from the pulpit, in the spirit of our Lord's words, " The Son of man came not to be ministered unto but to minister," let us dwell for a little on the *ethical* application of our message. The days have gone past when in well-trained evangelical congregations there was a strong prejudice against moral preaching. The prejudice was perfectly reasonable when moral duty was made to supplant the message of grace, when it was preached as a ground of acceptance with God, and when it was presented with a coldness and a dryness fitted to freeze and pulverise the soul.

But now may we not say that on the part of intelligent and pious laymen there is a desire for more ethical preaching instead of less ? Are not scenes often occurring in which men, nominally Christian, demean themselves in a most unchristian way ? Have none of us been at meetings, even of office-bearers of the church, at which we have had occasion to ask ourselves, Is the slightest particle of Christ's spirit present here ? Are there not dreadful evils, affecting whole counties, such as illegitimacy, against which all our efforts have hitherto not been able to prevail ? And who of us, when we hear of persons very zealous for religion, and very zealous for their church (perhaps for our church), can be sure that they shall be found to be persons of loving, generous hearts, upright and honourable, ever aiming to diffuse happiness, and studious never to give unnecessary pain ? Are we content that it should be possible for any one to say that Christian men are not more true and honourable, more generous, more sweet-tempered, more patient than others ? Why should it be possible to say that in any Christian society there is as much scandal and evil-speaking and bitterness as there is in the world ? Why should it be possible to charge a Christian merchant with winking at the dishonesties of trade ? Why should any one that has professed to renounce the world give occasion to the gleeful chuckles of those who, being behind the scenes, have their anecdotes of him to show that his spirit is yet steeped in greed ? Are not these evils very widely spread ? Is there not need for a new sort of total abstinence society, which all our people should be held bound to join—total abstinence from " all malice, and all guile, and hypocrisies, and envies, and all evil-speakings " ? Ought not those wonderfully compact and rigid summaries of Christian ethics which we have in the New Testament— the Beatitudes, the 12th of Romans, the 13th of 1 Cor., the 4th of Ephesians, and such like—be rung in our people's ears as rules for Christian life, till they begin to think that some attention ought to be paid to them—till there cease to be such overwhelming ground for our Master's retort, "Why call ye me Lord, Lord, and do not the things which I say?"

There may be exaggeration in a remark that has been made, but it is sad to think how much occasion has been given for it—that Christianity has been tried for more than eighteen hundred years, the religion of Christ, never. If only it could be said of the Church that it is Christ-like, what a number of baffling problems would be solved, what victories won! Semler justified his unbelief on the ground that he did not find that Christians paid more attention than other people to the command to love their enemies. Some one has said that if the whole Christian Church would but practise the thirteenth chapter of 1st Corinthians for one year, unbelief would vanish. That 'palace beautiful' in Bunyan's dream—where is it to be found? Those sweet chaste maidens, Discretion, Piety, Prudence, and Charity, where do they now dwell? That large upper chamber, whose window opened to the sun-rising, and whose name was Peace, who has now its key? We do not wonder at kindly men like Dean Stanley sighing for a Church with an atmosphere of serenity and peace, where jaded souls might find rest and refreshment, much though we differ from him as to how it is to be realised. Such a Church must be built on the foundation of the apostles and prophets, Jesus Christ Himself being the chief corner-stone; but it will never be found on earth till Christians on a great scale lay to heart the obligation to walk worthy of the vocation wherewith they are called. We may contend with the unbeliever in every field of argument, yet leave him an unbeliever still. The one argument which he cannot get over is the image of Christ reflected from His Church. There is great significance in the answer said to have been given by one who was asked under whose preaching he was converted. "Under the preaching of no one, but under the practising of my mother." Would only that such practising were universal! —that not individuals here and there, but the whole Christian community, presented such a character as to constrain the world to ask, "Who is she that looketh forth as the morning, fair as the moon, clear as the sun, and terrible as an army with banners?" Ought not every sermon, or at least every meeting for divine service, to contribute, in some marked degree, toward this result?

Once more, there are the *social* applications of Christianity. And here, too, Providence is opening out to us new and extensive fields. The conditions of modern life are imposing a new obligation to give great heed to the social relations of *the family*. Those vast conglomerations of modern life, our great cities, are fast disintegrating family life, drawing young men and young women everywhere from the country, and exposing them to temptations against which they have no domestic protection. To keep up pure family life where it is possible, and to find the best substitutes for it where it is not possible, are among the most imperative needs of our day.

Moreover, we are becoming familiar with social relations on a wider scale. The questions that have arisen are often delicate, and a preacher needs to be careful of the privilege of the pulpit. Questions between capital and labour; questions regarding the possession and the occupancy of land—why, the very mention of them sets suspicion on the edge, as if we were already trespassing on forbidden ground. And yet there is a deep conviction in fair and intelligent minds that Christianity has to do with these questions, and that there is something in its principles which is more favourable to the poor man than many of us preachers have had the courage to avow. Yes, in the heart of Christianity there is a spirit of brotherhood, a spirit hostile to all class interests, a spirit that aims at securing fair and comfortable conditions of life especially for the toiling multitude, a spirit of sympathy for the lonely and him that hath no helper. The relations of labour and luxury have not yet been finally adjusted. Is the pulpit, then, like the priest and the Levite in the parable, to pass by these social disturbances on the other side? Is it to be left to novelists like Mr. Walter Besant, to protest against the misery of the female worker, and preach to her a mere gospel of secularism, a paradise of mere worldly enjoyment? Are the perpetual struggles of labour to improve its condition to be set down to sheer greed and covetousness? If the pulpit shuts its eyes to all such matters, they will fall into other hands, and the Church itself will be classed among the institutions (as indeed it often is) which are hostile to labour, and ought therefore to be swept away. Was it not foretold in the seventy-second psalm as the blessed characteristic of the Messiah : " He shall deliver the needy when he crieth, the poor also, and him that hath no helper. He shall spare the poor and needy, and shall save the souls of the needy. He shall redeem their soul from deceit and violence, and precious shall their blood be in His sight"? The leaves of the tree of life are for the healing of the nations as well as individuals; and the Gospel as proclaimed from our pulpits ought to have a wide enough sweep to embrace all the sores and sorrows of humanity, and to justify the proclamation from the throne : " Behold, I make all things new."

Then there is the Temperance reformation, and the Social Purity movement, and Early Closing, and Sabbath Observance, all demanding a share of the preacher's thought and care. And there are some of the sections of

which congregations are composed—children and young
men and young women, masters and servants, whose
several dangers, opportunities, and responsibilities must
be considered and dwelt on.   Preaching to children is
becoming quite a recognised branch of pastoral duty.
And, in reference to all these applications of the Gospel,
we have to study, not only to place them on the true
evangelical basis, as fruits and tokens of union to Christ,
but also to set them forth in a bright, cheerful, attractive
spirit, not as fresh burdens for the weary back, but filial
services to be thankfully rendered to a gracious Father,
who has blessed us with all spiritual blessings in Christ
Jesus.

One other application of the Gospel we must bear in
mind in our preaching : what may be called its work of
harmonising, bringing out its proper place and true influence in relation to many important interests in the life
of man.   Ours is not the only voice that is uttering a
testimony in the name of truth, and calling on men to hear.
Nature, science, philosophy, art, literature, have all their
preachers, are all lifting up their voices around us, and
are all claiming the allegiance of men.   Are we then
living in a Babel ?   Or is it our business in the pulpit
simply to try to speak the loudest, and to reprove the
others for interfering with our work ?   We may be
tempted to do so when we are ourselves assailed, and our
office treated with open contempt.   But a true view of
the Christian pulpit will give a different result.   The
priests of nature and of art may mistake their true
message and deem it subversive of ours.   But for us the
conviction is immovable that there must be a true
harmony between the voice that sounds in the Gospel
and the voice that sounds from nature, and is interpreted, if only it be interpreted truly, in the art, the
science, the philosophy, and the literature of the age.

We may be quite unable to reduce the whole to harmony. But may we not hit on some harmonious notes; and is it not better to try to make something of this harmony than to intensify the discords? We may feel perplexity at some of the things we hear from men of science. But don't let us for this reason look askance on their work, or in our hearts curse the workers. Let our language rather be, Go on, brothers, with your investigations, the further the better; all we ask of you is to beware of premature conclusions; your work of searching nature we look on as honourable, useful, divine; part of what God gave to man when he bade him replenish the earth and subdue it; and if only you prosecute it in a becoming, filial spirit, God's blessing will rest on you, and He will establish the work of your hands.

Meanwhile let us give the more heed to another page of the book of Nature which is more easily read by us, and where we find our footing more sure. Though we may not adopt all of our friend Professor Drummond's theory of natural law in the spiritual world, we cannot but be struck with the numberless analogies, so beautifully unfolded in his book, between the ways of nature and the work of grace. We cannot but find a great deal of instruction, as solid as it is charming, in the nature-parables of one not less esteemed, our friend Dr. Macmillan. In the voice of many of the forces of Nature—the sun, the dew, the spring—we recognise echoes of grace. The only thing in the world against which the pulpit is called to declare war is sin,—perversion of God's work, resistance to God's will, subversion of God's order. Towards all that is not of this class our desire should be to harmonise and reconcile. The effect of sin is to create disorder; the effect of the Gospel is to gender harmony. The fruit of the one is discord—discord with God, with man, and with ourselves ; the fruit of the other is peace, good-will, and harmonious co-operation.   Jesus Christ is Lord of all ; Lord of nature and Lord of grace ; "it pleased the Father that in Him should all fulness dwell; and having made peace through the blood of the cross, by Him to reconcile all things unto Himself ; by Him, I say, whether they be things on earth, or things in heaven."

Having thus indicated some things that seem to be specially called for in the pulpit of to-day, we may now, by way of illustration, briefly advert to some of the contemporary preachers of Scotland, but to avoid invidious selection we shall limit ourselves to a trio whose published discourses have created unusual interest.

Among the men still living, who, after the death of Chalmers, followed closely in his wake, but adapted themselves more to the meridian of the present age, a prominent place is due to Dr. JOHN CAIRD, now Principal of the University of Glasgow.   The sermons in his early volume [1]—one of the most popular volumes of sermons of the age—are full of admirable qualities.   They rest, firm and square, on the evangelical foundations,—man's fall, the atonement of Christ, the regeneration of the Holy Spirit.   They are urgent in pressing the sinner to go to Jesus, and they are faithful in dealing with all on the momentous question whether or not they are born again.   They are almost Puritanic in their warning against all that tends to the sensuous in worship, and in dealing with that tone of careless gaiety which is often found in worldly men.   They have little originality or genius, but they show a marvellous felicity of structure ; great skill in placing truth in clear, plain, yet classical forms ; in the use of telling analogies and

[1] *Sermons.*   By John Caird, D.D.   Edinburgh: William Blackwood and Sons, 1858.

illustrations, homely in their source, but worked out with great skill and beauty; and in heaping arguments together, each adding something to that before it, and ending with a gush of eloquence which overwhelms the reader.

Moreover, the preacher shows remarkable tact in adjusting certain truths to each other which Chalmers had left in somewhat crude form ; quietly toning down exaggerations, and making evangelical teaching more exact and symmetrical ; bringing out the self-commending power of the Gospel, and harmonising it with other interests with which it has no necessary collision. In the way of application there is not much attempted in the direction of experimental godliness ; but in ethical following up good work is done ; and the view of " Religion in Common Life," the famous Balmoral sermon, that closes the later editions, has but one fault, though it is a serious one, that, unlike the earlier sermons, it is not seen to rest on the evangelical foundation. One can hardly set limits to the good that might have been done had the distinguished preacher continued through life on the lines which he occupied so well at the beginning. Nor is it easy to express the distress one feels when one finds such a man beginning the volume of *Scotch Sermons* with a couple of philosophico-religious essays which have no manner of communion with his earlier productions, and which appear to indicate that the blessed message of his youth is to him a Gospel no more.

The sermons of Dr. OSWALD DYKES[1] are in many respects similar to Dr. Caird's, but go further in carrying out the adaptations called for by the present age. There is the same compactness of plan and structure ; the same felicity and classical purity of style ; the same aptness of illustration ; and, though in a less degree, the same

[1] *Sermons.* By J. Oswald Dykes, M.A., D.D. London : Nisbet.

accumulation of argumentative force. They are remarkable for the fresh light they throw on some of the
doctrines of Scripture, and for their high tone of spiritual
earnestness. The harmonising tendency is conspicuous ;
the preacher would show the affinities of the Gospel to
whatever is yet true in the soul of man, and its power to
meet and satisfy all his legitimate aspirations. He brings
the voice of Jesus over the troubled sea of human life,
harmonising the discords and allaying the storm. Much
more emphatically than Dr. Caird, he fastens on sin as
the cause of all the discord and all the misery of the
world ; repudiates a theology that would make light of
it, that would heal the hurt of the daughter of Zion
slightly, that would attempt to get rid of it save by the
solemn work of Calvary, where the Son of God pours out
His soul an offering for sin. Though exercising his
ministry in England, and showing traces in some things
of English influence, Dr. Dykes holds by the old theology, and as a lecturer, both on the Old Testament and
the New, he favours the old plan of textual exposition.
Under his sermons one feels that there is nothing in
evangelical Christianity to repel the most cultivated man
of the age ; rather everything to satisfy him. The doctrines of the Cross harmonise with the truest exercise of
the reason. Philosophy and science have every encouragement to sit at the feet of Jesus. Nowhere can
the yearnings of the human spirit for a higher life be
fulfilled as Christ can fulfil them. Our eye and our heart
are lifted up to a higher and more beautiful world. The
harsh sounds of this troubled earth seem to give way to a
soft and serene music.

If anything is wanting, it is the homely element in
preaching. It is almost too high and too refined for the
masses—too high, too good, " for human nature's daily
food."

A third preacher of the day, whose loss we were lately called to deplore, is Dr. JOHN KER.[1] Some would say of him that he is not a Scotch preacher. Is he not quite a contrast to Ebenezer and Ralph Erskine, to Thomas Boston, not to mention John Knox or Richard Cameron ? In form, undoubtedly. In the use of the still small musical voice, where they spoke in thunder, undoubtedly. He differs in the soft, silvery trickle of his eloquence ; in the gentle spirit that seeks to move the soul without any hammer, by insinuating itself into its innermost chambers, rather than by smashing its doors and storming its barricades. But Dr. Ker *is* a Scotch preacher after all. The theology of the Scotch Church is his basement story, and again and again he shows how vain would be the effort to elevate the human soul into a Divine temple if it were not for the great foundation-stones of evangelical truth. The doctrinal and the practical are in vital synthesis. Dr. Ker would not dream of fostering a divine life in man till first by the atoning work of Christ he has been brought into a new relation to his offended God. He could find neither pith nor power in any motive to self-denial or holy living, till the living Spirit of Christ works in the soul and transforms it into His image. On these foundations his preaching rests. And its peculiar feature is that more than any other preaching it exemplifies the development and application of the Gospel in some of the directions where there is most need for it at the present day.

We would lay especial stress on the harmonising element in Dr. Ker's sermons. Read his sermon on the rain and the dew. See how the voice of nature is there harmonised with the voice of revelation. Nature is ever uttering the thoughts and feelings of God. It furnishes countless analogies to the operations of grace. And so

[1] *Sermons.* By Rev. John Ker, D.D. Edmonston and Douglas.

far as men are under Christ, all things are tending to final harmony. Man's heart is a medley—Christ is bringing all into unison. Society torn by sin is in a state of chaos—Christ, by subduing sin, and breathing over it His own spirit, would make all serene and peaceful. Round Christ as a centre gather all the features of human nature and all the graces of the Christian life. In the life of the best there is a conflict of joy and sorrow, and sometimes the sorrow is so keen and overwhelming that the joy seems driven out of it for ever; but let a man hope and patiently wait for the salvation of God and it will be seen that all is well. We do not consider that all the purposes of preaching are served by Dr. Ker's printed sermons. Though most really evangelistic, they are not directly or avowedly so, but we have no reason to suppose that the author would not have excelled in that department. They carry the spirit of the Gospel into a realm which few preachers have been able to reach. In a way of their own they bring out the aroma of divine truth, filling the whole house with the fragrance of its very precious ointment. They draw from the harp of grace a softer music, more like the gentle swell of an Æolian harp, than most fingers have been able to evoke. The style is alike chaste and beautiful, brightened by sparks of genius, rich in thoughts that breathe and words that burn; but amid all the music and poetry one glorious figure fills the eye, as the source of every comforting truth, and of all that is precious and blessed to the sons of men—" the Lamb in the midst of the throne."

But amid all the excellencies of these preachers it is to be remarked that they are preachers for the classes rather than the masses. They are valuable in their place, but their sphere is limited. We greatly need preachers for the people. A preacher to the people needs to be very clear in his views, homely in his style, full of illustration, direct and courageous in his application, rich in brotherly sympathy, and very warm and vigorous in his delivery. Alas! they are not common. I believe that if only every tenth student that passes through our hands were a man of this stamp, we should soon see a change on the face of society; we should not hear much longer of lapsed masses; and the glorious vision of Chalmers of a regenerated Scotland, which we are so apt to class with what were called Knox's devout imaginations, would become a reality before our eyes.

It is commonly said, and generally agreed, that preaching has two great purposes—to instruct and to persuade. Of instructive preachers there is no lack, but how seldom one falls in with any who have skill to persuade. And how seldom is the art of persuasion deliberately cultivated — the power that gets to close quarters with men, that touches their springs of action, that lays bare their poor aims and motives till they are ashamed, and that strives to turn them from the power of Satan unto God. Among our preachers there may be few Richard Baxters endowed by nature with this faculty; but it would mark something like a new era of pulpit power if preachers realised the obligation to persuade, and coveted this power as the best of pulpit gifts.

It is not possible to close the subject without glancing at that volume, now so famous, consisting of twenty-three sermons by twelve ministers of the Church of Scotland, entitled *Scotch Sermons*.[1] One thing we may say, that if intellectual ability and a command of clear and cultivated language could have commended a new theology to a people who have had so much cause to reverence the old, these sermons ought to have been a success. But what

[1] *Scotch Sermons.* Macmillan and Co., 1880.

X

gifts of genius, what tongue of men and angels could have prevailed to commend a set of opinions which ostentatiously set at nought the corner-stones of the Gospel, and deliberately substitute for them certain inherent qualities of the human soul ?   We know that every writer in the book is responsible only for his own opinions.   But in one or other of these sermons we find a rejection of the great Gospel message, the proclamation of which has been the glory of the Scottish Church in all her best and most effective periods.   We find, what in the days of Moderatism was hardly heard of, a systematic attempt to minimise the supernatural in Scripture, if not to deprive Christianity altogether of its supernatural character.   We find the great doctrine of eternal life, which in all ages has been such a wonderful stimulus to men serving God under painful conditions, spoken of with disparagement, as if it were much less to be valued than some present blessing, such as the improvement of character in the present life.   The atoning love that arrests and overcomes the prodigal ; the grace that sweeps away sin in one great act of forgiveness, and secures ever after the grateful allegiance of the accepted sinner ; the promises that sound like heavenly music in the ear of the dying, and that turn the shadow of death into morning, are all consigned to the *limbus patrum*—put away as among childish things.

A book like this may serve as a beacon to those, if such there be, who fancy that the evangelical pulpit has hitherto given a disproportionate place to Jesus Christ and Him crucified.   See what you come to, preachers, when He ceases to be the Sun in your firmament !   Recognise it as legitimate that the preaching of to-day should show some advance on the preaching of former generations.   But see that it is advance.   See that it is fair and loyal development and not revolution.   See that

it gives its due place to that message of grace, which
from the distant days of the saintly Columba in the
far-off Hebrides, onward through the times of Lollards
and Martyrs, of Reformers and Covenanters, of Seceders
and Evangelicals, has brought rest to the weary, peace
to the distressed, and life to the spiritually dead;
which has inspired the martyr with his heroic virtue,
comforted the widow in her night of weeping, animated
the missionary amid his solitary toil; which has made
the sons of labour patient, industrious, and honest, and
raised our country from savagery to an honourable place
among the nations. This is the heritage that has been
handed down from our fathers; and it is for the young
preachers of our country to say whether it shall now
be set aside, either respectfully or contemptuously; or
whether it shall not rather realise once more the emblem
of Milton :—

> "So sinks the day-star in the ocean-bed,
>   And yet anon repairs his drooping head,
>   And tricks his beams, and with new spangled ore
>   Flames in the forehead of the morning sky."

APPENDIX.

ON THE METHOD OF PREACHING ADAPTED
TO THE AGE.

[THE following paper bears so closely on the subject discussed in this volume that the author ventures to give it here. It was contributed by him to the *Homiletic Quarterly* for July 1878, as the introductory paper to a Symposium on the question, "What method of preaching is most calculated to render divine truth effective in this age of popular indifference and philosophical scepticism?" The other contributors were Professor H. R. Reynolds, D.D.; Professor J. G. Murphy, LL.D.; M. Edmond de Pressensé, D.D.; Canon J. J. S. Perowne; and Rev. J. Clifford, M.A., LL.B.]

IF a practical answer had been asked to this question, the city of Boston might have supplied it not unfitly, when Mr. Moody was holding meetings in his Tabernacle, and Mr. Joseph Cook was delivering his Monday lectures. The one preacher appeared not less capable of dealing with the popular indifference than the other with the philosophical scepticism of the age. Widely apart though their methods were, they had substantially a common basis. Both were servants of the same Master. Both derived their lineage from the Pilgrim Fathers. But while the one showed how the Gospel message might be brought to bear with awakening force

on the ordinary run of mortals, the other cleared a way
for it towards the souls of the philosophical and scientific
few.

Mr. Cook's work is more with the foundations than the
superstructure. He has to deal with an exceptional class,
and with a class placed in exceptional circumstances. His
lectures are Monday, not Sunday, lectures; and they are
directed mainly to the removal of objections and the establishment of the foundations of truth. Hence, while showing remarkably how special provision may be made for
a special want, they are not samples of the ordinary way
of bringing the Gospel to bear on the intellectual classes.
They serve in the end of the nineteenth century a purpose similar to that which the works of another Joseph—
Butler's *Analogy*, and *Fifteen Sermons*—served in the
beginning of the eighteenth. But even in his own day
no one would have recommended the discourses of Bishop
Butler as suitable for ordinary Sunday services. And
notwithstanding the much larger infusion of feeling and
imagination in Mr. Cook's lectures, no one, we presume,
would pronounce them models for the ordinary food of
even the most intellectual congregations.[1] Mr. Moody,
too, is in obvious respects an exceptional preacher. He
is an evangelist, not a pastor, and no one would more
readily acknowledge than himself that, however fitted to
rouse, his evangelistic addresses have not the fulness,
breadth, and depth needful for building up all classes
over a series of years in the Christian life.

----

[1] " The mode of preaching which has been affectedly termed ' the
intellectual' can hardly be made to consist with a bold, simple, and
cordial proclamation of the message of mercy. Its intention is not the
same ; and the fruit of it commonly will be an obtuse indifference in
regard to the most affecting objects of Christian faith. . . . Numbers
of those who come forth upon the Church as candidates for the
Christian ministry are fraught with all qualifications and all acquire-
ments rather than fervour and simplicity of spirit in proclaiming the
glad tidings of life."—*Saturday Evening*, by Isaac Taylor, p. 35.

Our practical answer, therefore, however tempting from its simplicity, and suitable in the circumstances, will hardly solve the problem put into our hands. We must look at it likewise from other points of view.

1. First, let us ask, What is the specific design of preaching? It is a Divine institution, we all believe; and, like all Divine institutions, it must have a Divine purpose. We need not spend time over this question. It will be allowed by all who take part in the present discussion that the immediate purpose of preaching is to convey to men the good news of the kingdom, the Gospel of Jesus Christ. Now, it will surely be admitted that the leading feature of the Gospel is its message of redemption. " God so loved the world that He gave His only-begotten Son, that whosoever believeth in Him should not perish, but should have everlasting life." If this be not allowed to be the heart and kernel of the Gospel of Jesus Christ, it is needless to go further. We cannot discuss methods of preaching with those who deem Christianity merely a brighter edition of natural religion. It has surely been well enough made out that " Christianity as old as the Creation" is essentially a deistical position. Buddhism, Islamism, Brahminism are religions; Christianity is more. These systems profess mainly to teach men how to worship; Christianity teaches them first how to be saved. According to Christianity, sin is not merely an imperfection, or disease, or disorder of some kind; it is ruin in every sense. Sin, besides involving condemnation, has broken up the normal relation of man to God; and while it is in the way, man is severed from God, and can never enjoy the numberless influences needed for his well-being and happiness that come from Him. Jesus Christ has come into the world to take away sin by the sacrifice of Himself. Whoever believes in Jesus has his sin taken away; the normal relation between him and God is

restored; and through that relation all Divine influences come to play upon his soul, so that he moves steadily onward towards the fulfilment of the great ends of his being.[1]

The design of preaching being thus, in the first instance, to convey the good news of redemption, and beseech men to be reconciled to God, no preaching can be worthy of the name of Christian which does not make this its first and most earnest endeavour. Preaching which leaves sin in the rear, and deals with man as if there were no gulf between him and God; as if all that was needed was to bring God's will to bear more forcibly upon him, and induce him to frame his life accordingly, is defective in the most essential of all the elements of the Gospel. Nothing will more effectively cause torpidity

---

[1] We must be allowed to express our fundamental difference from Dean Stanley, who, in a sermon preached at St. Andrews on the 18th March 1877, laid down *nine* points as the peculiar principles of Christianity, none of which either explicitly or implicitly contained redemption. Much more true was the late Miss H. Martineau's conception of what Christianity *professed* to be, and must be held to mean. Referring to her ancestors, she says in her Autobiography :—
" The first Martineaus were expatriated Huguenots, who came from Normandy after the revocation of the Edict of Nantes. Of course they were Calvinists, so fully admitting the Christian religion to be a scheme of redemption as to deserve, without limitation or perversion, the title of Christians. But their descendants passed by degrees, with the congregations to which they belonged, out of Calvinism into the pseudo-Christianity of Arianism first, and then of Unitarianism, under the guidance of pastors whose natural sense revolted from the essential points of the Christian doctrine, while they had not learning enough, Biblical, ecclesiastical, historical, or philosophical, to discover that *what they gave up was truly essential*, and that the name of Christianity was a mere sham when applied to what they retained" (vol. i. pp. 36, 37). Mr. Gladstone, in his address on Preaching, delivered in the City Temple on 22d March 1877, gave a much more emphatic place than Dean Stanley to the person and work of our Lord : " It is the preaching of Christ our Lord which is the secret and substance and centre and art of all preaching,—not merely of facts about Him and notions about Him, but of His Person, His work, His character, His simple but unfathomable sayings. Here, here, is the secret and art of preaching."

of conscience and feebleness of will than to represent the
disorder under which man labours as not malignant but
only functional, and tell him that a few mild tonics and
gentle stimulants are all that is needed to keep him in
spiritual health. A Gospel without redemption is not
only not a Gospel of salvation; it cannot be a Gospel of
power. Redemption has ever been the great dynamic in
the Christian Church. All the purely moral forces of the
world have been but as green withes compared to the
force of the conviction, "Ye are not your own, for ye are
bought with a price; therefore glorify God in your bodies,
and in your spirits, which are God's." All effective preaching must regard this, and the truths connected with it, as
the very key to the Christian position. "Truly the
Philistines would be upon us if we should ever be
tempted to abandon those solemn truths, which, uttered
in God's name, fasten themselves to the conscience, and
even when they do not lead to conversion, leave an awful
sense of their importance, and of the madness of trampling
them under foot. Far better no pulpit at all than a
pulpit that did not, as its chief business, solemnly address
men as lost sinners, summon them to repentance, faith,
and humility, and entreat them in Christ's stead to be
reconciled to God." [1]

Not only, in all faithful and powerful preaching, must
this view of redemption have the first place, but it must
also dominate and regulate all that is said on the more
practical aspects of life. Preaching, besides being doctrinal, is often described as experimental and ethical.
"Experimental" usually refers to the life of the spirit;
and "ethical" to the outer life, before the world. Each
term suggests an immense field for preaching. Experimental or spiritual preaching bears on the fellowship of
the soul with God, and the manner in which the Divine

[1] *For the Work of the Ministry*, p. 5.

influence may be most fully and constantly enjoyed. All
that tends to draw the soul away from God; all that it
suffers in consequence; all that brings nearness, confidence, and joy; the use and the abuse of the world, in
relation to the soul's prosperity or decline; the strange
thoughts, the subtle yearnings, the wayward impulses,
the doubts, the conflicts, the hopes and fears that make
up the chequered history of the spirit as it struggles upward, form a region of singular interest for the preacher
whose powers are adapted to it. But it is a region that
must be dominated by the great fact of redemption. To
delineate spiritual feelings which are in no way condi-
tioned by redemption, nor sought to be brought under
its influence, is not Christian preaching. Many an interesting thought, with a spiritual complexion, may pass
through even pagan minds. The natural heart has yearnings and longings upward, neutralised, however, by its
downward movements of much stronger force. To seize
hold on these yearnings and bring them under law to
Christ is a fine aim for a Christian preacher; to deal
with them quite apart from Christ and His redemption
is, to say the least, very perilous. Who that is acquainted
with the *Confessions* of Augustine can fail to recognise
the extraordinary interest of the soul's movements, even
before it has come to Christ? But it is a tantalising
interest—not comforting, but harrowing. What we
maintain is, that the whole sphere of the spiritual, in the
widest sense of the term, should come within the domain
of the evangelical preacher.

So should the equally wide sphere of the ethical. A
right relation to God is a relation in which the will of
God is the paramount authority over the whole realm of
practical life. To help in effecting such an object is
surely worthy of the best efforts of the Christian preacher.
"Teach them," said our Lord, "to observe all things

whatsoever I have commanded you." In prayer we are to say " Thy will be done on earth as it is in heaven." In daily life, our rule is, " Whatsoever ye do, whether in word or in deed, do all in the name of the Lord Jesus, giving thanks unto God, even the Father, by Him." The sphere is almost boundless. To establish the will of God as the great moral rule in every heart, every family, every social company ; in the sphere of business, the sphere of pleasure, the sphere of civil government ; to bind it upon masters and servants, parents and children ; upon artists, authors, men of science, philosophers, merchants, travellers, colonists, statesmen ; to feel that one's mission as a preacher is not at an end so long as there is one rebel heart in one's charge, or one rebel habit in any otherwise Christian life ; what a work is here for any preacher, what a spur and impulse to move him to the last hour of his life ! But how vain to enter on this undertaking likewise, apart from the great fact of redemption ! By what dynamic shall he move men to obey God's will, till, through experience of Christ's redemption, they come to know it in its sweetest bearings, and by the grace of the Holy Spirit the rebellion of their natural disposition yields to the feeling, " I delight to do Thy will, O my God " ?

The field which we thus find for evangelical preaching is very wide. Redemption at the basis and in the centre ; redemption as a substantive and outstanding element of the whole ; good news, through the work of Christ, to the chief of sinners ; grace abounding on every side ; but along with this a new, happy, filial relation to God, tending to all spiritual and ethical results ; manifold aid to the soul in all its endeavours after God, and motives innumerable to all manner of active obedience and passive submission to His will ;—this is our sphere for the preacher. We do think there is reason to blame many who never get beyond the simple elements of redemption. Texts all of the same class yield addresses all of the same character; a monotonous feeling gets into the very air; weariness lays hold of the best-intentioned listeners, and the only thing their admirers say of such preachers is that they faithfully preach the Gospel. So they do in its great central articles ; but not as a Gospel that evangelises the whole of life, that finds a place and a blessing for every legitimate movement of the human spirit, that sets on every true human interest the broad-arrow of the kingdom of heaven.

2. So much for what is designed to constitute the *substance* of preaching. Next let us ask for what reasons it has pleased the Head of the Church to employ *an order of living men* for the propagation of His message, instead of communicating it by other, and apparently easier, means.

The order of preachers is an original feature of the Gospel. No founder of any philosophical school made use of it. Preachers, be it observed, are essentially distinct from priests. Priests are ritualists, preachers are messengers. The originality of Christ's conception lay in employing a vast order of messengers to go into all the world, and keep delivering their message to the successive generations of men.

It seems at first sight a difficult, an expensive, a doubtful method. Will every succeeding generation furnish the needed men ? Will not their maintenance entail a great expense on honest industry ? Will they not embrace a great number of ineffectives ? And when a cheap and easily-worked printing-press comes into operation, will it not be better to communicate with men by means of it rather than by them ? [1]

[1] Mr. Gladstone says : "There are some who are connected with science who seem to think that it is a part of their mission to put an

In all these objections there is considerable force; and in setting them aside, and resorting after all to the order of preachers, our Lord was doubtless influenced by the paramount importance of a living agency—living, in the highest sense of the term; an agency penetrated by the message they were called to deliver; in lively sympathy with Him whose truth they proclaimed; with affectionate yearnings for the good of souls, for the reclamation of the erring, the restoration of wrecked lives, the re-establishment, in its pure and loving power, of the will of God; men whose words would not be those of the hireling nor of the formalist; men like Jeremiah, in whom God's word would be "like a burning fire in their bosom," or like Peter and John, who told the Council, "We cannot but speak the things which we have seen and heard."

Were all preachers really of this order, were all lips touched by seraph hands with a coal from off the altar, inquiries like that now before us would be much rarer. Were all preaching the obvious outcome of faith, accompanied with the tone and manner of deep conviction, warm with the glow of brotherly sympathy, and elevated by the awful thought of eternity, how comparatively easy would it be to overcome both popular indifference and philosophical scepticism! Popular indifference has never stood before this force, and has seldom given way to any other. And as to philosophical scepticism, there never was an age when it was more universal than that in which Christianity won its early triumphs. The enthusiasm of the Christian preachers and the manifest faith of the Christian community, the *certainty of conviction* which formed such a contrast to the wavering and restless spirit of the time, conquered many votaries of

end to preaching. My belief is, that as long as mankind subsists, preaching and science will both have their places in the field of life; and if I were to wager, I would as soon wager in favour of the longevity of preaching as I would on the longevity of science."

philosophical scepticism, and brought them to the feet of
Jesus.   "The first necessity of man's higher nature,"
says Isaac Taylor, "is TRUTH, and the despair of finding
it is indeed a darkness that may be felt." But when
Christianity appears, "everywhere we meet companies of
men, even multitudes, who have thrown off the listless-
ness of scepticism, from whose countenances the sullen-
ness of atheism has been dispelled, and who speak to us
in the decisive tones that spring from an accepted and
undoubted belief. . . . How cordially to be welcomed is
such a visitation, as of the morning, if it be the morning!
. . . The ear now catches the intelligible utterances of
men who say they have come into the possession of
CERTAINTY and of hope." [1]

There is another great reason why the Gospel should
be committed to the hands of living men.   In such hands
it is capable of being adapted to the ever-changing moods
of the human soul.   Ever-changing, we mean, within
certain limits.   In all ages the needs of man's spirit
are substantially the same, but in every age they
are circumstantially different.   To meet their substantial sameness, we have the same "everlasting
Gospel;" to meet their circumstantial diversity, there
is provided the vigilance, the insight, the elasticity of an
ever-changing ministry.   Now the more fully a preacher
is able to adapt his message both to the unchanging and
to the changing needs of the human soul, the firmer is
the hold he will take of it, and the more powerful the
impression that by God's grace his message will make on
his people.   If it were necessary to answer the question,
What are the *unchanging* needs of the soul of man? we
should be led to speak of what arise from his sense of
guilt, his troubled conscience, his separation from God,
his sorrows, his dissatisfaction and unrest, his inability to

---

[1] *Restoration of Belief*, pp. 50, 51.

realise his own ideal, the discord he feels in his soul, his dread of death and of the world to come. No preacher of the Gospel in any age can be powerful or successful who does not habitually address himself to these feelings, and strive to bring his message to bear on them. Essays however complete, disquisitions however elaborate, demonstrations of doctrine however unanswerable, are to little purpose, if they be not pointed at the actual wants and directed to fill the actual void of the soul. Neglect of this, neglect even of the unchanging needs of man, is doubtless the cause of a vast amount of inefficient preaching in every age. Dr. Macleod Campbell speaks of the extraordinary change which he found both in the facility, the interest, and the power of his preaching when he began to go among people and ascertain their wants, and when his sermons became the outpourings of what had accumulated in his heart during the week. In all ages preaching, to be efficient, must penetrate to the inner nature, take man up as he is, define to him his own feelings, declare God's judgment upon him, draw echoes from his own consciousness, and then present to him the glorious remedy, as furnished in the Gospel. The more thoroughly the preacher pursues this plan, arouses his hearer's consciousness, and shows himself acquainted with his needs, so much the deeper is the interest which he excites, and so much the heavier the blow he inflicts on popular indifference. Even if he do not travel much beyond the universal or unchanging needs, if he simply show skill in placing in his focus the outstanding features of man's moral malady, and applying the Gospel to them, he will be a great preacher, with an Orpheus-like power to command the ears of men.

But still more will this be so if he can adapt himself to the specially-felt needs of his individual age. That there are many such needs in the present age—perhaps that there never was an age more marked by them—will probably be disputed by few. The progress of physical science, establishing so firmly the reign of law, has created a crop of difficulties, and consequently of needs, not easily to be met. It has encompassed belief in the supernatural with difficulties which previous generations little knew. It has thrown shadows over the very being of God, the reality of Providence, the future life of the soul, even the existence of spirit. Criticism, too, has come and shaken the old impression of our infancy, that the Bible, as we have it, came from the hands of its Divine Author as complete in every part as the two tables of stone delivered to Moses in Sinai. Young minds, without wishing to break off, find it most difficult to share all the beliefs of their fathers. And this habit of mind seems more likely for some time to increase than to pass away. As science becomes more a popular study, the collision is likely to enlarge its area. And so the craving will become wider and louder for preaching that will be a real help out of the perplexities that are thus occasioned; preaching that will recognise the difficulties, or at least recognise the facts that cause them, but that will at the same time find a way through them for the Gospel stream, and enable the intelligent hearer to regale his soul in its waters without the feeling that in tasting the solace of religion he has broken the interdict of science.

Let us take another illustration of the special wants of the age. Men are impatient, in these days, of the hard and fast line that used to separate the domains of the secular and the sacred. They recognise Divine elements in many things where the rougher eye of their fathers saw them not. In science and art, for example. Does not science deal with the works of God, and is it to be called common or unclean? Is not art a reproduction of the natural, under forms of its own, and does it not often have for its special aim to bring out *the most Divine features* of nature, whether by music, or painting, or poetry? Why should it be relegated by preachers to the domain of paganism? There is no doubt that this is a very deep feeling in many earnest hearts at the present day. And there is truth in it. It is strong because it has a basis in truth. But it needs guidance. Unregulated, it flies off to pantheism; or perhaps it affirms that the culture of science and art is worship, is of the same quality as adoration, obedience, and prayer. The need arises of preachers who understand the feeling, sympathise with it in so far as it is just, but who divest it of all pantheistic tendency, not allowing it to climb to unlawful heights, or to interfere with the reality of Divine worship. It is not to be supposed that the most confident assertors of the *jus divinum* of art and science, in a religious point of view, are free from difficulties on it in their own minds. Their enthusiasm may just be a protest against general neglect, or against the denial of any claim or place to their favourite pursuits. Now to hear from a Christian pulpit any sound of sympathy, any recognition of their views, however limited, would to such souls be a singular refreshment. And under such guidance they might be found content to abate their claims; to allow that the term " sacred " may well be restricted to the more solemn and spiritual manifestations of God; that true worship is not æsthetic but moral; and that "the beauty of the Lord" which we are called to admire in the Bible is something infinitely deeper and more spiritually glorious than that faint material reflection of it which art delights to portray.

3. There is a third question which may serve to guide us to the true solution of our problem—Of what use is the *Bible* designed to be to the preacher? And

Y

how is it to be handled, so as most effectually to accomplish the ends of preaching?

The answer to this is very explicit. The Bible is the authoritative record of God's revelation; it is the record of that Divine Voice which at sundry times and in divers manners spake in time past to the fathers by the prophets, and in these last days has spoken to us by His Son. It is God's own repertory of all the truths and aspects of truth which it is essential for man to know and follow. It is the revelation of the new and living way to God, and it is an exposition, in a thousand varied forms, of all that is involved in a right relation to God; how that relation may be obscured and hampered, and how restored; what influence it is to have on the life and character, including all the aspects and relations of life, personal, social, ecclesiastical, and national. To the preacher, the Bible is at once an authority and a storehouse. It is his authority; for nothing that is not there can be spoken as a message from God. Not only so, but it is a great part of his business to get men to recognise and use the Bible as the authoritative record of God's will. But the Bible is also his storehouse. It furnishes numberless forms into which the message may be thrown. It provides a variety like the variety of nature; and the more fully he carries his people over its varied pastures, the more thoroughly he declares to them the whole counsel of God.

Most emphatically do we hold that preaching must be Biblical; and that, not merely because God knows better than we what truths men have most need to be told, but also because the power of the Holy Spirit may be expected to apply what is directly Divine truth, in a far higher degree than what is merely the offspring of the reflections of the human mind. Preaching must be Biblical, not merely in the sense of its having a text from the

Bible, but in the sense of its being really an exposition of Divine revelation, in something of its comprehensive fulness and variety.

But Biblical preaching, to be thoroughly effective, must be subject to two conditions : in the first place, the substance of it must be worked into the preacher's mind, digested, assimilated, and reproduced as from his own personal convictions ; and, in the second place, it must be so applied as to meet the needs of the hearers' souls — both the universal needs, common to all times and places, and the more especial needs, characteristic of the present time.

It must be digested by the preacher; for the freshness of all preaching depends on its coming out from a living soul, and if preaching be not fresh it cannot be interesting or powerful. The preacher must be an intense Biblical student; he should know the Bible exegetically, intellectually, and spiritually. What Lamartine said, but hardly with justice, of Bossuet must be true of him—he must show " the Bible transfused into a man." The Bible must be the man of his counsel, his meditation all the day. The condition is such, that without it he can hardly ever preach well ; with it, he can hardly ever preach ill. Such an acquaintance as that which we now require gives the material for sermons without number—makes his tongue like the pen of a ready writer.

Hardly less important is the condition that the Bible be so applied as to meet the needs, universal and special alike, of the souls of his hearers. No doubt this involves a somewhat rare power. But it may be rare only because it is not much cultivated. The Bible would not be the Bible if it did not contain materials capable of being applied in this way. We need not illustrate this in reference to the abiding and universal wants of the soul. But will it be maintained that the Bible is

capable of applications to meet the special features of
each new age? Were not those old leisurely Oriental
times in which it was written the very antithesis of our
rapid, rushing, daring, dashing nineteenth century? Is
it not wiser and more honest not to try to find guidance
in the Bible for such conditions of life, but, holding ever
to its general spirit, preach to the age through channels
more in unison with itself?

But this were to distrust the Word of God as Divinely
fitted for its great purpose to the end of time. " A Christian minister," it has been remarked, sometimes " thinks
he must meet the enemies of God's truth on their ground,
not on his. He must argue with the Materialist or the
Pantheist on purely scientific or metaphysical grounds.
He must enter the lists as a geologist, a biologist, or a
linguist. . . . But . . . we insist that the preacher is
uttering a revelation from God, and not acting as a philosopher of the schools. The Bible furnishes him with
quite strong enough weapons for any form of infidelity.
The battle can be fought out on the grand principles
enunciated in the Word, and need never be carried into
the detailed technics of a speciality. God made His
revelation a complete one for its purpose of saving man,
and there is a dishonouring of that revelation when the
imaginations of men are deemed a necessary *addendum*
to it." [1]

The power of finding the present in the past in the
pages of the Bible is a great power, and is the source
of much interest and originality in preaching. The
absence of it makes Biblical exposition very wearisome.
Some preachers would almost seem to count it a merit to
spend their whole time on the Hebrew soil, or among the
Hebrew people, as if their whole object were to reproduce
a scene two thousand years old. This is little better

[1] Rev. Dr. Howard Crosby, New York.

than a piece of dry antiquarianism. The real object is to illuminate the present by the lights of the past, and in some measure the past by the lights of the present. It is a power which may be given to some as an intuition, but, in the case of most, needs to be most diligently cultivated. It depends much on sympathy,—one of the chiefest of a true preacher's qualities. By means of sympathy he will read his Bible with and for his people, and see, as he reads, what will meet their wants. His people will never be far from his mind, and by his sympathy he will know their feelings almost as if they were his own. And when he meets them in the congregation he will be always *touching* them, coming into living contact with what is fresh and vivid, and *inquiring* in their hearts. It will be no painful effort to them to attend. We own to a suspicion of the preachers who are always urging on their people the duty of regularity—and hitting at absenteeism. It may be all right, possibly; but the question comes up, If their people found God's Word brought to bear on their actual wants, their sorrows, their bitternesses of soul, their weariness, their restless consciences, their unsatisfied hearts, would they not be more attracted, and not need to be scolded into regularity? God's Word is more to be desired than gold, yea, than much fine gold; sweeter also than honey and the honeycomb. But the preacher may utterly fail to bring it home, in the fulness of these qualities, to his congregation; is it wonderful that they get tired, fall asleep, or drop away?

To sum up our views of the preaching adapted to the age. It must, as its leading feature, bring to bear on men the redemption of Christ, as the basis of reconciliation, and of the re-establishment of that relation between man and his Maker on which the healthy exercise and development of his nature depends. On this basis it must enter the realm of the spiritual, and likewise that of the ethical, expounding the true conditions of spiritual prosperity and progress, and enforcing a thorough conformity to the will of God as the universal rule for the whole life of man. In the delivery of his message, the preacher must have his soul steeped in the truths he utters, his own manifest belief in them being one of the great factors for impressing his audience. Moreover, he must have skill to adapt his message to the needs of his hearers, both to the universal needs common to them with all the ages, and to those which more peculiarly mark the present time. Still further, he must use the Bible both as his authority and his text-book; appealing to it as the expression of a higher wisdom than his own, and using it as the foundation of the whole scope of his preaching. And in order to use it efficiently, he must seek to have it digested into the substance of his own soul, and at the same time endeavour to bring it to bear on the needs of the people. In his whole work he must deal with people rather than with topics, his great business being to fill hearts with Divine truth, and bring lives into conformity with the Divine will.

Our space is exhausted, and we must conclude hastily with three unconnected observations.

1. In the detailed work of preaching, we would strongly urge that the attempt be made systematically to reach the soul, not by one avenue only, but by all the avenues through which access can be found to it. Besides the reason (in its more restricted sense), approaches should be made through the conscience, the feelings, the imagination; each appeal, as far as possible, confirming the rest.

2. The preaching needed to break in on popular indifference is not *essentially* different from that ordinarily required to meet philosophical scepticism; that is to say,

the self-commending power of the truth of the Gospel is in both cases the most powerful weapon, only in the latter case occasions arise for special treatment and special dealing with the difficulties and perplexities of the age.

3. Our whole representation is based on the principle that in every case efficiency in the true sense, that is to say, the bringing of men, through Christ, into living fellowship with God, and under the habitual influence of His will, depends on a Divine Power; that the whole work of the preacher is to be carried on in dependence on this influence; that he is to regard himself as but an instrument, or vessel, through whom it pleases God to come into contact with other men; and that his supreme desire should be, that the vessel be so fitted for the Master's use as to do most good to men, and bring most glory to God.

NEW COLLEGE, EDINBURGH,
June 1878.

INDEX TO NAMES AND BOOKS.

THE END.